Introducing Kyoto in Temples and Shrines

Shikosha

装 幀 = 寄藤文平、古屋郁美

※本書は 2010 年に紫紅社から刊行された『寺社を歩けば京都がわかる』を改訂したものです。
本書の情報は 2019 年末時点のものです。拝観時間、拝観料などの記載情報は季節により変動することがあります。事前に各寺社にご確認ください。

AKIZ

英語で話す

「京都寺社ガイド」

Introducing Kyoto in Temples and Shrines

Shikosha
紫紅社＝編

日本の忘れものを訪ねる旅

精選した50余の寺社を巡る

旅を急ぐ人は特急列車に乗る。さらに急ぐ人は新幹線に乗る。しかし、都市と都市を結ぶだけで、旅情は淡い。では各駅停車か。となるとあまりに時間がかかりすぎる。

以前、準急という列車があって、特急が通過する二番手、三番手の駅にも停車した。そのため沿線の風景もよくみえた。

本書は京都を巡る準急列車のつもりである。50余りの「寺社」に停まりながら走った。というのは、本列車は通路を挟んで右に英語人の席、左に日本語人の席という編成だから、お互いの関心の度合を調和させつつ楽しい旅にしなければならないわけで、「京都」を堪能するためにほどよく快適な準急列車で、精選した寺社を周遊することにした。

濃密な京都の街

京都市の面積は、町村合併により現在827.9㎢というが、北域の左京区と北区、西域の右京区と西京区は大半が緑深い山地である。そのため京都市街は、大きな皿にわずかに注がれたスープほどの広さで、

Visiting the Things Japan Has Forgotten

More Than Fifty Selected Temples and Shrines

People in a hurry to travel take the limited express train, and people who are in even more of a hurry take the bullet train. But all that does is get you from departure point to destination, with little of the savor of travel. You can take a local train, but that takes too long.

In the past, there used to be a type of train known as a local express that would stop at many of the stations the limited express passed by. It also afforded a much better view of the landscape along the way.

This book is intended to be a local express around Kyoto, stopping at fifty or so temples and shrines. Furthermore, this local express seats English speakers on the right side of the aisle and Japanese speakers on the left, in the hopes of presenting an excursion that will suit the tastes and interests of both and give everyone a satisfying experience of Kyoto.

The Dense City of Kyoto

The city of Kyoto, having incorporated many surrounding towns and villages, now covers some 827.9 square kilometers, but the majority of its northern (the wards of Sakyō-ku and Kita-ku) and western (Ukyō-ku and Nishikyō-ku) areas are

そこに約147万人の人口のほとんどが暮らし、年間5000万人あまりの観光客を迎える。さらに約1680の寺院、約410の神社が建つ。京都市街というスープの濃度はまことに濃いのである。

つまり旅人にとって、京都の街を観光することは、人の背丈に合った適度な狭さと、歴史的資源(みどころ)の近接という好条件が得られるわけだ。さらにいえば、市街は皿の底の平坦地であるため、歩いて回っても、自転車を駆っても、さほど疲れることがない。次の寺社、さらに次へと足も伸びる。寄り道の愉しさもある。

千百年の都は甦生都市

本書に紹介した50余りの寺社はいずれも京都を知り、日本を知る重要な遺産で、千百年の永きにわたり都であった京都の歴史を物語るばかりでなく、日本美のミュージアムとして、日本人の美意識の源泉地であるのだ。それはとくに禅宗寺院の全容が京都ほど詳らかにみられる都市はほかにない、ということもある。ただ、私たちが留意しなければならないのは、京都は再建都市であるという点だ。

桓武帝が794年に京都に都を定め、都城の造営をはじめて以降、都は大火、戦火、地震、疫病、風水害にみまわれている。太郎・次郎焼亡（1177·78）、応仁の乱（1467～77）、天明の大火（1788）などで市街の建物は灰燼に帰した。そして、そのつど再建された。

thickly forested mountains. In this way, Kyoto resembles a soup bowl with just a small amount of soup at the bottom: a population of some 1.47 million residents, who each year greet approximately 50 million visitors. The soup is further thickened by the city's approximately 1,680 Buddhist temples and 410 *Shintō* shrines.

For visitors, then, the city affords a comfortable human element rich with historical resources, making for ideal tourism conditions. The flat area at the bottom of the soup bowl is easy to walk or bicycle around without getting tired. One can wander from one temple or shrine to the next, allowing the pleasure of serendipitous discovery.

A 1,100-Year-Old City Reborn

The more than fifty temples and shrines described in this book are not only important inheritances that are crucial for understanding the history of Kyoto and Japan, but they are also a museum of Japanese beauty, the fundamental sources of the aesthetic consciousness of the Japanese people. In particular, the full portrait of Zen temples cannot be seen anywhere but in Kyoto. But what we must keep in mind is that Kyoto is a rebuilt city.

Since Emperor Kanmu made Kyoto his capital in 794, the city has suffered fires, wars, earthquakes, epidemics, and terrible storms. The great Tarō-Jirō fires of 1177, 78, the Ōnin War (1467–77), the Tenmei Great Fire (1788), and other disasters reduced the buildings of the city to ashes and rubble, and each time the city was rebuilt.

焼失・再建がくり返されたのが京都の街で、それはもちろん寺社にも及んでいる。

東寺の五重塔は現在5代目であり、天龍寺は8回焼けている。清水寺、知恩院、相国寺、南禅寺、神護寺、伏見稲荷大社と枚挙にいとまがないほど、寺社は焼失と再建の歴史をもつ。

私たちが高仰する寺社の建物に平安期の面影を望むべきもないが、しかし、京都が千百年の都でありつづけたがゆえに人智が尽くされて甦った各寺社の姿と精神を見届けておくべきだろう。京都には私たちの忘れものがしっかり遺っている。

1644年に再建された東寺の五重塔
The five-story pagoda of Tō-ji (rebuilt in 1644)

Not only the city itself has been destruction by fire but many shrines and temples were damaged also.

The five-story pagoda of Tō-ji visible today is the fifth incarnation of that building. Tenryū-ji has been burned eight times. Kiyomizu-dera, Chion-in, Shōkoku-ji, Nanzen-ji, Jingo-ji, and Fushimi-Inari-taisha have all been reduced to cinders and rebuilt too many times to count.

We cannot see the image of the Heian period in the temples and shrines that we honor today, but what we can see is the image and spirit of the great human effort and knowledge that has been expended in preserving these temples over eleven hundred years. In Kyoto, the things we have forgotten still remain.

本書の読み方

本書は京都の寺社についての歴史、建物の特徴、建立の由来などを紹介したガイドブックです。左ページに日本語、右ページにはその対訳となる英語を掲載することで、英語学習の一助となるように構成されています。なお、英語は逐語訳ではなく、全体の意味に重点をおいた意訳になっています。

目　次

CONTENTS

京都市 宇治市
Kyoto City / Uji City

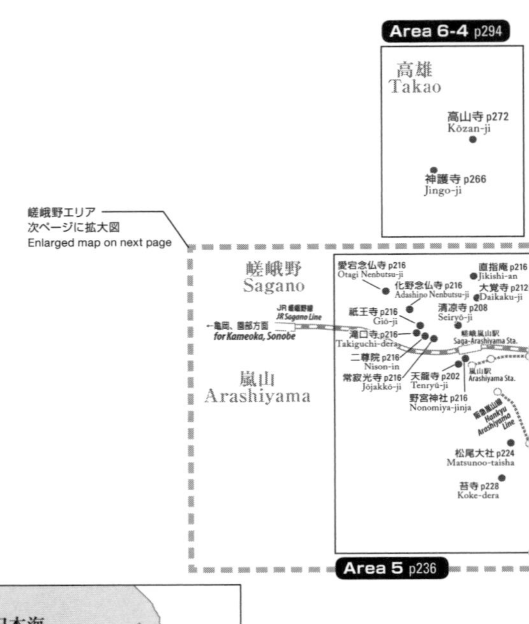

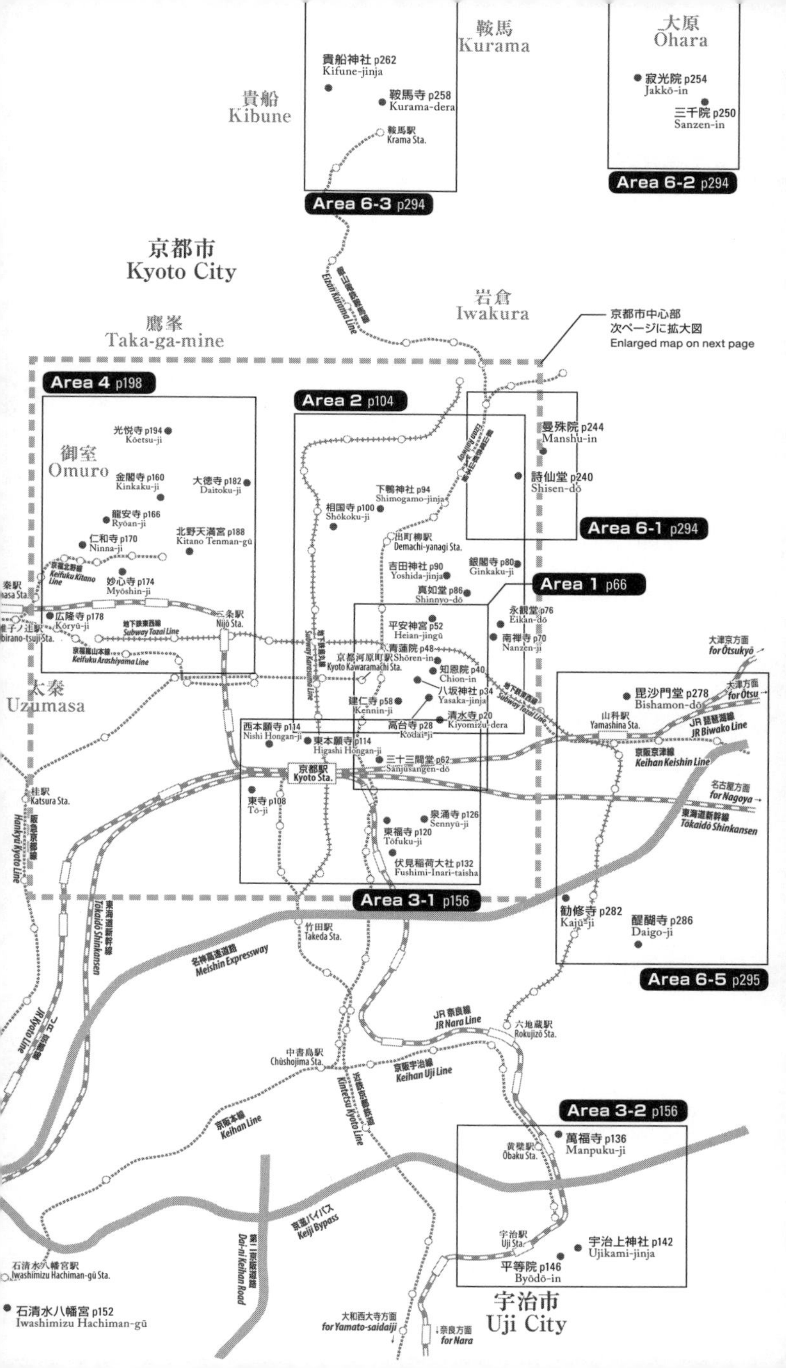

鞍馬
Kurama
大原
Ohara
貴船神社 p262
Kifune-jinja
鞍馬寺 p258
Kurama-dera
鞍馬駅
Krama Sta.
貴船
Kibune
寂光院 p254
Jakkō-in
三千院 p250
Sanzen-in
Area 6-3 p294
Area 6-2 p294
京都市
Kyoto City
Eizan Kurama Line
岩倉
Iwakura
京都市中心部
次ページに拡大図
Enlarged map on next page
鷹峯
Taka-ga-mine
Area 4 p198
Area 2 p104
光悦寺 p194
Kōetsu-ji
御室
Omuro
金閣寺 p160
Kinkaku-ji
大徳寺 p182
Daitoku-ji
龍安寺 p166
Ryōan-ji
仁和寺 p170
Ninna-ji
北野天満宮 p188
Kitano Tenman-gū
Keifuku Kitano Line
妙心寺 p174
Myōshin-ji
曼殊院 p244
Manshu-in
詩仙堂 p240
Shisen-dō
Eizan Railway
下鴨神社 p94
Shimogamo-jinja
相国寺 p100
Shōkoku-ji
Area 6-1 p294
出町柳駅
Demachi-yanagi Sta.
吉田神社 p90
Yoshida-jinja
銀閣寺 p80
Ginkaku-ji
真如堂 p86
Shinnyo-dō
Area 1 p66
永観堂 p76
Eikan-dō
南禅寺 p70
Nanzen-ji
広隆寺 p178
Kōryū-ji
地下鉄東西線
Subway Tozai Line
二条駅
Nijō Sta.
平安神宮 p52
Heian-jingū
青蓮院 p48
Shōren-in
京都河原町駅
Kyoto Kawaramachi Sta.
知恩院 p40
Chion-in
八坂神社 p34
Yasaka-jinja
Keifuku Arashiyama Line
Subway Karasuma Line
建仁寺 p58
Kennin-ji
清水寺 p20
Kiyomizu-dera
高台寺 p28
Kōdai-ji
大津京方面
for Ōtsukyō
太秦
Uzumasa
毘沙門堂 p278
Bishamon-dō
大津方面
for Ōtsu
山科駅
Yamashina Sta.
JR 琵琶湖線
JR Biwako Line
京阪京津線
Keihan Keishin Line
西本願寺 p114
Nishi Hongan-ji
東本願寺 p114
Higashi Hongan-ji
三十三間堂 p62
Sanjūsangen-dō
京都駅
Kyoto Sta.
桂駅
Katsura Sta.
Hankyu Kyoto Line
東寺 p108
Tō-ji
泉涌寺 p126
Sennyū-ji
東福寺 p120
Tōfuku-ji
伏見稲荷大社 p132
Fushimi-Inari-taisha
名古屋方面
for Nagoya
東海道新幹線
Tōkaidō Shinkansen
Area 3-1 p156
竹田駅
Takeda Sta.
勧修寺 p282
Kajū-ji
醍醐寺 p286
Daigo-ji
Area 6-5 p295
名神高速道路
Meishin Expressway
Tōkaidō Shinkansen
JR Kyoto Line
JR 奈良線
JR Nara Line
六地蔵駅
Rokujizō Sta.
中書島駅
Chūshojima Sta.
京阪宇治線
Keihan Uji Line
Kintetsu Kyoto Line
Area 3-2 p156
京阪本線
Keihan Line
萬福寺 p136
Manpuku-ji
黄檗駅
Ōbaku Sta.
京滋バイパス
Keiji Bypass
宇治駅
Uji Sta.
宇治上神社 p142
Ujikami-jinja
平等院 p146
Byōdō-in
石清水八幡宮駅
Iwashimizu Hachiman-gū Sta.
Dai-ni Keihan Road
石清水八幡宮 p152
Iwashimizu Hachiman-gū
大和西大寺方面
for Yamato-saidaiji
奈良方面
for Nara
宇治市
Uji City

京都市中心部
Center of Kyoto City

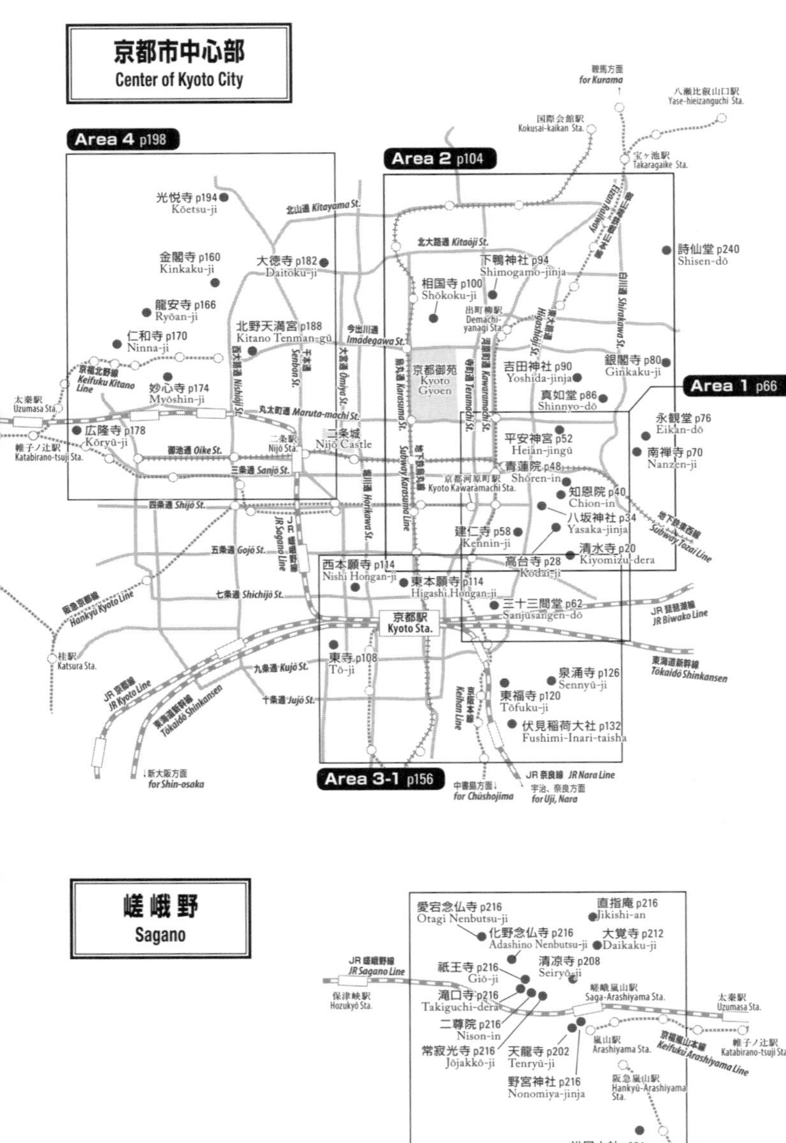

嵯峨野
Sagano

エリア 1
Area 1

京都の寺社観光のナンバーワンの地域
Kyoto's Number-One Area for Temple and Shrine Sightseeing

このエリアの中心はふたつある。ひとつは四条通の東端に建つ「八坂(やさか)神社」で、もうひとつが東山の深い緑黛(りょくたい)を背景にして広大な伽藍を構える「清水寺(きよみずでら)」だ。

このふたつの寺社はもちろん徒歩で行き来できる。足の便を考えれば、京阪電鉄の祇園四条駅に近い八坂神社から清水寺へ巡るのがいいだろうが、いったん山腹にある清水寺へ登ってしまえば、八坂神社方向へはずっと下り坂だから、汗をかかずにぶらりぶらりと楽しい散策になるだろう。

それに、「清水の舞台」から京都市街を眺めて、なるほど京都は盆地の底に広がる街だな、と実感するのも、京都観光の端緒としてはいい。

この清水寺からのルートを北に向かって歩けば、三年坂を下って、法観寺(ほうかんじ)の八坂の塔、「ねねの道」を通って円徳院(えんとくいん)、その東に建つ高台寺(こうだいじ)と見どころは多い。

高台寺から八坂神社はすぐである。桜の季節なら円山(まるやま)公園で花見をして、「八坂さん」に詣でてもいいし、さらに、知恩院(ちおんいん)、青蓮院(しょうれんいん)、そしてあでやかな朱塗りの平安神宮(へいあんじんぐう)と歩けば、まさに京都寺社巡りのゴールデンコースとなるわけで、十分に京都らしさを堪能できることになる。

もうひとつのルートは、八坂神社から、禅宗発祥の建仁寺(けんにんじ)、小さいながらも古い歴史を語る六道珍皇寺(ろくどうちんのうじ)や六波羅蜜寺(ろくはらみつじ)を参観して、五条通を南に渡って、七条界隈の妙法院(みょうほういん)、智積院(ちしゃくいん)、そして1001体の千手観音像が並ぶ三十三間堂(さんじゅうさんげんどう)の偉観を目前にするのもいい。

There are two centers in this area. One is Yasaka-jinja, at the eastern end of Shijō St., and the other is Kiyomizu-dera, the grand temple that is set off against a background of the green mountains of Higashiyama.

One can walk between Yasaka-jinja and Kiyomizu-dera. The most convenient route is to alight at Gion-Shijō Station on the Keihan Dentetsu Line, which is near Yasaka-jinja, and go from there. On the other hand, should you choose to visit Kiyomizu-dera first, then the walk to the shrine is a pleasant downhill stroll all the way.

Looking out from the "Kiyomizu stage" over the city of Kyoto will make it very clear that the city spreads out over the bottom of the basin, so it is a good starting point for exploring Kyoto.

Walking north from Kiyomizu-dera down Sannen-zaka, there are many things worth seeing, including Hōkan-ji's Yasaka-no-tō, Entoku-in via Nene no Michi street, and Kōdai-ji to the east.

From Kōdai-ji it is not far to Yasaka-jinja. If it is cherry-blossom time in the spring, you may want to go flower viewing and then visit Yakasa-san (Yasaka-jinja—Kyoto folk like to add the suffix *-san* to many sorts of things). You can also visit Chion-in, Shōren-in, and the elegant vermilion-lacquered Heian-jingū—this is the "Golden Course" of Kyoto tourism, and it will give you a real sense of the city.

Another route takes you from Yasaka-jinja to Kennin-ji, the cradle of Zen, and to the small but rich-in-history Rokudōchinnō-ji and Rokuharamitsu-ji. Then cross Gojō St. to the south to the Shichijō area, where you can visit Myōhō-in, Chishaku-in, and finally the Sanjūsangen-dō, with its 1,001 statues of thousand armed Kannon.

1

京都で最も人が訪れる寺

清水寺（きよみずでら）

京都市東山区清水1
075(551)1234
6時～18時
400円(春・夏・秋の夜の特別拝観は別料金)
www.kiyomizudera.or.jp
京都駅より市バス100・206系統　五条坂下車徒歩10分

二十数年連続で清水寺は京都を訪れる観光客の集客数第一位の栄冠に輝いている。それは修学旅行生の「定番」コースになっていることや、有名な寺社のなかでは最も早く午前6時から開門すること、さらに以前から夜のライトアップ拝観に力を入れていることなども要因として数えられるが、やはりこの清水寺の巨大な伽藍とその景観に魅力を感じる人が多いからだといえよう。

東山連山　比叡山から南へつづく京都市街の東側に連なる山系。36峰を数える。

京都市街の東を限る東山連山のひとつ音羽山（おとわやま）の麓から中腹にかけて清水寺の諸堂が展開し、境内にいたる坂道沿いには賑やかに茶店や土産物屋が軒をつらねる。清水坂、五条坂、茶碗坂、三年坂（産寧坂（さんねいざか））など清水寺に向かう道は、四季を問わず人波のとぎれることはない。

清水の舞台　「清水の舞台から飛び降りる」といえば、重大な決意をして事にあたるたとえ。

そして人々は清水寺が誇る「清水の舞台」へ足を早める。だが私たちは歴史を振り返りつつ、この大寺の堂塔をみていこう。

1. Kyoto's most visited temple
Kiyomizu-dera

Address: 1 Kiyomizu, Higashiyama-ku, Kyoto-shi
Tel: 075 (551) 1234
Hours: 6:00AM–6:00PM
Admission: ¥400 (Extra charge for spring, summer, and autumn night viewing)
www.kiyomizudera.or.jp/en/
10 min walk from Gojō-zaka bus stop, bus 100 or 206 from Kyoto Sta.

For more than twenty years, Kiyomizu-dera has had the distinction of attracting more visitors each year than any other temple or shrine in Kyoto. Reasons often cited for this include the temple's place as part of the itinerary of the standard Japanese school trip; the fact that Kiyomizu-dera opens at 6:00AM, earliest of all the well-known temples and shrines in Kyoto; and the effort it is putting into night-time illuminations. But the true reason is simply the sense of enchantment visitors experience amongst the temple's magnificent buildings and the beauty of its landscaping.

The temple's several halls spread up the hillside from the foot of Mt. Otowayama, part of the Higashiyama mountain chain marking the eastern boundary of urban Kyoto. The streets through the hills leading to the temple's grounds are lined with tea shops and souvenir vendors. You will find these streets—for example Kiyomizu-zaka, Gojō-zaka, Chawan-zaka, and Sannen-zaka (also known as Sannei-zaka)—filled with crowds of tourists regardless of the time of year.

Visitors often hurry to make their way to the main hall's vast veranda, or "stage"—the temple's centerpiece—but we would like to recommend a slower visit around the halls and pagodas, taking

清水寺の歴史

寺域の入口にまず朱色があざやかな仁王門が建つ。京都最大級の仁王像（像高365cm）が寺を護るように安置されている。石段を登ると鐘楼と八脚門の西門、そして優美な三重塔があらわれる。いずれも朱の塗り直しがおこなわれ、その朱色が音羽山の緑を背にして華やかである。経堂、そして田村堂とよばれる開山堂が建ち、そこには坂上田村麻呂夫妻、行叡上人、延鎮上人の清水寺の開創を物語る4人が祀られている。

778年（宝亀9）、大和（奈良県）の子島寺の延鎮上人は夢告によって東山山麓に赴き、音羽の滝で、白衣の行者行叡に出会う。そこで霊木から観音像を彫るようにいわれ、完成した観音像を滝上の草庵に祀ったのが、当寺のはじまりという。

さらに、798年（延暦17）に延鎮上人に帰依した征夷大将軍坂上田村麻呂（758~811）が金色の十一面千手観音像を造り、田村麻呂の夫人が807年（大同2）に仏堂を寄進して、その観音像を安置した。清水寺はそののちに、平安京を造営した桓武天皇（在位781~806）の御願寺となり、810年（弘仁元）には鎮護国家の道場となった。

桓武天皇 737～806。794年に長岡京より平安京へ遷都した天皇。

a look at some of the history of this magnificent temple as well.

The History of Kiyomizu-dera

At the entrance to the temple grounds stands the brilliant vermillion *niō-mon* gate, housing one of the largest *niō* statue (365 cm in height) in Kyoto. A climb up the stone steps brings the **bell tower**, the west gate, *Hakkyaku-mon*, and the elegant three-story pagoda into view. All of these have been repainted, and their vermillion creates a spectacular contrast against the green of Mt. Otowayama. This also affords a view of the temple's *kyō-dō* (storage hall for the sutras) as well as Tamura-dō, the initial hall (*kaizan-dō*) of Kiyomizu-dera's construction. Here are enshrined the spirits of the four central characters in the story of Kiyomizu-dera's beginnings: Sakanoue-no-Tamuramaro, his wife, Saint Gyōe, and Saint Enchin.

In 778, instructed by a dream, Saint Enchin left his own temple, Kojima-dera in Yamato (present-day Nara), and set out for the foot of Mt. Higashiyama. There, at Otowa Waterfall, he met the white-robed monk Gyōe, who instructed him to carve a statue of the Kannon from a sacred tree. When the statue was completed, they installed it in a grass hut at the top of the waterfall. This would be the beginning of the Kiyomizu-dera we see today.

Later, in 798, Shogun Sakanoue-no-Tamuramaro (758–811), who had been converted to Buddhism by Saint Enchin, had a golden thousand-armed Kannon statue made; and in 807 Sakanoue-no-Tamuramaro's wife dedicated a *butsu-dō* in which the Kannon was installed. Later, when the capital was moved to Heian-kyō (present-day Kyoto), Kiyomizu-dera served as Emperor Kanmu's dedicated place of worship, and in 810 the temple became a training hall for advocating government's reliance on Buddhism

南都六宗　奈良時代の仏教6宗派。三論・法相・華厳・律・成実・倶舎。

比叡山　京都市の北東に聳える(標高848m)。天台宗総本山の延暦寺の山号。「叡山」と通称。

清水寺はふるく北観音寺といい、南都六宗のひとつ法相宗として奈良興福寺に属していたため比叡山（北嶺）と「南都北嶺」の争いを生じ、たびたび堂塔は焼失したが、そのつど再建された。

本堂と「清水の舞台」

清水寺の本堂は1633年（寛永10）徳川3代将軍家光によって、今日私たちがみている正面約36m、側面約30mの巨大な建築物として再建された。寄棟造の本体に翼廊屋根を左右に付設した寝殿風様式で、屋根はすべてみごとな檜皮葺である。堂内は太い丸柱が並列して外陣と内陣を分けて、荘厳な雰囲気にみちている。

懸崖造　山際から木組によって前面に張り出した形の建築様式。舞台造ともいう。

そして、本堂の南に有名な**「清水の舞台」**が総檜張りで、空中に張り出して、新緑や紅葉の絶景となる錦雲渓とよばれる渓谷を見下ろす。懸崖造の代表的な建築物であるこの舞台は、高さ約13mで、下から見上げれば、縦横に組みあげられた豪壮な木組に驚嘆することだろう。

この大伽藍清水寺の全貌を眺めるには、本

for the protection of the nation.

Kiyomizu-dera, which in times past was known as Kitakannon-ji and is affiliated with the temple Kōfuku-ji in Nara through the Hossō sect of Buddhism, one of the Nanto roku-shū, or six major sects prominent. Several of the temples, halls, and pagodas were destroyed by fire in the fighting that broke out during the Nanto Hokuryō feud with the temple Enryaku-ji on Mt. Hieizan (Hokurei), but they were restored to their original appearance every time.

The Main Hall and the "Stage"

The main hall (*hondō*) we see today was magnificently rebuilt in 1633 by Tokugawa Iemitsu, third shogun of the Tokugawa dynasty, covering an area of approximately 36 meters across the front of the building by 30 meters across the sides. The structure employs a main hipped-roof construction with right and left transepts in the palatial shinden-zukuri style, and the roof is beautifully thatched with hinoki cypress bark. Inside the hall, rows of wide columns mark off the inner and outer sanctuaries, giving the hall an air of solemnity.

At the *hondō*'s south face we find **Kiyomizu-dera's** famed **veranda**, or "**stage**," with its all-*hinoki* cypress construction, suspended over the gorge Kin'un-kei, famous for its spectacular views of autumn leaves as well as the lush green of late spring and early summer. Standing at 13 meters in height, Kiyomizu-dera's veranda represents a classic of Japanese *kengai-zukuri* construction style (supporting a building over a hillside or over a body of water), and when viewed from the bottom, the latticework of beams supporting the stage is equally breathtaking.

For a full view of all of this spacious temple, we suggest having

堂の東に建つ同じ懸崖造の「奥の院」の舞台からか、南側の高台にある子安塔あたりからがいい。ほかの見どころをあげれば、奥の院の下の霊水「音羽の滝」、名庭をもつ子院の「成就院」、縁結びの神「地主神社」ということになろう。なお、清水寺から三年坂を下ると八坂の塔とよばれる法観寺の**五重塔**（高さ46m）が高々とみえてくる。

子安塔 清水寺子院泰産寺の三重塔（約15m）。安産祈願で知られる。

清水寺の全景
Panoramic view of Kiyomizu-dera

a look from either the *kengai-zukuri* veranda of the Oku-no-In to the east of the *hondō*, or from the hill to the south near the pagoda Koyasuno-tō. Other sights not to be missed include the Otowa Waterfall (Otowa no Taki), considered to be the holy water; the gardens of Jōju-in, one of the sub-temple of Kiyomizu-dera, and Jishu-jinja dedicated to the god of marriage. Also, walking down the hill Sannen-zaka as you leave Kiyomizu-dera will give you an impressive view of the **five-story pagoda** known as Yasaka-no-tō at the temple Hōkan-ji.

秀吉の正妻「ねね」の寺

高台寺

京都市東山区高台寺下河原町526
075(561)9966
9時〜17時30分
600円(円徳院・掌美術館を含む共通拝観券900円)
www.kodaiji.com
京都駅より市バス206系統　東山安井下車徒歩5分

高台寺は豊臣秀吉の没後、正妻である北政所（よび名はねね）が秀吉の菩提を弔うために草創した寺である。

秀吉の没年は1598年（慶長3）、ねねは落飾して高台院湖月尼と号する。秀吉の実子、秀頼を生んだ側室淀殿（茶々）が大坂城に入ったため、ねねは京都に隠棲して、亡夫の菩提寺とともに自らの終の栖となる寺院の建立を志した。

それを聞いた徳川家康は、秀吉の糟糠の妻で賢夫人、しかも孝養を尽くしたと評判の北政所を厚遇することは徳川家への反発をやわらげるために大いに利があると考え、東山の地に宏大な伽藍を建設して壮麗をきわめる高台寺を1606年（慶長11）に建立したのである。

伽藍と装飾の美

高台寺は東山連山の一峰、霊山の山麓に建

2. The temple of "Nene," wife of Hideyoshi, the man who unified Japan

Kōdai-ji

Address: 526 Kōdai-ji Shimokawara-chō, Higashiyama-ku, Kyoto-shi
Tel: 075 (561) 9966
Hours: 9:00AM–5:30PM
Admission: ¥600 (¥900 for full pass including Entoku-in and the Shō Museum)
www.kodaiji.com/e_index.html
5 min walk from Higashiyamayasui bus stop, bus 206 from Kyoto Sta.

After Toyotomi Hideyoshi's death, his legal wife Kita-no-Mandokoro (called "Nene") built the temple Kōdai-ji to pray for her husband's soul.

When Hideyoshi died in 1598, Nene left her life at court to become a nun and took the Buddhist name Kōdaiin. As the concubine Yodo-dono (Lady Yodo, also known as "Chacha"), who bore Hideyoshi's biological child Hideyori, had been installed at Osaka Castle, Nene retired to Kyoto, resolved to build a temple that would not only honor her husband, but also serve as a place to spend her final years.

When Hideyoshi's rival and soon-to-be shogun Tokugawa Ieyasu heard of this, he thought that doing good by Hideyoshi's old wife from the days before his rise to power, with her reputation of being a virtuous and loving wife, would help to soften any resentment of his grab at power. With his help, the enormous sanctuary was built in Higashiyama and the exquisite Kōdai-ji was completed in 1606.

The Beauty of Its Construction and Its Ornamentation

Kōdai-ji stands at the foot of Mt. Ryōzen, one of the

つ。庫裏の左手から境内に入ると、北側に建つ大雲院の瓦屋根と高楼の祇園閣が目の位置にみえ、この寺が名のごとく高台にあることが実感できる。

まず茶室の鬼瓦席や遺芳庵をみて、書院から方丈（仏殿）に上がる。方丈の前庭は勅使門を前にするすがすがしい**白砂の庭**で、方丈の東庭はふたつの池を囲む池泉回遊式庭園で小堀遠州作といわれる。

高台寺の伽藍の特徴は、橋廊によって諸堂がつながっていることで、いまは外側からしかみられないが、方丈と開山堂、さらに霊屋にまで「楼船廊」や「臥龍廊」という屋根つきの廊下がくねるようにあがっている。

開山堂は中興の僧三江を祀る。この堂の天井が見どころで、入口近くには秀吉が使用した船の天井、奥には北政所の御所車の天井が用いられている。よく目を凝らせば、その文様や色彩の華やかさがみてとれる。

開山堂から一段高いところにある霊屋には北政所の遺骸を葬っており、須弥壇の右に秀吉坐像、左に北政所坐像、中央に随求菩薩像を安置する。この須弥壇の柱や扉、勾欄、階段部分には有名な黒漆塗りに金色の蒔絵が施されている「高台寺蒔絵」がみられる。

大雲院　織田信長・信忠を弔うため正親町天皇が創建。通常非公開。

祇園閣　大倉財閥の大倉喜八郎が1927年に建てた高さ34mの祇園祭の鉾を模す高閣。

池泉回遊式庭園　池と築山を中心にした回遊して観賞する庭園。

小堀遠州　1579～1647。江戸時代前期の茶人・造園家。多様な造園で知られる。伏見奉行を勤めるなど有能な役人でもあった。

Higashiyama mountain chain. When entering the temple grounds from the left-hand side of the monks' quarters, the tile roof of Gion-kaku and the great tower of Daiun-in lie visible to the north, allowing one to appreciate how the temple got its name kōdai (lit. "high plateau").

We recommend first visiting the tea-ceremony rooms Onigawara no Seki and Ihō-an, and next walking up from the *shoin* (study-cum-living room) to the *hōjō* (Buddhist sanctum, main hall). The **white-sand gardens** of the *hōjō* lie before the *chokushi-mon* gate (imperial messenger's gate), and the *hōjō's* east garden, which encircles two ponds, is said to be the design of Kobori Enshū and is of the round pond style.

The distinctive feature of Kōdai-ji's construction is the bridge-like hallways that connect it to the temple's other halls. Now they can only be viewed from the outside, but the hallways, with names like Rōsen-rō and Garyō-rō, wind their ways from the *hōjō* to the patriarch's memorial hall (*Kaizan-dō*), and even to the mausoleum (*tamaya*).

The *Kaizan-dō* enshrines the spirit of the priest of restoration, Sankō. The ceiling is of particular interest. Part of it near the entrance was made from the boat used by Hideyoshi, and the rear section of the ceiling was constructed from the ox-drawn coach used by Kita-no-Mandokoro. A close examination reveals the splendor of their design and color.

One level above the *kaizan-dō*, the mausoleum (*tamaya*) kept the remains of Kita-no-Mandokoro. To the right of the altar sits an image of Hideyoshi, and to the left an image of Kita-no-Mandokoro, with the Zuigu bodhisattva (*Zuigu bosatsu*) installed in the center. The columns, doors, railings, and steps of the altar offer a glimpse of the famous Kōdai-ji *maki-e* technique of gold

円徳院　北政所の死後、甥の木下利房が木下家の菩提寺として創建。

さらに山腹をのぼると、内部が傘(からかさ)を開いたように竹を放射状に組んだところから「傘亭(かさてい)」とよばれる茶室、入母屋造(いりもやづくり)で二階建の茶室「時雨亭(しぐれてい)」が建っている。なお、高台寺の西側にかつて北政所の住居（化粧御殿(けしょうごてん)）があった地に円徳院(えんとくいん)が建つ。

円徳院の北庭
Entoku-in temple, looking for the north garden

powder decorations on **black lacquer**.

Further up the mountainside, one can also visit the **tea-ceremony rooms** Kasa-tei (lit. "umbrella room") with its radial-thatched bamboo reminiscent of an opened paper umbrella, and the two-storied Shigure-tei with its gable and hip roof (*irimoya-zukuri*). To the west of Kōdai-ji, the temple Entoku-in now occupies the site of Kita-no-Mandokoro's former residence (Keshō-goten).

3

町衆の熱気が満ちる神社

八坂神社

京都市東山区祇園町北側625
075(561)6155
境内参拝自由(祈禱は9時～16時)
www.yasaka-jinja.or.jp
京都駅より市バス100、206系統　祇園下車2分

京都人はものの名に「さん」をつけてよぶことが多い。「お揚げさん」から「天皇さん」とさまざまである。とくに寺社の名に「さん」をつける。「弘法さん」(東寺)、「天神さん」(北野天満宮)、「お西さん」(西本願寺)、「お東さん」(東本願寺)と別称や略称を用いる場合もあれば、「建仁寺さん」「清水さん」と本名に「さん」をつけることもある。八坂神社はその両方で「八坂さん」とよばれたり、「祇園さん」とよばれたりする。京都の中心地に住む人たちに最も親しまれている神社といっていい。

京都市街を東西に走る大通りのなかでいちばん賑やかな四条通の東の突き当たりに「八坂さん」は位置する。西の端は松尾大社で、ふたつの古社が四条通の両端を押さえているわけだ。

「八坂さん」の草創

八坂神社の創建については諸説があって、一説には656年に高麗国から来朝した八坂氏

3. The shrine that abounds with the spirit of the people of Kyoto

Yasaka-jinja

Address: 625 Kitagawa, Gion-machi, Higashiyama-ku, Kyoto-shi
Tel: 075 (561) 6155
Hours: 24 hours a day (Prayer requests accepted from 9:00AM–4:00PM)
Admission: Free
www.yasaka-jinja.or.jp/en/
2 min walk from Gion bus stop, bus 100 or 206 from Kyoto Sta.

The people of Kyoto often put the suffix *-san*, expressing deference, dearness, or politeness, to the names of things ranging from fried tofu (*o-age-san*) to the emperor himself (Tennō-*san*). In particular, one often hears this -san attached to the names of temples and shrines in Kyoto. Sometimes a variation of the name is used, such as "Kōbō-*san*" for Tō-ji, "Tenjin-*san*" for Kitano Tenman-gū, "O-nishi-*san*" for Nishi Hongan-ji, and "O-higashi-*san*" for Higashi Hongan-ji. Sometimes the full name of the temple is used, like in "Kennin-ji-*san*" and "Kiyomizu-*san*." Yasaka-jinja enjoys two alternate names, one of each type: "Yasaka-*san*" and "Gion-*san*," and is by far the best-loved shrine of the residents of central Kyoto.

Yasaka-san lies at the eastern end of Shijō St., busiest of the boulevards that run from east to west through Kyoto. The western end of Shijō St. is also bounded by one of Kyoto's oldest shrines, Matsunoo-taisha.

The Beginnings of Yasaka-san

There are many theories as to the origins of Yasaka-jinja. One theory states that in 656, ancestors of the Yasaka clan who came to

の祖が朝鮮の牛頭山に祀られていた素戔嗚尊の霊を移して、八坂の地に奉じたといわれる。素戔嗚尊はインドの祇園精舎の守護神である牛頭天王と同一視され、薬師如来の垂迹（仮の姿）とされる。また一説に、876年（貞観18）興福寺の僧円如が牛頭天王を迎えて、藤原基経の寄進により堂宇を建てたことがはじまりともいう。牛頭天王は疾病退散の神として祇園信仰が深まり、以来、厄除け、商売繁盛にご利益があるとされて多くの参詣客を集めている。

正門は下河原町通に面する南門だが、四条通の東端、東大路通に面した賑やかな西楼門のほうになじみがあろう。この西楼門は応仁の乱ののち1497年（明応6）に再建されたそのままの優美な姿をいまに伝えている。この楼門には蜘蛛の巣が張ることがなく、また雨だれの跡もつかないという不思議な話が伝わる。

八坂神社の境内と祇園祭

西楼門をくぐり境内に入ると、祇園のお茶屋や料亭などが奉納した提灯がぶら下がる華やかな**舞殿**があり、その北に、南をむいて建つ**本殿**は、**拝殿**と合わせてひとつの屋根で覆ったもので、ほかではみられない特殊な建築様式のため「祇園造」とよばれている。

現本殿は1654年（承応3）の再建で、2002年に修復された。本殿下には龍穴があって、

court from Koguryo established a new place of worship for Susanoo, a God revered on Mt. Gozusan in Korea. Susanoo is syncretized with Gozu Tennō, the guardian deity of Jetavana in India, and is considered to be the Shinto manifestation of the Yakushi nyorai (healing Buddha). Another theory places the shrine's beginnings in 876, with the main hall being built through a donation from Fujiwara-no-Mototsune when Kōfuku-ji monk Ennyo embraced faith in Gozu Tennō. As belief in Gozu Tennō's power to heal disease spread, this Gion Shinkō, or Gion faith, grew to include prayers for protection during life's critical times as well as for business prosperity and went on to claim more and more adherents.

The main gate to the shrine faces the boulevard Shimo-kawaramachi St. to the south, but most people are more familiar with the bustling "west two-story gate" (Nishi-rōmon) facing Higashiōji St. at the east end of Shijō St. This western gate has been in its present state since 1497, when it was rebuilt following the Ōnin War. An odd legend holds that spiders will not spin their webs on the gate and that raindrops leave no marks.

Yasaka-jinja's Grounds and the Gion Matsuri

Entering the grounds through the west two-story gate, one comes to the **stage hall** (*Bu-den*) hung with lanterns given as offerings to the shrine by the teahouses and *ryōtei* (traditional Japanese restaurants) of Gion. To the north of that stands the southward-facing the **main sanctuary** (*hon-den*), which shares a common roof with the **worship hall** (*hai-den*). This represents a unique design not to be found anywhere else, and thus is referred to as the Gion-zukuri style of construction.

The current main sanctuary was rebuilt in 1654 and underwent renovations in 2002. The main sanctuary sits on a *ryūketsu* (lit.

神泉苑　平安京遷都と同時期に、当時の大内裏の南に造営された庭園の遺構。

日本三大祭　ほかに東京日枝神社の山王祭（神田神社の神田祭とも）、大阪天満宮の天神祭。

京都三大祭　ほかに上賀茂神社と下鴨神社の葵祭、平安神宮の時代祭

その穴は神泉苑や東寺までつながっているという伝説がある。

京都の夏をさらに熱く彩る祇園祭は、八坂神社の祭礼で日本三大祭、京都三大祭のひとつに数えられている。この祭は、平安時代の初期、都に**疫病**が蔓延したさい、これを退散させるために、神泉苑に長さ2丈（約6m）の鉾66本をたてて厄災の除去を祈ったことがはじまりといわれている。

その後、一時中断したが、1500年（明応9）に町衆たちの手により復興した。7月1日から1カ月間にわたっておこなわれる祇園祭は、とくに16日の宵山、17日の山鉾巡行に大勢の見物客が集まる。

また大晦日の白朮詣では、キク科の植物で薬草の白朮で焚かれた火を吉兆縄に移し、家に持ち帰って**神棚**の灯明に点したり、その火を元火にして元旦の雑煮を炊くと1年間無病息災で過ごせるといわれている。深夜の初詣のあと、クルクルと火縄を回しながら家に戻る人も多くみられ、八坂神社独特の正月風景である。

円山公園　1886年開園。八坂神社の東に位置する86,600㎡の京都市最古の公園で桜の名所。

長楽寺　古くは「洛中随一絶景の霊地」といわれた時宗の寺。

春、夜桜見物の人で賑わう円山公園や市街を一望できる長楽寺も八坂神社の東側にあって、足を延ばしたいところだ。

"dragon hole" which is said to extend to the temples Shinsen-en (the Imperial Palace garden) and Tō-ji.

The Gion Matsuri is Yasaka-jinja's holy festival. This staple of Kyoto summer culture is not only one of the three great festivals of Kyoto, but is also counted as one of the three great festivals of Japan. The festival began during the early Heian period when an **epidemic** was sweeping across the city, and 66 floats, or *hoko*, each 2 *jō* (approx. 6 meters) in length, were erected at Shinsen-en as an offering to pray for an end to the plague.

In subsequent years the festival was temporarily suspended, but in 1500 the festival was brought back to life through the work of the townspeople. The festival is now a month-long event beginning July 1, with the yoiyama festival on July 16 and the parade of decorated floats (called *yama* and *hoko*) on July 17 attracting the greatest crowds of spectators.

A New Year's Eve event unique to Yasaka-jinja is the Okera Mairi (lit. "Atractylodis Prayers"). Atractylodis, a medicinal plant of the daisy family, is used to prepare a bonfire with which the faithful light specially prepared ropes to take the fire home and light the candles of their **household Shintō altars**. It is also believed that using fire from this flame to cook the New Year's *zōni* soup (rice-cake soup) the following morning will bring the family good health for the coming year. The sight of people making their way back home after New Year's prayers, twirling their burning ropes as they make their way through the night, is something you can only experience by spending New Year's here.

Yasaka-jinja is also frequented in spring by visitors making their way to Maruyama Park for night cherry-blossom viewing and to the temple Chōraku-ji, which offers an expansive view across all of Kyoto, both of which are located to the shrine's east.

浄土宗総本山としての偉容

知恩院（ちおんいん）

京都市東山区林下町400
075(531)2111
9時～16時
境内参拝自由（方丈庭園400円、友禅苑300円、共通券500円）
www.chion-in.or.jp
京都駅より市バス206系統　知恩院前下車徒歩5分

知恩院は全国に7000余もの寺院と約600万人の信者を擁する浄土宗（じょうどしゅう）の総本山で、すべてにおいてスケールの大きな寺院である。東山連山のひとつ華頂山（かちょうざん）を背後にして、7万3000坪という広大な境内をもつ。

三門　三は「空」「無相」「無願」を意味し、この門をくぐることで三つの解脱を得る。

まず豪壮な三門（さんもん）（国宝）。これは1621年（元和7）に徳川2代将軍秀忠（ひでただ）が建立した高さ24m、横幅50mの現存する木造門では日本最大のもので、高い**石段**上に建つためにいっそうその姿を大きくみせている。楼上中央に「華頂山」と霊元（れいげん）上皇の宸筆（しんぴつ）をいただき、内部には宝冠釈迦如来（ほうかんしゃかにょらい）坐像、十六羅漢（じゅうろくらかん）像などを安置する。

法然と知恩院の創建

この三門をくぐり、正面の男坂（おとこざか）とよばれる急峻な石段を登ると、広々とした境内に出る（右になだらかな女人坂（にょにんざか）がある）。御影堂（みえいどう）（国宝）

4. The majesty of the head temple of Jōdo Sect

Chion-in

Address: 400 Rinka-chō, Higashiyama-ku, Kyoto-shi
Tel: 075 (531) 2111
Hours: 9:00AM–4:00PM
Admission: Free (Hōjō garden ¥400, Yūzen-en ¥300, full ¥500)
www.chion-in.or.jp/en/
5 min walk from Chion-in-mae bus stop, bus 206 from Kyoto Sta.

As the head temple of the Jōdo sect (Pure Land sect), which has over 7,000 temples throughout Japan and approximately 6 million followers, Chion-in is big in every sense of the word. Against the backdrop of Mt. Kachōzan, one of the Higashiyama mountain chain, Chion-in boasts expansive grounds spanning 73,000 tsubo (approx. 24 hectares).

Let us begin with the grand *san-mon* gate (Main gate, national treasure), which was built in 1621 by Hidetada, second shogun of the Tokugawa dynasty. Standing 24 meters in height and 50 meters across, this is the largest surviving wooden gate in Japan today, and it looks even bigger set at the top of its **stone staircase.** The upper tier of the gate bears the inscription "Kachōzan" in the calligraphy of former Emperor Reigen, and inside there are statues including those of the crowned seated Buddha (*shaka nyorai*) and the sixteen Arhat.

Hōnen and the Founding of Chion-in

The steep stone staircase known as *Otoko-zaka* (lit. "man hill") lying directly beyond gives way to the wide expanse of the temple's grounds (to the right lies the more gentle *Nyonin-zaka*, lit. "woman

が南面して建ち、ここでは一度に2000人もの信者が集うことができるという。この浄土宗最大の堂宇は1639年（寛永16）に徳川3代将軍家光（いえみつ）によって建立され、開祖の法然（ほうねん）像を祀っている。

1133年（長承2）美作国（みまさかのくに）（岡山県）に生まれた法然（源空（げんくう）・1133〜1212）は9歳のとき父を失い、その遺言により13歳のとき比叡山で仏門に入る。のちに延暦寺三塔のひとつ西塔黒谷（さいとうくろだに）の叡空（えいくう）に師事して修行をかさねる。

延暦寺三塔　ほかに東塔、横川。

43歳のとき、ひたすら「南無阿弥陀仏（なむあみだぶつ）」と念仏を称えることによりすべての人が救われるという「専修（せんじゅ）念仏」の教えを確立して、比叡山を下りるのである。この1175年（承安5）を浄土宗開宗の年とする。

法然による浄土宗の教えは広く人心をとらえ、証空（しょうくう）や親鸞（しんらん）といった高弟を輩出して大教団となっていく。しかし旧来の仏教界から反発を招き、法然は四国へ、親鸞は越後へ配流されてしまう。法然は79歳で許されて京都に戻り、いま、知恩院境内の東側に建つ勢至堂（せいしどう）あたりに禅房を建てて住まうが、翌1212年（建暦2）に80歳で入寂（にゅうじゃく）する。

今日の知恩院の基礎となったのは、1234年（文暦元）に門弟の源智（げんち）が法然の**廟堂**をこの地に再建し、あわせて仏殿や御影堂などを建て

hill"). The *miei-dō* (national treasure) enshrining the temple's founder stands facing south and is said to be capable of accommodating two thousand worshippers at one time. This largest of all Jōdo sect sanctuaries was built in 1639 by Iemitsu, third shogun of the Tokugawa dynasty, and houses the statue of the sect's revered founder, Hōnen.

Born in Mimasaka Province (modern-day Okayama Prefecture) in 1133, Hōnen (Genkū 1133–1212) lost his father at age nine. At age thirteen, in accordance with his father's will, he became a monk at Mt. Hieizan (Enryaku-ji) and would later go on to receive instruction from Eikū.

At age forty-three, he left Mt. Hieizan and established the teaching of *Senju Nembutsu* (pray to Amida Buddha exclusively), which teaches that any person can achieve salvation by single-mindedly reciting the Nembutsu prayer: *Na Mu A Mi Da Bu Tsu*, or "I seek refuge in the Amitabha of Immeasurable Light and Eternal Life." It is this year, 1175, which is considered the founding year of Jōdo sect.

This new teaching captured the hearts of the people and developed into a great religion, producing disciples such as Shōkū and Shinran. But the new teaching provoked resentment among the Buddhist establishment of the day; Hōnen was exiled to Shikoku, and Shinran to Echigo Province. At the age of seventy-nine, Hōnen received pardon and was finally allowed to return to Kyoto. He set up his dwelling in the area now occupied by the Seishi-dō in the eastern part of Chion-in, but the following year (1212), he died at the age of eighty.

The foundations of today's Chion-in were laid by the disciple Genchi, who in 1234 rebuilt Hōnen's **mausoleum** (*byō-dō*) on these grounds and also established a Buddhist sanctuary and the

華頂山知恩教院大谷寺と号したことによる。

応仁の乱 1467～77年（応仁元～文明9）足利将軍家の相続問題と管領家による戦い。京都は焼き尽くされて甚大な被害を被った。

それらは応仁の乱などで焼失するが、その後、織田信長や豊臣秀吉により寺領が与えられ、また江戸時代に入って徳川家康が生母伝通院の菩提を弔うために、多大な援助をして大伽藍を完成させた。ところが1633年（寛永10）の火災で三門と経蔵を残してすべての諸堂を焼失してしまう。しかし、3代将軍家光が再興して旧観に戻すのである。

知恩院七不思議と梵鐘

広大な境内には、三門、御影堂、知恩院最古の建物の勢至堂、経蔵、唐門、方丈庭園など見どころは多い。また、「知恩院七不思議」がある。

御影堂正面裏に名工左甚五郎が魔除けに置いた「忘れ傘」は火災の守りで、御影堂から大方丈、小方丈につづく550mの「**鶯張りの廊下**」は、そこを歩くたびに鶯が鳴くような音をたてるので、警護のためのものといわれる。大方丈入口廊下の梁上に置かれた重さが30kgもある「大杓子」のほか、襖絵の雀があまりにもリアルに描かれたため飛び立ったといわれる大方丈菊の間の「抜け雀」、どこからみても目があう大方丈廊下の杉戸に描かれた「三方正面真向の猫」、そして知恩院が建てられる前からあったという「瓜生石」は黒門の西に残り、植えたはずのない瓜が一夜にして

miei-dō to honor his master. The complex was given the name "Kachō-zan Chionkyō-in Ōtani-dera."

These were burned during wars such as the Ōnin War, but land was later set aside for a new temple by Oda Nobunaga and Toyotomi Hideyoshi. Soon after the start of the Edo period, for the memorial services of his biological mother, Dentsūin, Tokugawa Ieyasu provided tremendous assistance and completed the great sanctuary. Fire would again burn all but the *san-mon* gate and the scripture house (*kyōzō*), but the third Tokugawa shogun, Iemitsu, would later restore Chion-in to its original splendor.

The Seven Wonders of Chion-in and the Temple Bell

There is no shortage of sights to see within the temple's spacious grounds: the *san-mon* gate, the *miei-dō*, the *seishi-dō* (oldest of the temple's buildings), the scripture house, the Chinese style *kara-mon* gate, the *hōjō* garden. But there are also the "Seven Wonders" of Chion-in.

Beneath the front eaves of the *miei-dō* is the Wasure-gasa (lit. "forgotten umbrella") placed there by the master craftsman Hidari Jingorō as a charm to protect against fire; stretching 550 meters from the *miei-dō* to the *ō-hōjō* (lit. "greater *hōjō*") to the *ko-hōjō* (lit. "lesser *hōjō*") is the **Nightingale Floor Corridor** (*uguisubari-no-rōka*), which gets its name from the chirping sound the floor makes when walked across. This is said to have been designed as a kind of security system. There is the 30-kilogram *ō-shakushi* (lit. "Great Rice Paddle") above the beams of the *ō-hōjō* entrance corridor; the tree sparrows known as *Nuke-suzume* (lit. "escaping sparrows") of the *ō-hōjō*'s Chrysanthemum Room (Kiku-no-Ma), which are so lifelike it is often said they have flown off the *fusama* (Japanese sliding doors) they are painted on; the "Ever-watching

伸びるという伝説をもつ。

さらに三門の楼上には三門の建築を命じられた大工五味金右衛門（ごみきんえもん）夫婦の**木像**がおさめられている「白木の棺（しらきのひつぎ）」がある。五味は建築予算を超えたときには自刃するつもりでいたが、後世に誇るものを建てようとしてやはり超過してしまい、夫婦で果てる。その夫婦の冥福を祈るために現在の場所に白木の棺がおかれたといわれる。

また、1636年（寛永13）に鋳造された**梵鐘（ぼんしょう）**は高さ3.3m、直径が2.8m、重さが約70tと巨大なもので、日本三大梵鐘のひとつである。除夜の鐘では、撞木（しゅもく）につながれた子綱を16人の僧侶が引き、親綱をもったひとりの僧侶が仰向けになって鐘に撞木をぶつける。京都の師走の歳時記である。

日本三大梵鐘　ほかに京都東山の方広寺と奈良東大寺の梵鐘。

Cat" (Sanpō Shōmen Mamuki no Neko) painted on the cedar doors in the *ō-hōjō* corridor, whose eyes are said to follow you regardless of the angle from which it is observed; and, predating Chion-in, the rock known as Uryū-seki, which legend holds can sprout gourds overnight despite no one ever having planted seeds.

At the top of the gate can be found the "plain wood coffin" containing **wooden statues** of the builder of the *san-mon* gate, Gomi Kin'emon, and his wife. Gomi vowed to kill himself if he went over budget on the construction project. When he exceeded his budget, despite having created a building that would be celebrated in posterity, he and his wife both fulfilled his promise. To ensure their happiness in the next world, the plain wooden casket was placed in its current location.

The **temple bell**, forged in 1636, is one of the largest in Japan, at 3.3 meters in height, 2.8 meters in diameter, and about 70 tons in weight. On New Year's Eve, sixteen monks are needed to pull back the rope holding the wooden bell hammer while a seventeenth monk holds the restraining rope on the bell. The resulting tone is one of the defining elements of New Year's Eve in Kyoto.

5

寺格の高さと佇まいの美

青蓮院

京都市東山区粟田口三条坊町69
075(561)2345
9時〜17時　500円　(春と秋の夜間拝観は別料金)
www.shorenin.com
京都駅より市バス5系統　神宮道下車徒歩3分

美しい寺院である。まず、その青蓮院という寺名。そして静謐な建物と庭。さらには三条神宮道へ抜ける道沿いの東側の景色は、楠の巨樹が青蓮院の石垣の上の土塁にしっかりと根を張り、大きく枝を広げて緑陰をつくるようすが、ここ青蓮院独特の佳景である。

青蓮院の**住持**は妙法院、三千院とともに叡山(天台)座主を兼ねるため天台宗のうち、叡山の三門跡寺院として寺格は高い。

妙法院　高倉天皇の皇子が入寺して以来門跡寺院となる。1614年(慶長19)から七条の現在地に移る。

門跡寺院　皇子や皇女、また貴族の子弟が住職となった寺院。

かつては比叡山僧坊のひとつで、最澄が草創、往時の場所の近くにあった青蓮池にちなんで青蓮坊といい、1150年(久安6)関白藤原師実の子、僧行玄が住持して院名に変わった。そののち、いまの粟田口三条坊に移り、鳥羽上皇(在位1107〜23)の皇子覚快法親王が第2世で入寺、天台座主となり、当院は門跡寺院として、粟田御所、東山御所とよばれることになる。

5. A temple with high status and beautiful grounds

Shōren-in

Address: 69 Awadaguchi Sanjōbō-chō, Higashiyama-ku, Kyoto-shi
Tel: 075 (561) 2345
Hours: 9:00AM–5:00PM
Admission: ¥500 (Additional fee for evening entry in spring and fall)
www.shorenin.com/english/
3 min walk from Jingu-michi bus stop, bus 5 from Kyoto Sta.

This is a beautiful site, starting with its name, which means "Temple of the Blue Lotus," and continuing with the serenity of its buildings and gardens. The landscape on the eastern side of the street that runs off of Sanjō-jingū St. is lined with giant camphor trees that spread their green canopies wide, a unique feature of Shōren-in's grounds.

The head of the Tendai sect is chosen from among the **chief priests** of Shōren-in, Myōhō-in and Sanzen-in. These are three of the Tendai *Monzeki* temples, which were taken care of by members of the imperial family, so the status of this temple is considered to be very high.

A priest formerly from Mt. Hiei named Saichō founded the temple, naming it after the nearby *Shōren* pond, and in 1150, the monk Gyōgen, the son of Fujiwara-no-Morozane, became head priest and changed the name to Shōren-in. Subsequently the location of the temple was moved to what is now known as Awataguchi Sanjōbō, and the son of former Emperor Toba (r. 1107–23), Prince Kakukai, became the second head of the temple after Gyōgen. The prince became the head priest of the Tendai sect, and the temple became known as a *Monzeki* temple, also called Awata Palace or Higashiyama Palace.

青蓮院の名僧と名庭

青蓮院の名を高めた僧がふたりいる。ひとりは、4度も天台座主になった慈円（慈鎮）で、全7巻におよぶ歴史書『愚管抄』を著し、日本の歴史を仏教的な世界観で解釈した。

親鸞が9歳で出家するさいも青蓮院において慈円の得度を受けている。そのため本願寺との関係は深く、歴代の本願寺法主はこの寺で得度したのである。

もうひとりの僧は伏見天皇（在位1287〜98）の皇子尊円法親王で、書に優れ、青蓮院流をおこす。江戸時代にこの流派が御家流となり、公文書はこの流派の書体を用いた。

そのような高僧たちが住持した青蓮院も応仁の乱で焼失、その後、再建と焼失をくり返し、江戸時代には知恩院の造営により寺域を割譲した。そして不幸なことに1893年（明治26）9月の火災で諸堂をことごとく失ってしまった。いま私たちがめぐる建物は、明治中期以後の建築である。

しかし、寺宝は貴重なものが多く残り、宸殿浜松の間の**襖絵**、廊下杉戸の祇園会山鉾図、さらに「青不動」とよばれる不動明王二童子画像は、日本三不動のひとつとして著名である。

日本三不動　ほかに三井寺の黄不動と高野山明王院の赤不動。

庭園も小堀遠州作といわれる「霧島の庭」。これは山の斜面に霧島躑躅を一面に植えたもので、また、好文亭前の**苔の庭**、相阿弥作と伝えられる林泉庭園もともに名園として知られている。

Famous Priests and Gardens of Shōren-in

Two priests in particular made the name of Shōren-in famous. One was Jien (Jichin), who was the head of the Tendai sect for four times and wrote the seven-volume work of history, the *Gukanshō*, which interpreted Japan's history from a Buddhist point of view.

When Shinran who became the founder of the Jōdo Shinshū sect was nine years old, he entered religion under Jien, so the relationship between Shōren-in and Shinran's temple, Hongan-ji, are deep.

Another famous priest at Shōren-in was Son'en, a son of Emperor Fushimi (r. 1287–98), who was highly skilled at **calligraphy** and inaugurated the Shōren-in style. In the Edo period, this style became known as the *Oie* style and was used as the style of calligraphy for official documents.

Yet despite these famous head priests, Shōren-in too was burned down during the Ōnin War. It was destroyed and rebuilt several times subsequently, and in the Edo period, Shōren-in was forced to cede territory for the construction of Chion-in. Then, in 1893, an September fire destroyed nearly all the buildings of Shōren-in, so the structures we see today were all built since the mid-Meiji era.

However, many of the temple's treasures were preserved, including the **screen paintings** in the *Shinden*, Hamamatsu-no-ma, the Gion Festival's *Yama-hoko* float drawings, and the "Blue Fudō, (Acala)" a drawing of the Buddhist deity that is considered one of the three finest in Japan.

The garden is a Kirishima garden created by Kobori Enshū, with Kirishima azalea covering a steep mountainside. The *rinsen* (forest and water) garden—said to have been created by Sō ami—and the **moss garden** in front of the Kōbuntei tea-ceremony room are also famous.

6

平安京最初と最後の天皇を祀る

平安神宮

京都市左京区岡崎西天王町97
075(761)0221
6時〜17時(時期により変動あり)　境内参拝自由
神苑は8時30分〜16時30分(時期により変動あり) 600円
www.heianjingu.or.jp
京都駅より市バス5系統　京都会館・美術館前下車1分

平安京は794年（延暦13）から1869年（明治2）の東京奠都までつづいた。日本の都のなかで最も永く繁栄した都であった。

しかし、天皇や公卿らが東京に移ると、京都は衰退の兆しをみせる。そこで考えられたのが京都市民共通の祭神として平安京の建設者であった桓武天皇を祀る平安神宮の建立であった。1895年（明治28）の平安遷都千百年の年に創建、さらに1940年（昭和15）平安京最後の孝明天皇も合祀された。

孝明天皇　在位1846〜66。公武合体を支持し、皇妹和宮の降嫁を容認した天皇。

時代祭　平安神宮創建の年にはじまった祭礼。10月22日に時代風俗行列が都大路をめぐる。

三条通から神宮道を北に上がると、まず高さ約24m、柱の直径は3m強の朱塗りの巨大な**鳥居**が目に入る。この大鳥居をくぐり、正面に碧瓦に朱塗りの柱が華やかな応天門をみて、広々とした境内に入ると、その先に、碧瓦と朱色の大極殿、東の蒼龍楼、西の白虎楼が、ゆったりと横列している。この景色は、やはり平安朝の流麗さというべきである。これらの建物は平安京政庁の中心的建物朝堂院

6. The shrine for the first and last emperors of Heian-kyō

Heian-jingū

Address: 97 Okazaki Nishi-tennō-chō, Sakyō-ku, Kyoto-shi
Tel: 075 (761) 0221
Hours: Grounds: 6:00AM–5:00PM;
gardens: 8:30AM–4:30PM (May vary depending on season)
Admission: Grounds: free; gardens: ¥600
www.heianjingu.or.jp
1 min walk from Kyoto Kaikan/Bijutsukan-mae bus stop, bus 5 from Kyoto Sta.

Heian-kyō, now Kyoto, was the imperial capital from 794 until 1869, when the emperor's seat was transfered to Tokyo, the longest period any Japanese city has served as capital.

But when the emperor and his court moved to Tokyo, Kyoto began showing signs of decay. One response to counter this decline was the establishment of the Heian-jingū to dedicate to Emperor Kanmu, the founder of Heian-kyō, as the patron saint of the people of Kyoto. Built in 1895, which was the 1,100th anniversary of the establishment of the capital at Kyoto, the shrine also deified Emperor Kōmei in 1940, who was the last emperor to reign in the city.

As you walk north up Jingū-michi St. from Sanjō St., the first thing to strike your eye is the enormous 24-meter-tall *torii* gate (**sacred gate**), with its vermilion painted columns 3 meters in diameter. Passing under the *torii*, you are greeted by the Ōten-mon gate, with its blue-green tiles contrasting with the bright vermilion of its columns, and the wide, open space of the temple grounds. Other temple buildings, including the similarly blue-tiled and vermilion-columned *daigoku-den* outer sanctuary, the Shōryū-rō to the east and the Byakko-rō to the west stretch out before you,

を模して、8分の5のスケールで造られたものである。

平安神宮４つの神苑

白虎楼の北に神苑の入口がある。この神苑は社殿を背後から取り囲むようにして、右回りに南西中東の4つの庭からなり、約1万坪におよぶ日本庭園である。

南神苑は八重紅枝垂桜の名所であるとともに、平安時代庭園の特色である野筋（入り組んだ細道）と遣水（流れ込む小川）が設けられ、また「平安の苑」は『源氏物語』や『枕草子』といった平安時代の書物に登場する草木が植えられて、その作品の一節とともに観賞することができる。

南神苑の樹林を抜けると白虎池のある西神苑へとつながる。この池畔には花菖蒲が群生し、中神苑の蒼龍池には周囲に約千株の杜若が植栽され、池の水面には睡蓮が浮かんでいる。ここにある「臥龍橋」とよばれる**飛び石**はかつての三条大橋と五条大橋の橋脚が用いられたものだ。

さらに東へと歩くと、東山を借景にして、尚美館、泰平閣の姿を水面に映す栖鳳池がみえる。池には中国の伝説の仙郷「蓬莱山」をあらわしたという「鶴島」と「亀島」を造る。泰平閣とよぶ橋廊を渡り、そこから東、また西方向を眺めると、それぞれに異なった表情をみせ、とくに春には鏡のように静かな水面

evoking the graceful style of the Heian period. These buildings were all modeled on the *chōdō-in*, the main administrative building of Heian-kyō government, although slightly smaller (5/8 scale).

The Four Shrine Gardens

The entrance to the shrine gardens is to the north of the Byakko-rō. Providing a backdrop to the shrine buildings, the four gardens—South, West, Middle, and East—total approximately 10,000 *tsubo* (33,000 square meters) of Japanese gardens.

The South Garden, in addition to being famous as a site for *yaebenishidare* cherry-blossom viewing, also contains landscaping characteristic of the Heian period, a *nosuji* arrangement of narrow paths and an *yarimizu* network of small streams. You will also find the Heian-no-Sono garden, containing plants and trees that are mentioned in famous Heian-period literary works such as *the Tale of Genji* and *the Pillow Book* of Sei Shōnagon.

Passing out through the grove of the South Garden, you can make your way to the West Garden, with the *byakko* pond. The pond is noted for its flowering irises and flags, as is *sōryū* pond in the Middle Garden. The surface of this pond is also covered with floating water lilies. The **stepping stones** in *sōryū* pond, known as the *garyū-kyō*, were formerly used as bridge supports for the Sanjō-Ōhashi and Gojō-Ōhashi bridges in the center of the city.

Walking into the East Garden, you will see reflected in the surface of the *seihō* pond the forms of the Shōbi-kan and Taihei-kaku halls against the background of the Higashiyama mountains. In the pond lie two small islands, *tsuru-shima* and *kame-shima*, which are said to depict Mt. Hōraisan of Chinese legend. When you cross the bridge of the Taihei-kaku, it is possible to look east and west for two very different views. This is particularly striking

に桜花がいっせいにそのあでやかな姿を映すのである。桜の名所として京都の春を代表するのが、ここ平安神宮である。

平安神宮の神苑
The shrine garden of the Heian-jingū

in the springtime when the cherry blossoms blanket the mirror-like surface of the pond in a most bewitching manner. This is one of the scenes that makes the Heian-jingū a totemic location for Kyoto's springtime blossom viewing.

京都で最初の禅寺

建仁寺

京都市東山区大和大路通四条下ル
小松町584
075(561)6363
10時〜17時
境内参拝自由(伽藍拝観500円)　www.kenninji.jp
京都駅より市バス100、206系統　東山安井下車徒歩5分

日本の**禅宗**は、臨済宗、曹洞宗、黄檗宗の三宗で、建仁寺は日本臨済宗の宗祖栄西（ようさい）が京都で最初に建てた**禅寺**である。それは栄西が2度におよぶ入宋後の1202年、元号でいえば建仁2年で、それにより寺名とした。

しかし当初は比叡山など旧仏教からの反発を減じるため、天台、真言、禅の三宗兼学の寺としており、1265年（文永2）、11世住持の蘭渓道隆によって禅刹として定まった。

なお、栄西は中国から日本に茶の種を持ち帰り、茶の効用と栽培方法を広め、『喫茶養生記』を著した僧として知られる。

その後、建仁寺は室町幕府3代将軍足利義満が定めた**京都五山**の第三位となり、大いに隆盛するが、たびたびの火災で堂宇を失い、そのたびに再建をくり返す。明治維新までは約5万4000坪という寺域の広さを誇っていたが、上知令によって半分以下に減らされてしまった。

五山（京都五山）
1386年に足利義満が新たに制定した臨済宗の五大寺。天龍寺、相国寺、建仁寺、東福寺、万寿寺の順位で、南禅寺を「五山の上」とした。

7. Kyoto's first Zen temple
Kennin-ji

Address: 584 Komatsu-chō, Yamatoōji-dōri Shijō-sagaru, Higashiyama-ku, Kyoto-shi
Tel: 075 (561) 6363
Hours: 10:00AM–5:00PM
Admission: Free (Entry to temple: ¥500)
www.kenninji.jp/english/
5 min walk from Higashiyamayasui bus stop, bus 100, 206 from Kyoto Sta.

Japanese **Zen Buddhism** is divided into three major sects: Rinzai, Sōtō, and Ōbaku. Kennin-ji, founded by Eisai (also called Yōsai), the founder of the Rinzai sect, was the first **Zen temple** in Kyoto. This was in 1202, the second year of the Kennin era, which gave the temple its name.

Initially, under pressure from the powers of the old Buddhism of Hieizan (Tendai Sect), Kennin-ji followed the practices of Tendai, Shingon and Zen, but in 1265, the temple focused on Zen practice under the leadership of the eleventh head priest, Rankei Dōryū.

Eisai is famous for bringing back knowledge about the uses and cultivation of tea from China to Japan, and wrote a well-known book on the subject entitled the *Kissa Yōjōki*.

Subsequently, Kennin-ji was named the third of the Five Great Kyoto Rinzai Zen temples defined by the third Muromachi shogun, Ashikaga Yoshimitsu and enjoyed the ensuing prosperity. However, it repeatedly suffered fires that destroyed various buildings, which were repeatedly reconstructed. By the time of the Meiji Restoration it had amassed holdings of approximately 54,000 *tsubo* (178,524m^2), but this was reduced by more than half during, Jōchi-rei, Meiji land reforms.

禅寺の伽藍と寺宝

四条通に弁柄色の壁をみせる「一力」の角を南に、お茶屋が建ち並ぶ花見小路通をゆくと、建仁寺の裏門から境内に入ることができるが、正統な拝観順路とはいえない。できればまず八坂通に門を開く勅使門に佇んで、その勅使門から放生池、三門、法堂、方丈と並び、東西に境内塔頭を配する禅宗伽藍の迫力ある景観をぜひみていただきたい。

三門の先に建つ法堂は、1765年（明和2）の建設と伝える。重厚さを二層の大瓦屋根で示し、枯淡さを初層の白壁と火頭窓であらわす。

方丈は1599年（慶長4）に安芸国（広島県）の安国寺から移築したもので青緑色の銅板葺の屋根がゆったりとして端正な姿をみせている。この方丈前庭は白砂敷に砂紋を描き緑苔と巨石を配してのびのびとした造園である。

建仁寺には美術品も多く、法堂の天井画「双龍図」、また方丈内の襖絵には1940年（昭和15）に橋本関雪が描いた「生々流転」「伯楽」があり、さらに方丈の裏の部屋には有名な「風神雷神図」が陶板複製となって置かれている（実物は京都国立博物館に寄託）。

なお、建仁寺の南、松原通付近に盂蘭盆会の「精霊迎え」で知られる六道珍皇寺と空也上人由来の六波羅蜜寺がある。とくに六波羅蜜寺の宝物館に展示される仏像肖像群は傑作。

六道珍皇寺　この寺の前を「六道の辻」といい、人間が善悪の業により、地獄、餓鬼, 畜生、修羅, 人間、天のいずれかに赴く分岐点とされる。

六波羅蜜寺　市中をめぐり踊念仏をおこなった空也上人が建てた仏堂が前身の寺。

The Zen Temple and Temple Treasures

Although it is possible to enter Kennin-ji through the back entrance on Hanamikōji St. amid the teahouses of Shijō St., if at all possible we recommend that you enter through the *chokushi-mon* gate on Yasaka St. Entering this way, one can appreciate the striking array of buildings stretching from east to west through the temple precincts, in between there are *hōjō* pond, the *san-mon* gate, the *hattō* (Dharma hall), and the *hōjō* (abbot's quarters).

Across the *san-mon* gate, the *hattō* built in 1765 is there. Its two-story tiled roof shows its solidity, while the white walls of the first story and the distinctively shaped "*katō*" windows express its elegant simplicity of style.

The *hōjō* was transported to its present site in 1599 from Ankoku-ji in Aki (Hiroshima prefecture); its green copper roof has a calm, noble appeal. The garden in front of the *hōjō* is notable for its design of white sand and the easy grace of its arrangements of green moss and large stone megaliths.

Kennin-ji also possesses many important works of art, including the **ceiling painting** "*Sōryū-zu*" (twin dragons) in the *hattō* and the screen paintings in the *hōjō*, "*Seisei Ruten*" and "*Hakuraku*," painted in 1940 by Hashimoto Kansetsu. In a rear room of the *hōjō* is a ceramic replica of the famous "Wind and Thunder Gods" (the original is in the Kyoto National Museum).

Just south of Kennin-ji, near Matsubara St., are two temples, Rokudōchinnō-ji (known for its celebration of Ullambana which honors the spirits of the dead) and Rokuharamitsu-ji, which boasts some masterpieces of statues and portraits of the Buddha displayed in its treasure hall.

8

創建当時の姿を残す
三十三間堂

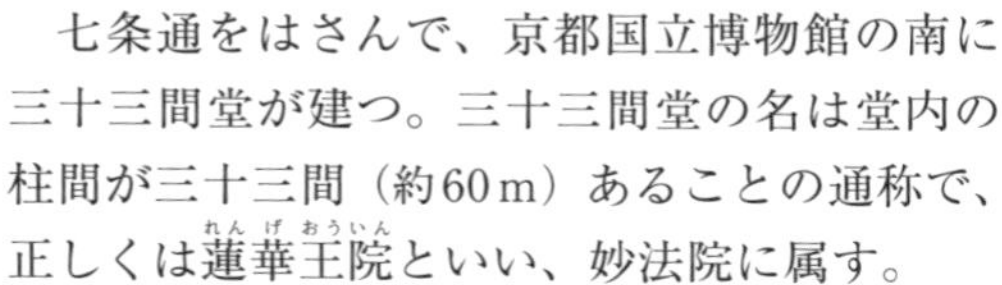

京都市東山区三十三間堂廻り町
075(561)0467
8時～17時(11月16日～3月31日は9時～16時)　600円
www.sanjusangendo.jp
京都駅より市バス206・208系統　博物館三十三間堂前徒歩1分

七条通をはさんで、京都国立博物館の南に三十三間堂が建つ。三十三間堂の名は堂内の柱間が三十三間（約60m）あることの通称で、正しくは蓮華王院といい、妙法院に属す。

後白河上皇はこの地周辺に法住寺御所を造営され、そこに平清盛の援助で蓮華王院という寺を建てた（1164年）。その寺の本堂が三十三間堂である。一度火災にあうが1266年（文永3）に再建されて旧観をとり戻す。その姿を私たちはいまみているのだ。

熱烈な信仰心のあらわれ

三十三間堂の外観は、総檜の入母屋造で本瓦葺、正面の長さは約120m、幅は約17mと異様な長さである。

そして、驚くのが堂内部である。内陣を広くとって、中央に丈六の大きな千手観音坐像を安置し、その左右に10段の段を設け、それ

8. Retaining the form of its initial construction

Sanjūsangen-dō

Address: Sanjūsangen-dō Mawari-chō, Higashiyama-ku, Kyoto-shi
Tel: 075 (561) 0467
Hours: 8:00AM–5PM (November 16–March 31: 9:00AM–4:00PM)
Admission: ¥600
www.sanjusangendo.jp
1 min walk from Hakubutsukan/Sanjūsangen-dō-mae bus stop, bus 206 or 208 from Kyoto Sta.

Sanjūsangen-dō stands just south of the Kyoto National Museum, spanning Shichijō St. Its name comes from the thirty-three bays between the columns of its main hall. The official name of the temple of which the Sanjūsangen-dō is a part is Rengeō-in, which is attached to the Myōhō-in, a Tendai temple.

Former Emperor Goshirakawa ordered an imperial palace to be built on the site, and with the help of Taira-no-Kiyomori, built the temple Rengeō-in in 1164. The Sanjūsangen-dō was the main hall (*hondō*) of the temple. It burned down once but was rebuilt in 1266 to match its original appearance. That is the building that we see today.

A Demonstration of Passionate Faith

The exterior of the Sanjūsangen-dō is of all-*hinoki* cypress in the gable and hip style with a tiled roof. The façade is 120 meters long, with a width of approximately 17 meters, an unusual length.

A truly surprising scene awaits the visitor inside the main hall. In the wide inner hall stands a large (approx. 4.85 meters high) statue of the thousand-armed Kannon, surrounded on both sides

ぞれ500体の正しくは「十一面千手千眼観世音」という観音立像が立ち並ぶ。

堂内は東面の障子越しの日射しがあって、この1001体という圧倒的な数の仏像を鈍く金色に光らせている。息をのむ偉観である。1001体の仏像の前をゆっくり歩いて眺めてもいい、また両端に立って横列する仏像群の迫力を瞼に焼きつけてもいい。熱烈な信仰心とはこのような驚くべき造形物を生み出し得るということを実感する。

また観音は33に化身するということから、この三十三間堂の仏は3万3033体になるのだともいう。また堂内の両端にひときわ高く置かれる**風神**と**雷神**像、観音立像の前に並ぶ二十八部衆の姿もじつに優れた彫刻である。

この横長な堂を利用して、「通し矢」が毎年1月におこなわれ、京都の歳時記には欠かせない行事である。

この界隈には、天台宗門跡寺院として格式のある妙法院と真言宗智山派の総本山である智積院が寺域を広げている。智積院の収蔵庫には桃山時代を代表する画家長谷川等伯父子の**障壁画**が展示されているのでみておきたい。さらに三十三間堂の東に建つ養源院には、俵屋宗達の**杉戸絵**「白象」が残っている。

通し矢　本堂西側の約60mの射場で直径1mの的を射る。江戸時代には120m先の的に一昼夜かけて弓を引く大矢数が競われた。

智積院　1603年(慶長8)に再建の全容が整って、真言宗の教学を伝える「学山智山」としての地位をもつ。

養源院　浅井長政の長女で豊臣秀吉の側室となった淀君が父の菩提を弔うため1594年(文禄3)に建立。

by one thousand statues of Kannon, each with eleven faces and one thousand arms and one thousand eyes.

When the sunlight streams through the screens on the eastern façade, the 1,001 statues are bathed in a soft golden light. It is truly a breathtaking sight. You may choose to stroll slowly before the statues or let the overwhelming array of statues to your left and right strike your eyes where you stand. This is an opportunity to appreciate the passion of religious feeling that could create such an amazing display.

Since Kannon is said to be manifested in thirty-three different forms, the 1,001 statues in this hall actually represent 33,033 bodies of the Kannon. The statues of the **wind and thunder gods** placed high in the hall and the twenty-eight other Buddhist deities in front of the Kannon are also superlative examples of wood carving.

Every year in January the great length of the hall is used to hold the *tōshiya* archery contest, a Kyoto seasonal event that is not to be missed.

Nearby are two important temples, the Myōhō-in, a major *monzeki* temple of Tendai sect, and Chishaku-in, the head temple of the Shingon Sect Chizan school. Chishaku-in boasts **wall paintings** panels and screens painted by Hasegawa Tōhaku, the representative painter of the Momoyama period, and his son. To the east of the Sanjūsangen-dō is Yōgen-in, where one can see **cedar-panel paintings** of white elephants by Tawaraya Sōtatsu.

エリア 1　Area 1

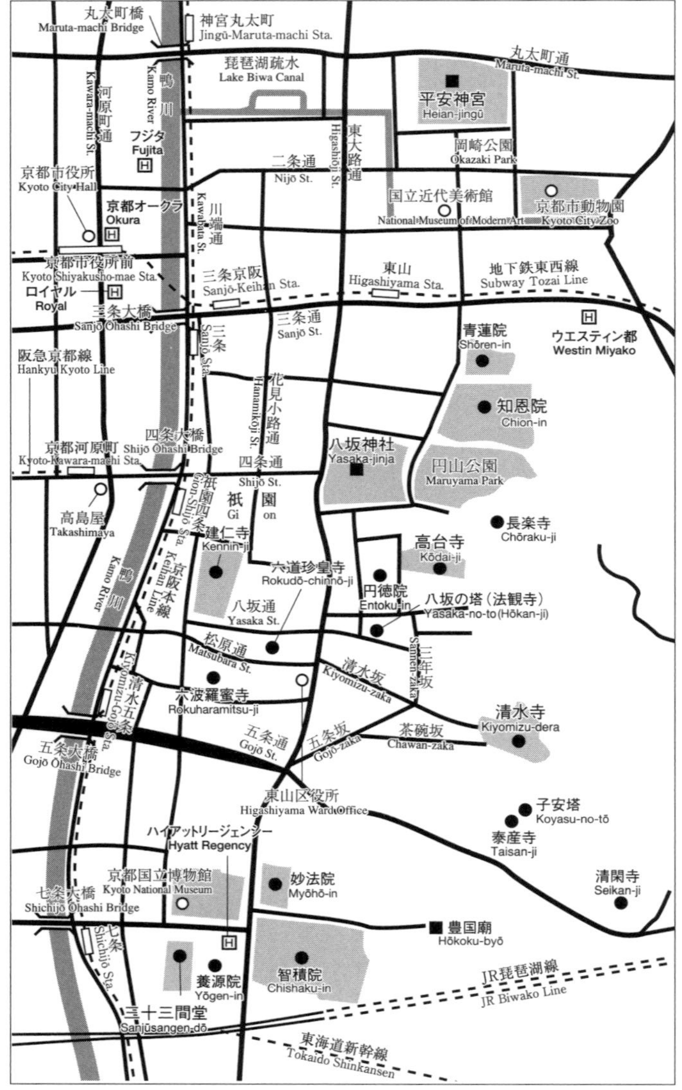

丸太町橋
Maruta-machi Bridge
神宮丸太町
Jingū-Maruta-machi Sta.
丸太町通
Maruta-machi St.
琵琶湖疏水
Lake Biwa Canal
平安神宮
Heian-jingū
河原町通
Kawara-machi St.
鴨川
Kamo River
フジタ
Fujita
東大路通
Higashiōji St.
岡崎公園
Okazaki Park
二条通
Nijō St.
京都市役所
Kyoto City Hall
国立近代美術館
National Museum of Modern Art
京都市動物園
Kyoto City Zoo
京都オークラ
Okura
川端通
Kawabata St.
京都市役所前
Kyoto Shiyakusho-mae Sta.
三条京阪
Sanjō-Keihan Sta.
東山
Higashiyama Sta.
地下鉄東西線
Subway Tozai Line
ロイヤル
Royal
三条大橋
Sanjō Ōhashi Bridge
三条
Sanjō Sta.
三条通
Sanjō St.
青蓮院
Shōren-in
ウエスティン都
Westin Miyako
阪急京都線
Hankyu Kyoto Line
花見小路通
Hanamikōji St.
知恩院
Chion-in
四条大橋
Shijō Ōhashi Bridge
京都河原町
Kyoto-Kawara-machi Sta.
八坂神社
Yasaka-jinja
円山公園
Maruyama Park
四条通
Shijō St.
祇園四条
Gion-Shijō Sta.
祇園
Gion
高島屋
Takashimaya
長楽寺
Chōraku-ji
建仁寺
Kennin-ji
高台寺
Kōdai-ji
京阪本線
Keihan Line
六道珍皇寺
Rokudō-chinnō-ji
円徳院
Entoku-in
八坂の塔（法観寺）
Yasaka-no-to (Hōkan-ji)
八坂通
Yasaka St.
松原通
Matsubara St.
三年坂
Sannen-zaka
清水坂
Kiyomizu-zaka
清水五条
Kiyomizu-Gojō Sta.
六波羅蜜寺
Rokuharamitsu-ji
清水寺
Kiyomizu-dera
五条大橋
Gojō Ōhashi Bridge
五条通
Gojō St.
五条坂
Gojō-zaka
茶碗坂
Chawan-zaka
東山区役所
Higashiyama Ward Office
子安塔
Koyasu-no-tō
泰産寺
Taisan-ji
ハイアットリージェンシー
Hyatt Regency
京都国立博物館
Kyoto National Museum
妙法院
Myōhō-in
清閑寺
Seikan-ji
七条大橋
Shichijō Ōhashi Bridge
豊国廟
Hōkoku-byō
七条
Shichijō Sta.
養源院
Yōgen-in
智積院
Chishaku-in
JR琵琶湖線
JR Biwako Line
三十三間堂
Sanjūsangen-dō
東海道新幹線
Tokaido Shinkansen

エリア 2
Area 2

緑深い山麓の寺社から糺ノ森へ足を延ばす
Venturing from the Temples and Shrines of the Green Foothills Up to Tadasu-no-Mori

むかし、東海道を歩いてきた旅人たちは、日ノ岡の峠を越え、蹴上に立って、京都の街並をはじめて目にした。その京都の入口は東山連山の万緑のなかにある。私たちは、その緑の山麓を北に向かって古刹を訪ね歩くことにしよう。

まず、ひときわ高く緑林の上に三門の大瓦屋根をみせる南禅寺。京都五山の上に位された大禅刹であるが、その高名さほど人出の少ない静かな山内だ。南禅寺の塔頭の塀沿いに鹿ヶ谷道をゆくと「秋はもみじ」の永観堂。山崖に貼りつくような堂宇をめぐり、「見返り阿弥陀」を拝する。

坂をあがると若王子神社。そこから有名な「哲学の道」が琵琶湖疏水のゆるやかな流れに沿って約2km、銀閣寺橋につづく。凡人に哲学は縁遠いが、流れに浮かぶ落花や紅葉のようすを眺めれば、いささかなりと旅情は深まる。天皇の女御たちの悲話が残る安楽寺、寂びた山門と白沙段の庭に法然の教えが伝わる法然院に立ち寄れば、閑静な京都の寺の良さを知ることだろう。

しかし、銀閣寺の参道に入ると、あまりに多い人波と櫛比する土産物屋にその旅愁はみごとにうちこわされる。京都寺社めぐりの鉄則は朝早いうちに有名寺社を訪れ、拝観開始と同時に境内に入ることで、そうすれば人に背を押されずにすむ。

ただ銀閣寺の庭園は変化に富んで、掃き清められた苑地をめぐれば、日本人の伝統の一端が理解されよう。

今出川通を西に、吉田山の山中に鎮座する吉田神社、賀茂大橋を渡れば、北に「糺ノ森」と奥に下鴨神社、西に相国寺が松林のなかに建つ。

In the old days, travelers on Tōkaidō Road would come over the Hinooka pass, reache Keage where they would catch their first glimpse of the city of Kyoto. That entrance to Kyoto was in the lush forest of the Higashiyama mountain chains. Let us set off northward from the foothills of those mountains to visit some old temples.

First, we will see the great tiled roof of the *san-mon* gate (Main gate) of Nanzen-ji in the high woods. The greater of the Five Great Kyoto Rinzai Zen Temples of Kyoto (Kyoto Gozan), this Zen temple's renown belies the quiet emptiness of its grounds. We walk on Shishigatani Rd. along the earthen walls of Nanzen-ji's sub-temples to Eikan-dō, famous for its autumn colors. Observe the temple buildings that somehow cling to the mountain cliffs, and pay your respects to the Backward-Looking Amitabha.

Here we climb the hill to Nyakuōji-jinja, and from here the famous Philosopher's Walk takes us about 2 kilometers along the gentle stream of the Lake Biwa Canal to Ginkaku-ji Bridge. For most people, philosophy is something removed from their daily lives, but gazing at the flowers and leaves floating on the surface of the water may deepen the mood of your journey. Make a stop at Anraku-ji where the sad stories of court ladies linger, or Hōnen-in, where the teachings of Hōnen were shared in the antique-look *san-mon* gate or the white gravel garden, and you will begin to know the real appeal of the quiet temples of Kyoto.

However, when you enter the approach path of Ginkaku-ji, with its crowds of people and welter of souvenir stands, the melancholy feeling is completely swept away. The iron rule of Kyoto temple-and-shrine tourism is to visit the famous sites early in the morning if you want to avoid the crush.

However, when you walk around the clean-swept parks of Ginkaku-ji, you can gain some understanding of the traditions of the Japanese people.

Across Imadegawa St. to the west, on the slopes of Mt. Yoshidayama, stands Yoshida-jinja. If you cross at the Kamo-Ōhashi bridge, to the north is the Tadasu-no-Mori forest, which shelters the Shimogamo-jinja, and to the west is Shōkoku-ji amid the pines.

1

絶景の三門で知られる林間の禅刹

南禅寺

京都市左京区南禅寺福地町86
075(771)0365
8時40分～17時(12月～2月は16時30分・12月28日～31日は閉門)
境内拝観自由(方丈庭園と三門は各500円)
www.nanzen.net
地下鉄東西線　蹴上下車徒歩10分

南禅寺を紹介するときに、よくいわれることは、歌舞伎の舞台「楼門五三桐」で大泥棒の石川五右衛門が南禅寺の三門に昇り「絶景かな」といい、見得を切ったということで、それが今日まで広く伝わっている。ただし、これは作者並木五瓶の巧みな創作であって、三門は五右衛門が釜茹の刑で死んだ30数年後(1628年)に江戸期の大名藤堂高虎によって建てられたものである。

藤堂高虎　1556～1630。安土桃山から江戸前期の武将。豊臣秀吉に仕え、のち徳川幕府の大名。築城に秀でる。

といっても「絶景かな」はいまもたしかに絶景であって、南禅寺の三門は珍しく拝観者に開放されているので、ぜひ楼上に昇って四方を見晴らす眺めを楽しんでみたい(上写真)。西方向は松林越しに平安神宮から鴨川の西域の市街を望み、東側に回れば東山の一峰南禅寺山の深々とうねる緑黛が間近で、南や北方向は眼下に専門道場や塔頭の**瓦屋根**をみることになる。

1. The Zen temple in the forest known for its splendid *san-mon* gate

Nanzen-ji

Address: 86 Nanzen-ji Fukuchi-chō, Sakyō-ku, Kyoto-shi
Tel: 075 (771) 0365
Hours: 8:40AM–5:00PM (Closes at 4:30PM December–February; closed December 28–31)
Admission: Free (¥500 fee to enter hōjō garden and san-mon gate respectively)
www.nanzen.net/english/
10 min walk from Subway Tozai Line Keage Sta.

When we introduce Nanzen-ji, we often think of a famous moment in the Kabuki play "Roumon-gosan-no-Kiri," when the master thief Ishikawa Goemon mounts the stairs up to the *san-mon* gate (main gate) of Nanzen-ji and declares, "A peerless view," striking a distinctive *mie*, or pose. However, this is a bit of a stretch on the part of playwright Namiki Gohei, since in fact the *san-mon* gate was not built until 1628, more than thirty years after Goemon was executed (by being boiled alive). The gate was constructed at the behest of the Edo period *daimyō* (feudal lord) Tōdō Takatora.

In any case, the *san-mon* gate still affords a peerless view. It is one of the few such gates that is open to the public, and a climb to the top to enjoy the 360° view is well worth the effort (see above photo). To the east, over the pine forest, one can see from the Heian-jingū to the city on the west side of the Kamo River, and a turn toward the west reveals the green hills leading to Mt. Nanzen-ji-yama, the highest of the Higashiyama mountain chains. To the south and the north, one can see the **tiled roofs** of a study hall and sub-temples.

南禅寺の創建と寺域

1264年（文永元）亀山天皇はこの林間の地に離宮禅林寺殿（ぜんりんじでん）を造営した。しかし、それ以前にあった古寺の死霊が出没したため、亀山帝は数々の名僧に祈禱をさせたが、その効き目はなく、東福寺3世の無関普門（むかんふもん）を請じたところ死霊は退散した。それにより普門に深く帰依した亀山法皇は1291年（正応4）離宮を禅寺に改めた。これが南禅寺の創建となる。

亀山法皇は南禅寺の住持になる僧は法脈を問わず「器量卓抜（きりょうたくばつ）」のものを選ぶように文書を残した。これによって各門流の名僧が南禅寺に集まった。

なお、足利義満によって京都五山の順位が定められたとき、南禅寺は「天下五山之上（てんかござんのうえ）」として五山の上位におかれたのである。

三門の眺めを楽しんだのち、林間のなかを山側に歩くと、まず法堂（はっとう）（仏殿）が中央に建つ。南禅寺の諸堂はたびたびの火災で江戸期に再建されたものだが、この法堂だけは1895年（明治28）に焼け、1909年（同42）に再建されている。

さらに右手奥に歩くとアーチ型構造の「水路閣（すいろかく）」がみえてくる。京都近代化の偉業である琵琶湖疏水（びわこそすい）を通す陸橋で、いまも橋の上には勢いよく水が流れる。古色な煉瓦色がこの禅寺の景色によく溶けこんでいる。

琵琶湖疏水　琵琶湖の水を引き入れ、電力発電に用いる。1890年に完成。若い土木工学者の田辺朔郎（さくお）が設計。

Nanzen-ji's Origins and the Temple Grounds

In 1264, Emperor Kameyama commissioned the construction of an Imperial villa for his retirement in this wooded area. However, as the story goes, the ghosts of the residents of an ancient temple that had stood on the spot had been disturbed, and despite retaining the services of many famous monks to exorcise the ghosts, the emperor was unable to rid his villa of them. Finally he engaged the Tōfuku-ji head priest Mukan Fumon, who successfully banished the ghosts. This convinced the emperor to convert to Fumon's teachings, and in 1291, he turned the remote villa into a Zen temple that would be the foundation of Nanzen-ji.

In his will, the former Emperor Kameyama commanded the head priest of Nanzen-ji to select monks of talent and taste, regardless of school, to serve at the temple. For this reason, monks from many different schools gathered at Nanzen-ji.

Subsequently, when Ashikaga Yoshimitsu named the five great Zen temples of Kyoto, he declared Nanzen-ji the greatest of all.

After enjoying the view from the *san-mon* gate, if you stroll through the forest toward the mountain, you will come first to the *hattō*, or Dharma hall. Many of Nanzen-ji's buildings were destroyed by fire and rebuilt during the Edo period, but the *hattō* was the most recently destroyed, in 1895. It was rebuilt in 1909.

Continuing onward on the right-hand path, the arch-shaped Suirokaku comes into view. This viaduct bringing water from Lake Biwa is one of the great feats in the modernization of Kyoto. The water still flows merrily overhead, and the antique colors of the tiles melt pleasingly into the scenery of the temple.

第一級の美術館と名庭

山際に位置する本坊の各建物も見どころで、庫裏から堂内に入ると、単層、寝殿造で柿葺の大方丈につづく。数多くの部屋をもち、各部屋は狩野元信や永徳の障壁画で飾られ、建物とともに超一級の美術館といっていい。つづく小方丈にも狩野探幽作の「群虎図」などの傑作がある。

狩野派　室町幕府御用絵師の狩野正信にはじまる日本画最大の画派。元信、永徳、探幽など。

大方丈の庭園は、山麓の緑樹を背景に、庫裏の瓦屋根や五筋の築地を前景にして、広縁からゆったりと眺められる。砂紋を描く白砂が美しく、奥まって「虎の児渡し」という巨石群と植栽、刈込が一カ所にまとめられ、格調高い**借景庭園様式**をみせている。

また、庫裏大玄関先の景色は、山際に建つ玄関口に参道の敷石が吸いこまれていくような遠近法の構図が印象深い。

南禅寺の代表的な塔頭を紹介すれば、徳川家康の政僧として暗躍した以心崇伝が再興した「金地院」と、南禅寺の開山無関普門の塔所として建立、のちに細川家の菩提寺となった「天授庵」、さらに南禅寺の別院で亀山法皇の離宮の遺構である「南禅院」があげられる。この三寺院はいずれも庭園の美を誇り、訪れる価値はおおいにある。

以心崇伝　1569～1633。臨済宗の僧で徳川家康から３代家光までの政治的側近。

First-Class Museum and Gardens

The buildings of the temple are also well worth seeing. Entering via the *kuri*, or living quarters, one continues to the *dai-hōjō*, or cental hall, a single-story building in the *shinden-zukuri* style with a shake-shingled (*kokera-buki*) roof. There are many rooms, all decorated with screens painted by Kanō Motonobu and Kanō Eitoku. In addition to the building itself, it is fair to say the *hōjō* ranks as a first-class museum as well. Continuing to the *shō-hōjō*, the smaller hall, one can see masterpieces by Kanō Tan'yū, such as his tiger screens.

One can enjoy the gardens of the *dai-hōjō* from the veranda with the green trees of the mountain foothills as a backdrop and the tiled roof of the *kuri* in the foreground. The gardens feature beautifully rippling white sands and the arrangement of giant stones known as "tiger cub crossing the river." When combined with a view of the neighboring hills, it is a prime example of the **"borrowed scenery garden" style.**

Also impressive is the composition of the view from the entryway of the *kuri*. The perspective through the entryway opening causes the gravel path leading to the shrine to seem to flow into the mountain ridge.

Nanzen-ji's subsidiary temples include Konchi-in (founded by the Tokugawa shogunal adviser and monk Ishin Sūden), Tenju-an (family temple of the Hosokawa family), and Nanzen-in (originally the imperial villa of the former Emperor Kameyama). All three of these temples boast beautiful gardens and are well worth visiting.

2

見返り阿弥陀と紅葉の寺

永観堂（えいかんどう）

京都市左京区永観堂町48
075(761)0007
9時〜17時
600円
www.eikando.or.jp
地下鉄東西線　蹴上下車徒歩10分

永観堂は通称で、正しくは禅林寺（ぜんりんじ）という浄土宗西山（せいざん）禅林寺派の総本山である。南禅寺の北に寺域を接するように位置する。

ここ永観堂はふたつのことで有名である。ひとつは「見返り阿弥陀（みかえりあみだ）」とよばれ、うしろを振りむくように首を左にむけた高さ77㎝あまりの小さなご本尊である。この仏像の由来はこうだ。1082年（永保2）2月15日の早朝、禅林寺7世住持の永観は、念仏を唱えながら行道（ぎょうどう）していると、壇上から本尊の阿弥陀如来がおりてこられ、永観を先導するように歩きはじめられた。驚いて立ちつくす永観に、阿弥陀如来はふり返り「永観遅し」と声をおかけになったのである。この姿を彫ったのが本堂阿弥陀堂に安置されている「見返り阿弥陀」である。なお、このことから永観は禅林寺の中興（ちゅうこう）の祖とされ、当寺の通称名となった。

行道　仏道の修行のため仏堂や仏像の周囲をめぐり歩くこと。

もうひとつ「秋はもみじの永観堂」と京都人の口の端にのぼる紅葉の名所であることだ。いま境内の楓（かえで）は3000本を超えるといい、紅葉

2. Temple of the Backward-Looking Amitabha and autumn colors

Eikan-dō

Address: 48 Eikan-dō-chō, Sakyō-ku, Kyoto-shi
Tel: 075 (761) 0007
Hours: 9:00AM–5:00PM
Admission: ¥600
www.eikando.or.jp/English/index_eng.html
10 min walk from Subway Tozai Line Keage Sta.

Although it is commonly known as Eikan-dō, the formal name of this temple is Zenrin-ji, and it is the head temple of the Seizan-Zenrin-ji sect of Jōdo. It is located just north of Nanzen-ji.

Eikan-dō is famous for two things. The first is a 77-centimeter-tall statue of the Amitabha (*amida-nyorai*) with his head turned to the left as if looking behind him known as the Amitabha looking back. The story has it that early in the morning on the fifteenth of February in 1082, Eikan, the seventh head priest of Zenrin-ji, was performing his morning meditation when the Amitabha arose from the altar and began walking, beckoning to Eikan to follow him. Surprised, the priest stood up, and the Amitabha statue looked back at him and said, "Eikan, you are slow!" A statue of the Amitabha's pose was installed as the temple's principal statue of the Amitabha, and it came to be known as the Amitabha looking back (Mikaeri Amida). Furthermore, the event marked Eikan as the progenitor of Zenrin-ji's revival, giving it its commonly used name.

The second thing Eikan-dō is famous for is its autumn colors, giving rise to the Kyoto expression, "Autumn means the autumn leaves of Eikan-dō." There are said to be more than three thousand

時には境内が真紅に染まる。

寺の創建と山際の諸堂

禅林寺の創建は853年（仁寿3）空海の高弟真紹が、文人で書家として知られる藤原関雄の山荘を真言密教の道場にしたことによる。その後、火災で諸堂を失うが、5世深覚とその弟子の永観が再興した。その後の住持が法然に帰依して13世紀初めに真言宗から浄土宗へ正式に改めた。

ふたたび応仁の乱などで伽藍諸堂を焼失するが、1497年（明応6）から永正年間（1504～21）にかけて御影堂、書院、方丈、回廊が建てられ、1607年（慶長12）には阿弥陀堂が完成して今日の寺観となった。

放生池　仏教の不殺生の思想に基づき、魚類を放ち慈悲のおこないをするための池。

永観堂は総門を入って放生池の周辺を散策しているときは気がつかないが、本坊の大玄関から諸堂内をみてまわり、御影堂から先の階段をのぼりはじめると、この寺の堂宇はまさに山崖に貼りついて建っていることがわかる。少しでも山が崩れれば永観堂の建物は無事ではすまないと怖れるほどである。とくに斜面をかけ上がる「臥龍廊」と名づけられた回廊をめぐるとそのスリリングな構造がよくわかる。

五山の送り火　京都のお盆の伝統行事（8月16日）。京都を囲む5つの山にそれぞれ「大文字」「左大文字」「船形」「鳥居形」「妙・法」の形に火を灯す。

また、御影堂の脇から多宝塔にのぼれば、京都市街が一望できて、京都御苑や双ケ丘、左大文字をひろびろと見晴らすことができる。

maple trees in the precincts of the temple, and in the autumun the grounds are dyed crimson.

The Founding of the Temple, and the Halls on the Ridge of the Mountain

Zenrin-ji was founded in 853, when Shinshō, a leading disciple of the famous priest Kūkai, founded a temple dedicated to the esoteric Shingon teaching in the mountain villa of the writer and calligrapher Fujiwara-no-Sekio. Later, many of the buildings were destroyed by fire, but the fifth head priest, Shinkaku, and Eikan, his disciple, were able to rebuild the temple. A later head priest, influenced by Hōnen, led the change of the temple from Shingon to Jōdo (Pure Land) sect.

More temple buildings were destroyed by fire during the Ōnin War and other disturbances, but during the Meiō and Eishō era (from 1497 to 1521), the *miei-dō*, the *shoin* (study-cum-living room), the *hōjō*, and the hallways were constructed, and in 1607 the *amida-dō* was completed, achieving the form of the temple that we see today.

As one enters the main gate of Eikan-dō and strolls around the hōjō pond, it is easy to miss the fact that the temple compound is built on the edge of a series of cliffs. If the mountains become even slightly restless, it is unlikely that the buildings of Eikan-dō will escape unharmed. In particular, a stroll around the Garyū-rō corridor, built on the side of a diagonal face, clearly illustrates the remarkable nature of this structure.

Climbing the *tahōtō* tower next to the *miei-dō* affords an excellent view of all of the city of Kyoto, including Kyoto Gyoen National Garden, Narabigaoka Hill, and Mt. Hidari Daimonji.

3

室町八代将軍義政の隠棲地

銀閣寺(ぎんかくじ)

京都府左京区銀閣寺町2
075(771)5725
8時30分〜17時(12月〜2月は9時〜16時30分)
500円
www.shokoku-ji.jp/ginkakuji/
京都駅より市バス5・17系統　銀閣寺道下車徒歩5分

室町幕府のふたりの将軍は退位後にそれぞれ山荘を造営する。3代足利義満(よしみつ)は衣笠山(きぬがさやま)の東麓に北山殿(きたやまどの)を建て、8代義政(よしまさ)は東山連峰の月待山(つきまちやま)西麓に東山殿(ひがしやまどの)を建てる。

義満の北山殿の象徴が「**金閣**」であり、義政の東山殿のそれは「**銀閣**」となる。将軍職を子の義持(よしもち)に譲ったのちも権勢を誇った義満に比べ、政治的に孤立した義政であるから、おのずから「銀閣」には枯淡な風態がみてとれる。

義政は隠棲地を岩倉(いわくら)、嵯峨(さが)あたりに探して、洛東のかつて天台宗浄土寺(じょうどうじ)の寺域が広がっていた山麓に定めた。1483年(文明15)に常御所(つねのごしょ)ができて義政はさっそく移り住まう。その後、東山殿は着々と諸堂を整え、最後に観音殿(かんのんでん)(銀閣)が1489年(長享3)2月に完成する。しかし、義政はその翌年没してしまう。

3. The retirement villa of Yoshimasa, the eighth Muromachi shogun

Ginkaku-ji

Address: 2 Ginkakuji-chō, Sakyō-ku, Kyoto-shi
Tel: 075 (771) 5725
Hours: 8:30AM–5:00PM (December–February: 9:00AM–4:30PM)
Admission: ¥500
www.shokoku-ji.jp/en/ginkakuji/
5 min walk from Ginkaku-ji-michi bus stop, bus 5 or 17 from Kyoto Sta.

Two of the Muromachi-era shogun built mountain villas after retiring. The third shogun, Ashikaga Yoshimitsu, built Kitayamadono in the eastern foothills of Mt. Kinugasayama, and the eighth shogun, Yoshimasa, built Higashiyamadono in the western foothills of Mt. Tsukimachiyama in the Higashiyama mountain chain.

The defining symbol of Yoshimitsu's Kitayamadono was the Kinkaku (**Golden Pavilion**), and the symbol of Yoshimasa's Higashiyamadono was the Ginkaku (**Silver Pavilion**). Compared to Yoshimitsu, who passed his political power on to his son Yoshimochi and gloried in his influence, Yoshimasa was politically isolated, and his Ginkaku reveals his own refined simplicity attitude.

Yoshimasa considered Iwakura or Saga area for the location of his retirement villa, and eventually chose the area around the Jōdō-ji of the Tendai sect. In 1483, as soon as his palace was completed, Yoshimasa moved in. More buildings were gradually added to the compound, concluding with the *kannon-den* (Ginkaku) in February 1489. Unfortunately for him, Yoshimasa died the following year.

夢窓疎石 1275〜1351。鎌倉後期から南北朝期の臨済僧。天龍寺の項参照（202ページ）。

義政の遺命によって東山殿は寺となり、相国寺から住持を迎えて義政の法号、慈照院から慈照寺と名づけ追請開山は夢窓疎石とした。ただ残念なことにのちの兵火によって銀閣と持仏堂（東求堂）および庭園以外は焼亡してしまう。

銀閣とその見事な庭園

銀閣寺の総門を入るとすぐに参道は右に折れ、下部は石垣、中段は竹垣（左側）、上段は椿の生け垣の意匠がみごとな銀閣寺垣が左右に高々として中門につづく。

中門の先に円錐形に砂を盛りあげた「向月台」、その左に一段高く砂をならして太い筋文様を入れた「銀沙灘」が造られて、錦鏡池を前にして「銀閣」（観音殿）が建つ。銀閣寺の独特の静謐な庭園構成が広がっている。

東の展望所まではわずかな坂道で、そこにあがると銀閣寺の諸堂と庭園が一目にとらえられ、山内を囲む林のうえに吉田山の緑と周囲の街並が浮かぶようにみえる。

銀閣は義満が建てた金閣と対比されて、江戸時代以降、そうよばれているが、銀箔でおおわれていたというわけではない。正式には観音殿といい、正面四間、側面三間の重層で宝形造、上層は**禅宗様式**で「潮音閣」、下層は

In accordance with Yoshimasa's dying wish, Higashiyamadono was turned into a temple named Jishō-ji guided by the spirit of the late priest Musō Soseki. However, all the buildings except for the Silver Pavilion, the Buddha hall (Tōgu-dō) and the gardens were burned in the fires of subsequent wars.

The Silver Pavilion and Its Spectacular Gardens

After entering the main gates of the temple, the approach turns to the right. The lower portion of the fence along the approach is stone, the middle portion is bamboo (on the left side), and the top portion is hedge of camellias. This distinctive type of fencing, known as "Ginkaku-ji fence," towers high above as you approach the inner gate of the temple.

In front of the central entrance towers a cone of sand called the Kōgetsu-dai, or "Moon-Viewing Platform," and to its left is an arrangement of raked sand in a thick stripe pattern, called the Ginshadan, or "Sea of Silver Sand." The Silver Pavilion (Ginkaku), also called the *kannon-den* (Kannon Hall), stands on the other side of the Kinkyō pond. The uniquely tranquil organization of Ginkaku-ji's gardens stretch out before you.

A short incline leads to the eastern viewing point. When you ascend to this point, you can see all of Ginkaku-ji's buildings and gardens spread out around you. The green of Mt. Yoshidayama seems to float above the trees that surround the temple.

Since the Edo period, the Silver Pavilion has been compared to Yoshimitsu's Golden Pavilion (Kinkaku), but in fact it was never covered with the intended silver foil. It is formally known as the *kannon-den*. It is a two-story structure built in the *hōgyō* (square) style. The top floor, in a **Zen motif**, is called the Chōon-kaku, and

住宅様式で「心空殿（しんくうでん）」という。閣上に金銅の鳳凰をいただく。

もうひとつの古堂、東求堂（持仏堂）は三間半方形の単層で入母屋造、南に板の間と方二間の仏間、北に六畳と四畳半の部屋がある。この四畳半の部屋は「同仁斎（どうじんさい）」とよばれ、草庵茶室の源流とされる造りである。

銀閣寺の全景。奥の緑は吉田山
Ginkaku-ji, the overall view. A green at the back is Yoshidayama.

the lower floor, intended for living, is called the Shinkū-den. Atop the hall stands a statue of a **phoenix** made of gilt bronze.

The other remaining old building is the Tōgū-dō. It is a single-story rectangular building in the gable and hip roof (*irimoya-zukuri*), with a wooden-floor room and a small room for Buddhist images (*butsuma*) on the southern end and two small *tatami*-floor rooms in the northern part of the building. The smaller of these is known as the *Dōjinsai*, and is constructed in the *sōan-chashitsu* (thatched style tea-ceremony room) style.

4

ゆるやかな参道と端正な本堂

真如堂（しんにょどう）

京都市左京区浄土寺真如町82
075(771)0915
9時〜16時
500円
shin-nyo-do.jp
京都駅より市バス5・17系統　真如堂前下車徒歩8分

平安神宮の北域には、東西に走る丸太町（まるたまち）通と南北の白川（しらかわ）通が山裾の道となるように小高い丘陵地があって、この丘にふたつの名刹が建っている。

ひとつは京都人に「黒谷（くろだに）さん」とよばれる金戒光明寺（こんかいこうみょうじ）で、法然（ほうねん）が比叡山での修行を終えて小庵を設けたことを草創とする浄土宗の四カ本山の大寺である。高仰な山門をくぐると、さらに高い境内に御影堂（みえいどう）が堂々として構えている。

金戒光明寺　御影堂の内陣に法然自作という像を安置。また堂の廊下からは市街を一望する。

もうひとつの寺が真如堂である。金戒光明寺の御影堂の左手から北にあがる道は、同寺の子院が一段低い西側の斜面に建ち並び、東側は丘上に墓所を見上げる土肌の道で、人影もなく静まりかえっている。雨のあとなど、水溜まりをよけながら歩いていると、ひとり旅の寂寥感が身にしみいるような道である。

一条天皇　在位986〜1011。平安時代中期の天皇。

一条天皇の勅願寺

その道はやがて金戒光明寺の北門を抜け、

4. A gentle approach to the handsome main hall

Shinnyo-dō

Address: 82 Jōdoji Shinnyo-chō, Sakyō-ku, Kyoto-shi
Tel: 075 (771) 0915
Hours: 9:00AM–4:00PM
Admission: ¥500
shin-nyo-do.jp
8 min walk from Shinnyo-dō-mae bus stop, bus 5 or 17 from Kyoto Sta.

North of the Heian-jingū, where Marutamachi St., running east–west, and Shirakawa St., running north–south, both turn into small foothill roads, stands a small hill. On top of this hill are two famous temples.

One of these is Konkaikōmyō-ji, known to locals as "Kurodani-san," where Hōnen went after finishing his training at Hieizan (Enryaku-ji). He built a small hermitage that would become one of four head temples of Jōdo sect. When you pass under the breath taking *san-mon* gate, the grand *miei-dō* hall stands above you in the broad temple precincts.

The other temple on the hill is Shinnyo-dō. The path that heads north to the left of the *miei-dō* of Konkaikōmyō-ji passes between some sub-temples built high on a hillside to the west and a cemetery above to the east. When walking along this path with no one else present, avoiding the puddles, one can truly feel the loneliness of the solitary traveler.

A Temple Built at the Order of Emperor Ichijō

Eventually, the path winds out of the northern gate of

そのまま100mほど進むと、真如堂の**参道**が東側にみえてくる。ゆるやかな上り勾配で幅も広い石段は、三重塔を右に、本堂を正面にみるじつにゆったりとした気持のいいアプローチで、寺社の参道としては京都市内でも五指に数えて間違いない。

真如堂、正式には真正極楽寺（しんしょうごくらくじ）といい、その創建は、992年（正暦3）比叡山の戒算（かいざん）上人が一条天皇の母、東三条院藤原詮子（ふじわらのせんし）の女院離宮（元真如堂の地）に一宇を建て、延暦寺にあった阿弥陀如来を安置したことによると伝える。

一条天皇の勅願寺となり、やがて天台宗の巨刹として荘厳な伽藍を誇ったのだが、応仁の乱の兵火でいっさいの諸堂を失い、その後、寺地は近江坂本、市中の一条町など転々として、足利義政（あしかがよしまさ）の寄進で1484年（文明16）いまの地に再建された。そして、およそ20年後には天台宗から浄土宗へ改宗して、また一条町に戻るなど移転をくり返し、ようやく1693年（元禄6）に現在地に定まり、ふたたび天台宗に改宗した。

なだらかな参道に低く枝を伸ばす樹々の先に本堂が端然と建ち、右手には高い樹木に囲まれて三重塔が親しみやすい存在感を示している。いま真如堂を大寺という人はないが、伽藍配置の整然としたようす、それぞれの建物の落ちついた佇まい、緑の多い境内が、訪れる人々の呼吸とよくあって、しみじみとした気分にさせてくれる。

Konkaikōmyō-ji, and continuing on about 100 meters, one sees the **approach** to Shinnyo-dō on the east. Mounting the gentle rise of the broad stone staircase, the three-storied pagoda is visible on the right and the main hall (*hondō*) is straight ahead. The relaxed, pleasant atmosphere of this approach is certainly one of the top five in the city.

Shinnyo-dō, formally Shinshōgokuraku-ji, was founded in 992 by the priest Kaizan of Hieizan (Enryaku-ji), on the site of a women's Imperial villa belonging to Fujiwara-no-Senshi, the mother of Emperor Ichijō. A statue of the Amitabha (*amida-nyorai*) brought from Enryaku-ji was installed.

As a temple created by Emperor Ichijō's order, eventually Shinnyo-dō became a major Tendai institution boasting splendid buildings, but all of them were destroyed in the conflagration of the Ōnin War. Subsequently, the temple was forced to move several times within Kyoto. Eventually a donation from Ashikaga Yoshimasa allowed construction at the current site in 1484. Some twenty years later, the temple switched from Tendai to Jōdo sect, and after several more moves, at last, in 1693, settled at the current setting, and converted back to Tendai sect.

Just beyond the edges of the branches that sweep low over the gently sloping approach to the temple, the *hondō* stands proper, the three-story pagoda bordered by trees to the right. Today no one would call Shinnyo-dō a big temple, but the tidy array of its grounds and the soothing appearance of all the buildings amid their green precincts seem to blend smoothly with the breath of all who visit, encouraging quiet contemplation.

5

緑深い丘陵に鎮座する八百万の神

吉田神社

京都市左京区吉田神楽岡町30
075(771)3788
境内参拝自由(祈禱受付9時〜17時)
www.yoshidajinja.com
京都駅より市バス206系統　京大正門前下車5分

銀閣寺から今出川通を西に向かう。この通りはなだらかな下り坂で、南に緑林に覆われた丘陵が盛り上がってみえる。標高約105mの吉田山である。

吉田山は京都市街にあって、船岡山や双ケ丘とともに独立した山稜で、神楽岡ともよばれ、山は緑樹を被り、京都市街を湖とすれば、水面に浮かぶ中島のような景色である。西麓には京都大学のキャンパスが広がる。

船岡山　標高約112m。都人の遊行地であり、山頂に建勲神社が建つ。

この吉田山に鎮座するのが吉田神社で、山名も神社名からのものである。吉田山には四方から登れるが、京都大学の時計台を左手にみながら、東一条通を東に進んで、白い砂利道を歩いてゆくと、**本殿**へとつづく石段に突きあたる。これが吉田神社の表参道となる。

吉田神道　森羅万象すべては神の意志であるとして、儒教・仏教・道教・陰陽道などを融合した神道説を唱えた。

春日神から吉田神道の本拠地へ

桓武天皇が794年（延暦13）平安京に都を定めたさい、吉田山は都の**鬼門**（北東）にあたるとして比叡山とともに王城鎮護の山とさ

5. Myriad gods enshrined atop a hill in the deep forest

Yoshida-jinja

Address: 30 Yoshida Kaguraoka-chō, Sakyō-ku, Kyoto-shi
Tel: 075 (771) 3788
Admission: Free
www.yoshidajinja.com
5 min walk from Kyōdai-seimon-mae bus stop, bus 206 from Kyoto Sta.

From Ginkaku-ji, head west along Imadegawa St. As the street slopes gently downhill, to the south you can see a hill surrounded by forest. This is Mt. Yoshidayama, with an elevation of approximately 105 meters.

Like Mt. Funaokayama and Narabigaoka hills, Mt. Yoshidayama is an independent mountain within the city limits. Also called Kaguraoka, it wears a mantle of green trees; if the city of Kyoto were a lake, it would peek just above the surface. On Mt. Yoshidayama's western edge, the campus of Kyoto University unfolds.

Mt. Yoshidayama is named for Yoshida-jinja. It is possible to ascend the mountain from any direction, but we recommend that you begin by keeping the clock tower of Kyoto University on your left and walking east on Higashi-ichijō St. The white gravel approach will bring you to the stone steps of the **main sanctuary** *(hon-den)*. This is the front approach to Yoshida-jinja.

From the God of Kasuga to the Headquarters of Yoshida Shinto

In 794, when Emperor Kanmu chose Heian-kyō as his capital, Mt. Yoshidayama was considered to stand in an **unlucky direction** (the northeast, called the demon's gate), so along with Mt. Hieizan,

れた。859年（貞観元）に、中納言藤原山蔭がこの吉田山の地を選び、藤原氏の氏神である大和の春日神を勧請した。これがもともとの吉田神社の創建で、その後、吉田兼倶がとなえた唯一神道の吉田神道の本拠地となる。

吉田神社の本殿は朱塗りの4棟の社殿からなり、奈良春日大社の春日造を継承する。応仁の乱の兵火にかかり、以来いくたびもの修造を重ねている。

春日造　春日大社本殿の建築から名づけられた神社本殿形式のひとつ。

ふだんの日は、境内にある幼稚園児らの声が聞こえるくらいで、静寂な社域であるが、当社の節分祭は京都の一大行事として知られ、節分の当日を中心に前後3日間は大勢の参拝者で境内は埋め尽くされる。表参道はもちろんのこと、境内、本宮から大元宮までの坂道にも露店が立ち並び、いつもの静寂さとはうってかわって賑わいをみせるのである。

節分祭では、**疫神**を鎮める「疫神祭」、平安初期より宮中ではじめられた**悪鬼**を払う「追難式」、参拝者が持参した古い御札を焼く「火炉祭」がおこなわれる。

なお、大元宮とは、日本国内すべての神を祭神とする吉田神道の根本殿堂である。

この吉田山の地は古来霊域として崇められ、お菓子の神を祀る菓祖神社、料理・飲食の神を祀る山蔭神社など多くの社がある。

it was named as a guardian mountain of the city. In 859, Fujiwara-no-Yamakage, an imperial councilor, selected Mt. Yoshidayama as the location where God of Kasuga in Yamato (Nara), the patron god of the Fujiwara clan, would be enshrined. This was the inception of the Yoshida-jinja, which under Yoshida Kanetomo, would later become the stronghold of the Yoshida Shinto movement.

The main sanctuary is composed of four buildings in the *kasuga* style structure, modeled after the Kasuga-taisha in Nara. Beginning in the Ōnin War, the shrine has had to be repaired and rebuilt numerous times.

On normal days, the shrine is peaceful enough so that one can hear the voices of the children in the kindergarten on the shrine grounds, but the shrine's annual Setsubun Festival is one of Kyoto's most famous events, which fills the shrine grounds with sightseers for three days. The approach to the shrine and the precincts are lively with stalls during this event (February 2–4).

At the Setsubun Festival, various rituals are performed, including the Ekishinsai ritual to pacify the **spirits of plague**, the Tsuinashiki ritual for chasing away **evil spirits**, which was practiced in the imperial court since the early Heian period, and the Karosai, in which shrinegoers burn old charms.

The Daigengū is the fundamental shrine of Yoshida Shinto, and all the enshrined Shinto deities from all over Japan can be worshipped here.

In addition, because the ground of Mt. Yoshidayama has been recognized as sacred ground since time immemorial, Kaso-jinja (where the god of sweets is honored), Yamakage-jinja (honoring the god of food and drink), and other shrines can also be found here.

6

平安京以前の京都で最も古い社

下鴨神社（しもがも）

京都市左京区下鴨泉川町59
075（781）0010
6時〜18時（時期により変更）
境内参拝自由
www.shimogamo-jinja.or.jp
京都駅より市バス4・205系統　下鴨神社前下車徒歩１分

糺ノ森と下鴨神社

吉田山の密生した緑林をふり返りながら、京都大学の校舎に沿って今出川通を西に向かうと、賀茂大橋を渡ることになる。この賀茂大橋に佇んで北側を眺めると、目の下には東北から流れてきた高野川（たかのがわ）と北西からの賀茂川が合流するようすがみえ、この三角州から目を上げると、京都が都になるはるか以前の植生を残す「糺ノ森（ただすのもり）」のうっそうとした樹林がみえる。

糺ノ森とは偽りを糺す神域の森を意味していたと考えられる。昔は、両川の河岸まで約150万坪という広大な森であったというが、いまは住宅地に迫られ、3万6000坪に縮小している。往古にくらべ狭くなったとはいえ、空を隠すさまざまな種類の大木が葉を茂らせて、都会においては実感できない森の深さを、その樹木や草の匂いとともに伝えてくれる貴重な場所である。

この糺ノ森のほぼ中央を一直線に下鴨神社

6. A shrine that was here before Heian-kyō itself

Shimogamo-jinja

Address: 59 Shimogamo Izumigawa-chō, Sakyō-ku, Kyoto-shi
Tel: 075 (781) 0010
Hours: 6:00AM–6:00PM (May vary depending on season)
Admission: Free
www.shimogamo-jinja.or.jp/english/
1 min walk from Shimogamo-jinja-mae bus stop, bus 4 or 205 from Kyoto Sta.

The Tadasu-no-Mori Forest and Shimogamo-jinja

Leaving the dense forest around Mt. Yoshidayama behind, head west on Imadegawa St. along the Kyoto university campus, and you come to Kamo-Ōhashi bridge. If you stand on the bridge and look north, you can see the confluence of the Takano River flowing from the northeast and the Kamo River flowing from the northwest. Just above the convergence stand the dense trees of Tadasu-no-Mori forest, which has been growing there since long before Kyoto became the capital.

Long ago, the Tadasu-no-Mori forest is said to have covered about 4,959,000m^2 of land, up to the banks of both rivers, but now it has been reduced by residential construction and has shrunk to some 119,016m^2. Although it may be much smaller than it once was, it is still a precious place, sheltering many kinds of trees large enough to blot out the sky and offering the feeling of the deep forest here within the city.

One can follow the approach to Shimogamo-jinja through the

への参道がつづき、道の東側には清流の泉川が流れていて､清涼感に満ちた森の道である。この約500mの参道は朱塗りの明神鳥居にいたる。

下鴨神社は正式には「賀茂御祖神社」と称する（上賀茂神社は「賀茂別雷神社」)。祭神は賀茂建角身命とその娘玉依姫命。賀茂建角身命は神武東征のおり、神武帝が熊野から大和に入る案内役の八咫烏に化した神といわれ、鴨（賀茂）県主の祖となる。

神武東征　日本神話において、神武天皇が日向国を発ち、大和を征服して橿原宮で即位するまでの話。

また、その娘の玉依姫命は瀬見の小川（賀茂川）で川遊びをしているとき川上から丹塗りの矢が流れてきて、それを床に置いて寝たところ懐妊したという。その子が賀茂別雷神で上賀茂神社の祭神となった。

下鴨神社と上賀茂神社は朝廷からの尊崇をえて、正一位の神階が贈られる。また時代は下るが源頼朝をはじめとする武家からの信仰も篤かった。

明神鳥居をくぐると白砂敷の境内には朱塗りの鮮やかな楼門が建ち、その奥に平安時代の配置と変わらない社殿が華麗に棟を並べている。本殿は1863年（文久3）の造替で、三間社流造、**檜皮葺**の東西二殿からなる。

center of Tadasu-no-Mori, with the cool waters of the stream flowing to the east. After about 500 meters, the approach brings us to the vermilion columns of the *myōjin torii* gate.

The formal name of the shrine is Kamomioya-jinja (Kamigamo-jinja's formal name is Kamowakeikazuchi-jinja). The shrine honors Kamotaketsunumi-no-Mikoto and his daughter, Tamayorihime-no-Mikoto. Kamotaketsunumi is said to have led Emperor Jinmu's army in its journey from Kumano (Wakayama) to Yamato (Nara) in the form of a crow, Yatagarasu.

The legend continues that Kamotaketsunumi's daughter, Tamayorihime was playing by the side of the river when she saw a vermilion arrow come floating down the stream. When she took it home, placed it on the floor, and went to sleep, she became pregnant. The child she bore was Kamowakeikazuchi, the patron deity of Kamigamo-jinja.

Shimogamo-jinja and Kamigamo-jinja were venerated by the imperial court, and their enshrined deities were placed in the highest rank of the gods. In later periods, many samurai families, beginning with Minamoto-no-Yoritomo, devoutly worshipped at these shrines.

After you enter under the *myōjin torii* gate, you will see the gaily painted two-story gate and the white sands of the shrine grounds. The buildings, their layout unchanged since the Heian period, stretch out splendidly before you. The *hon-den*, or main sanctuary, last rebuilt in 1863, is in *sangensha-nagare* style structure with **cypress shingle** *(hiwada-buki)* **roof** and consists of an eastern and a western section.

上賀茂神社　北区上賀茂本山 339
075(781)0011
境内参拝自由。

上賀茂神社へ詣る

下鴨神社からいったん賀茂川の左岸に出て、府立植物園の森をみながらさかのぼること約3kmで上賀茂神社にいたる。上賀茂神社の社伝では677年に社殿造営と記しており、下鴨神社の成立は750年ころとするが、いずれも遠い昔のことで詳らかではない。

斎院　賀茂社に奉仕した未婚の皇女。

810年（弘仁元）嵯峨天皇の第九皇女有智子内親王が初代斎院となり、以来、未婚の内親王を斎院とする（伊勢神宮は斎王）制度がはじまり、それは後鳥羽天皇の皇女まで約400年つづいた。いまは5月15日におこなわれる「葵祭」でそれに扮した女性の姿をみることができる。

一の鳥居の先は広い芝生地で、空が広く、下鴨神社とは好対照のアプローチである。二の鳥居をくぐると正面に拝殿（細殿）、舞殿（橋殿）と土屋（到着殿）がみえ、拝殿の前には砂を三角錐に形づくった砂盛がふたつ並ぶ。舞殿は御手洗川に架かる橋になり、それを渡ると朱塗りのあざやかな楼門が目前だ。

社殿の多くは江戸初期、1628年（寛永5）の建築で、本殿と権殿は1863年（文久3）の造替で、両殿とも三間社流造で檜皮葺、東に本殿、西に権殿と並ぶ。権殿は本殿が支障をきたしたときの仮本殿である。

Visiting Kamigamo-jinja

Crossing over to the left bank of the Kamo River, one can reach Kamigamo-jinja by walking 3 kilometers through the forests belonging to the municipal botanical garden. Kamigamo-jinja's legend tells that it was founded in 677, even earlier than Shimogamo-jinja (750). In any case, they are clearly both extremely old.

In 810, Princess Uchiko, the ninth daughter of Emperor Saga, became the first *saiin*, or ceremonial maiden, beginning the tradition of unmarried princesses performing these duties that would continue for approximately 400 years. Today you can see a young woman dressing up to observe the rituals on May 15 in the Aoi (Hollyhock) Festival.

Through the first *torii* gate lies a broad expanse of lawn open to the sky, a stark contrast to the approach to Shimogamo-jinja. Passing through the second *torii* gate, one can see the worship hall (*hai-den*), the stage hall (*mai-den*), and the Tsuchiya. There are two pyramids of sand in front of the *hai-den*. The *mai-den* is a bridge spanning the Mitarai stream. After crossing it, one can see the vermilion-lacquered two-story gate.

Many of the buildings date back to the early Edo period, having been built in 1628. The *hon-den* and the *gon-den* buildings were rebuilt in 1863, both in the *sangensha-nagare* style structure with cypress shingle roofs, the *hon-den* to the east and the *gon-den* to the west. In the event that the main *hon-den* building is damaged or unavailable, the *gon-den* is used in its place.

7

御苑の北、松林に囲まれた禅境

相国寺

京都市上京区今出川通烏丸東入ル
相国寺門前町701　075(231)0301
10時～16時30分
境内参拝自由(春と秋に方丈・法堂・浴室の特別拝観あり　800円)
www.shokoku-ji.jp
京都駅より地下鉄烏丸線　今出川下車徒歩5分

足利幕府の絶頂期の将軍であった三代義満は1378年（永和4）に「花の御所」とよばれる広大な室町殿を造営した。

花の御所　足利義満は室町殿に多くの花を植えたことでこうよばれた。

さらに、義満はその室町殿の東側に大禅院を建立する。それが相国寺である。義満はすでに故人であったが夢窓疎石に深く帰依しており、疎石の弟子である春屋妙葩と義堂周信を開創の中心として1382年（永徳2）からおよそ10年間をかけて伽藍を完成させた。

さらに1386年（至徳3）に義満は南禅寺を五山の上として格上げし、相国寺を天龍寺につぐ第二位に列した。さらに、禅宗寺院を統轄して僧侶の人事権をもつ僧録司の職を相国寺の住持に兼務させた。

足利家の威信をかけた大禅刹

そのような大禅刹も完成から2年後に出火により諸堂を焼失、そして諸大名から費用を徴収して2年後には再建、また、1399年（応永6）には高さ約109mという七重大塔も建立

7. A Zen temple surrounded by Pine Grove north of the Imperial Gardens

Shōkoku-ji

Address:	701 Shōkoku-ji Monzen-chō, Imadegawa-dōri Karasuma Higashi-iru, Kamigyō-ku Kyoto-shi
Tel:	075 (231) 0301
Hours:	10:00AM–4:30PM
Admission:	Free (Spring and fall entry to hōjō, hattō, and bathhouse: ¥800)

www.shokoku-ji.jp/en/

5 min walk from Subway Karasuma Line Imadegawa Sta.

The greatest of the Ashikaga shoguns, Yoshimitsu, built the Muromachi-dono palace in 1378, also known as the Flower Palace (Hana-no-Gosho).

On the east side of the palace, Yoshimitsu had a great Zen temple constructed, which was named Shōkoku-ji. Yoshimitsu had greatly respected the late priest Musō Soseki and requested Soseki's disciples Shun'oku Myōha and Gidō Shūshin to lead the temple, which was completed after ten years of construction in 1392.

In 1386, having placed Nanzen-ji above the Five Great Zen temples, Yoshimitsu ranked Tenryū-ji first, followed by Shōkoku-ji. He also made the head priest of Shōkoku-ji the *sōrokushi*, or administrative head of all Zen temples.

The Great Zen Temple of the Ashikaga Clan

Despite its high stature, only two years after its completion many of the buildings at Shōkoku-ji were destroyed in a fire. Several feudal lords joined to pay the cost of reconstruction two years after that, and in 1399, the 109-meter-tall seven-story pagoda

する。しかし、それも4年後に落雷により焼失、そしてふたたび再建するも、1416年（応永23）に、やはり塔頭からの出火で寺域の主要諸堂は全焼してしまう。

　足利幕府の威信をかけた再建事業は義満、義持、そして義教と引きつがれていったが、応仁の乱では相国寺は東軍の陣となり兵火で伽藍は全壊する。しかし次に8代将軍義政が再建に着手、永正年間（1504～21）には旧観を復するまでになった。が、またしても細川晴元と松永久秀の戦いで全焼。そののち中興の祖となる西笑承兌が豊臣秀吉や徳川家康の寄進を受け再建。天明の大火で、法堂、浴室など以外を焼失するが、文化年間（1804～18）にはやっと今日みる伽藍が整った。

天明の大火　1788年（天明8）1月に1424町を焼いた江戸期京都で最大の火事。

　総門を入ると、西側に勅使門があり、その前に立つと、放生池にかかる天界橋、そしていまは松林になっている三門跡、仏殿跡の先に法堂（本堂）がみえる。この法堂は、1605年（慶長10）豊臣秀頼の寄進の堂々とした桃山様式の代表的仏堂で、いま残る最大の法堂建築である。屋根は本瓦葺、内部は敷瓦で天井には狩野光信筆の龍が描かれている。

　法堂の右手に夢窓疎石像を安置する開山堂、奥には廊下でつながる方丈と庫裏が建ち、この一角の景色は、大禅院としての寺観がよくみてとれる。

was erected. Sadly, only four years later this structure too was burned due to a lightning strike, and although it was reconstructed, it was from that sub-temple that another fire started in 1416, which destroyed most of the temple buildings.

The successive rebuilding of Shōkoku-ji attracted the passion of Yoshimitsu, Yoshimochi, and Yoshinori, but in the Ōnin War, Shōkoku-ji was used as a camp by the Eastern Army and ultimately was completely burned once again. Then the eighth shogun, Yoshimasa, took on the task of rebuilding and through the Eishō period (1504–21) brought the temple back to its old form. Again it was burned during the battle between Hosokawa Harumoto and Matsunaga Hisahide. It would be the priest Seishō Jōtai who would once again rejuvenate Shōkoku-ji with the support of Toyotomi Hideyoshi and Tokugawa Ieyasu. In the great Tenmei fires all the buildings of the temple but the *hattō* (dharma hall) and the bath-house would be burned again, but during the Bunka era (1804–18), at last the temple that we know today was completed.

If you enter the main gate and look to the west you see the *chokushi-mon* gate (imperial messenger's gate). Standing in front of this gate, one can take in the *tenkaibashi* bridge over *hōjō* pond, the remains of the *san-mon* gate, now nearly hidden in a grove of pine, and the remains of the Buddha hall. Just beyond them the *hattō*, the main temple building is there. The *hattō*, built in 1605 with the support of Toyotomi Hideyori, is a classic example of the grand Momoyama style of architecture and is the largest existing *hattō* building. The roof is tile and the interior is also covered in tile. The ceiling boasts a famous painting of a dragon by Kanō Mitsunobu.

To the right of the *hattō* is the *kaizan-dō*, which contains a statue of Musō Soseki. A hallway connects to the *hōjō* and the *kuri*, providing a representative view of a great Zen temple.

エリア 2　Area 2

至 上賀茂神社
To Kamigamo-jinja
北山
Kitayama Sta.
北山通
Kitayama St.
松ヶ崎
Matsugasaki Sta.
府立植物園
Kyoto Botanical Garden
修学院
Shūgaku-in Sta.
高野川
Takano River
叡山電鉄
Eizan Railway
北大路
Kitaōji Sta.
北大路通
Kitaōji St.
一乗寺
Ichijō-ji Sta.
詩仙堂
Shisen-dō
賀茂川
Kamo River
下鴨神社
Shimogamo-jinja
茶山
Chayama Sta.
鞍馬口
Kuramaguchi Sta.
糺の森
Tadasu-no-Mori
白川通
Shirakawa St.
元田中
Mototanaka Sta.
相国寺
Shōkoku-ji
賀茂大橋
Kamo Ōhashi Bridge
叡山出町柳
Eizan-Demachiyanagi Sta.
今出川
Imadegawa Sta.
京阪出町柳
Keihan-Demachiyanagi Sta.
今出川通
Imadegawa St.
銀閣寺
Ginkaku-ji
吉田山
Mt. Yoshidayama
京都大学
Kyoto University
地下鉄烏丸線
Subway Karasuma Line
吉田神社
Yoshida-jinja
法然院
Hōnen-in
京都御苑
Kyoto Gyoen
京阪本線
Keihan Line
東大路通
Higashiōji St.
真如堂
Shinnyo-dō
神宮丸太町
Jingū-Marutamachi Sta.
哲学の道
Philosopher's Walk
丸太町
Maruta-machi Sta.
河原町通
Kawara-machi St.
金戒光明寺
Konkaikōmyō-ji
丸太町通
Maruta-machi St.
烏丸通
Karasuma St.
平安神宮
Heian-jingū
永観堂
Eikan-dō
烏丸御池
Karasuma Oike Sta.
京都市役所前
Kyoto Shiyakusho-mae Sta.
金地院
Konchi-in
南禅寺
Nanzen-ji
三条京阪
Sanjō-Keihan Sta.
東山
Higashiyama Sta.
南禅院
Nanzen-in
烏丸御池
Karasuma Oike Sta.
鴨川
Kamo River
三条
Sanjō Sta.
青蓮院
Shōren-in
蹴上
Keage Sta.
天授庵
Tenju-an
烏丸
Karasuma Sta.
知恩院
Chion-in
阪急京都線
Hankyu Kyoto Line
三条通
Sanjō St.
祇園四条
Gion-Shijō Sta.
八坂神社
Yasaka-jinja
地下鉄東西線
Subway Tozai Line
四条
Shijō Sta.
京都河原町
Kyoto-Kawara-machi Sta.
建仁寺
Kennin-ji
高台寺
Kōdai-ji
東山ドライブウェイ
Higashiyama Driveway
五条通
Gojō St.
清水五条
Kiyomizu-Gojō Sta.
五条
Gojō Sta.
清水寺
Kiyomizu-dera
至 山科
To Yamashina

エリア 3
Area 3

篤い信仰に支えられた豪壮かつ精緻な寺社
Splendid and Elegant Temples and Shrines
Supported by Deep Devotion

日本最大の仏教宗派、浄土真宗のふたつの大伽藍が京都市街の中央にでんと構えている。西本願寺と東本願寺で、双方とも空の半分を隠すほどの巨大な御影堂と阿弥陀堂をもつ。

西本願寺をはじめ、この章で紹介する寺社には、とくに豪壮な建築物が多く、それらは、殿上貴人や庶民らの篤い信仰によって建立されたものである。

東寺の五重塔——空海が造営に着手し、現5代目となる日本古塔中最高（55m）の塔である。東福寺の三門——禅刹中日本最古、最大の重層門である。泉涌寺——日本で唯一「御寺」とよばれる皇室の菩提寺には、四条天皇（在位1232～42）の月輪陵以下25の御陵が鎮まる。

そして、千本鳥居が全山を巡る伏見稲荷大社は日本四万社の「お稲荷さん」の総本社であるし、極楽浄土の世界を具現した平等院鳳凰堂も篤い信仰の賜物である。

京都駅近くの両本願寺と東寺を訪れたのち、JR奈良線の各駅近くの寺を巡ってみよう。東福寺駅はもちろん東福寺と泉涌寺に近く、稲荷駅は伏見稲荷大社の大鳥居の前である。さらに南下をすれば、黄檗駅の東に中国寺院の趣が残る萬福寺が建ち、宇治駅からは平等院、宇治川を北に渡れば宇治上神社がある。

同じように電車を利用するならば、三十三間堂近くの京阪電鉄七条駅から乗車して、東福寺駅、伏見稲荷駅、京阪黄檗駅、京阪宇治駅と回ってもいい。最後に紹介する石清水八幡宮も京阪宇治駅から中書島経由で、わずかな時間で着く。

Two great temples of Japan's largest Buddhist sect, Jōdo Shinshū, stand in the middle of the city of Kyoto. Nishi Hongan-ji and Higashi Hongan-ji both possess massive *goei-dō* and *amida-dō* that seem to obscure half the sky.

Beginning with Nishi Hongan-ji, the temples and shrines introduced in this chapter are notable for their splendid buildings, attesting to the strong devotion of the aristocrats and common people who built them.

Tō-ji's five-story pagoda, whose construction was started by Kūkai and is the fifth incarnation of the tallest of Japan's old temple pagodas, stands 55 meters tall. Tōfuku-ji's *san-mon* gate (Main gate) is the oldest and largest multi-story gate at a Zen temple in Japan. Sennyū-ji with its Tsukinowa Mausoleum—only being called an ancestral temple in Japan—is the resting place of twenty-five emperors, beginning with Emperor Shijō (r. 1232–42).

The thousand *torii* gate (sacred gate) covering the mountain at Fushimi-Inari-taisha, the head shrine of forty thousand "O-inari-san" shrines across Japan, and the Hōō-dō (phoenix hall) at Byōdō-in, embodying the land of Perfect Bliss, also are testament to the deep faith of their supporters.

After visiting the two Hongan-ji (Nishi and Higashi) and Tō-ji near Kyoto Station, we recommend looking at several temples along the JR Nara line. Tōfuku-ji Station is near (of course!) Tōfuku-ji and Sennyū-ji, while Inari Station is in front of the great *torii* gate of Fushimi-Inari-taisha. Traveling south, just east of Ōbaku Station is Manpuku-ji, retaining the flavor of a Chinese temple, while near Uji Station is Byōdō-in and, across the Uji River to the north, Ujigami-jinja.

Similarly, starting from the Keihan Dentetsu Shichijō Station near Sanjūsangen-dō, you can easily reach Tōfuku-ji Station, Fushimi-inari Station, Keihan Ōbaku Station, and Keihan Uji Station. Iwashimizu Hachiman-gū is also not far from Keihan Uji Station via Chūshojima Station.

1

奈良時代様式の豪壮な伽藍

東寺

京都市南区九条町1
075(691)3325
8時～17時(開門は5時。9月20日～3月19日は16時30分まで)
境内参拝自由(金堂・講堂・五重塔の入場は500円)
toji.or.jp
近鉄京都線東寺駅下車徒歩5分

京都駅に降りても、あわてて東山や嵯峨野周辺の寺社へ向かうことはやめて、まず駅近くの三つの大寺をじっくり訪れてみよう。そのひとつが、正式には教王護国寺と称する東寺である。

794年に開かれた平安京は、都城の中央南端に羅城門を構え、そこから北へ一直線に朱雀大路を大内裏まで走らせた。本来は新都の外周を羅城でとり囲むつもりであったようだが、それは果たせず、羅城門の東西に官寺を同じ規模で建て、東寺、西寺と称した。

大内裏　天皇の住まいの内裏を中心に、政務や儀式をおこなう建造物が集まる宮城。

823年(弘仁14)、東寺に空海が入り、真言密教の道場とした。同年、西寺は守敏に与えられたが、平安中期の焼亡後は廃され、いま跡碑が残るだけである。また、羅城門も平安中期には、地震や風水害にともなう都の騒乱によって、荒れるにまかせ、それは芥川龍之介の『羅生門』に描かれるような有様になって、やがて瓦解した。そのため、平安京造営時の

1. A dynamic temple in the Nara-period style
Tō-ji

Address: 1 Kujō-chō, Minami-ku, Kyoto-shi
Tel: 075 (691) 3325
Hours: 8:00AM–5:00PM (Gate open: 5:00. September 20–March 19: 8:00AM–4:30PM)
Admission: Free (¥500 to enter Kondō, Kōdō, five-story pagoda)
toji.or.jp/en/index.html
5 min walk Kintetsu Tō-ji Sta. from Kintetsu Kyoto Sta.

When you alight from the train at Kyoto Station, don't rush off too quickly to see the temples and shrines in the Higashiyama and Sagano areas. First I recommend that you take the time to visit the three great temples very close to the station. One of these is Tō-ji, formally known as Kyōōgokoku-ji.

Heian-kyō was founded in 794. At the center of its southern edge stood the *rajō-mon* gate, and directly northward from here the broad Suzaku-Ōji avenue ran up to the Dai-dairi (Inner Enclosure). Originally, the gate was intended to be part of a perimeter wall around the entire capital, but this was never completed. To the east and west of the gate stood two great temples, Tō-ji (East Temple) and Sai-ji (West Temple).

In 823, the priest Kūkai came to Tō-ji and made it a temple of the Singon esoteric Buddhist teachings. In the same year, Sai-ji was granted to another priest, Shubin, but the middle of the Heian period the temple was burned, and today only monument stone remain. The *rajō-mon* gate also fell into ruin due to earthquakes and floods the middle of the Heian period, as depicted in Akutagawa Ryūnosuke's story "*Rashōmon*." Today all that remains of the period when Heian-kyō was being constructed is Tō-ji,

遺構としては、数度の再建を経た東寺だけが今日に遺る。

東寺の諸堂

東は大宮通、南は九条通に沿う幅広い堀や堂々とした築地塀が、まずこの悠揚たる大寺の偉容を示す。東寺の境内には東西南北それぞれの大門から入ることができるが、寺域の中央に、金堂、講堂、食堂が一直線に並ぶ奈良時代様式の伽藍配置を眺めるには南大門から足を踏み入れるべきだ。

南大門から入って、北に歩き、食堂近くの受付で拝観料をおさめて、五重塔を含む中央のエリアを見学する。

まず講堂に入る。この建物は外観も内部もまだ朱塗りの木肌をあざやかに残している。堂内は思いのほか明るい。内陣は広く、中央の如来部に大日如来、向かって右の菩薩部には、金剛波羅密多菩薩、左の明王部には不動明王の各座像を囲むように、21体の仏像が「**立体曼荼羅**」の世界をあらわして、真言密教の具現をみることができる。

内陣　寺の本堂や神社の本殿で、本尊や神体を安置する部分。

曼荼羅　仏の悟りの境地を表現し、一定の形式で諸仏の集合図を描いたもの。

金堂は、講堂より一段と大きく、堂々とした東寺の本堂で、中央の本尊薬師如来の光背の上には十分な余裕がみられるほどの高さである。こちらは木組の朱色はすっかり淡くなり、それゆえに仏堂の荘重さがいっそう拝観者に伝わる。

which has been reconstructed many times.

The Buildings of Tō-ji

The wide moats and splendid roofed walls along Ōmiya St. to the east and Kujō St. to the south attest to the calm grandeur of this great temple. It is possible to enter the grounds of Tō-ji through the great gates from the east, west, south, or north, but I recommend starting through the *nandai-mon* gate in the south in order to fully appreciate the layout of the temple in the Nara-period style, with the central main temple area containing the *kon-dō* and *kō-dō* halls and the *jiki-dō*, refectory, arrayed in a straight line.

From the *nandai-mon* gate, walk north, and pay the entry fee at the reception near the *jiki-dō*, which allows you into the central area, including the five-story pagoda.

First, enter the *kō-dō*, which boasts decoration in vermilion-lacquered bark both inside and out. The brightness of the interior of the hall will surprise you. Twenty-one statues of Buddhas form a "**three-dimensional mandala**," including the central *nyorai* area with a statue of *Dainichi Nyorai*, the *Bosatsu* area to the right with a *kongōharamitsuta bosatsu*, and the *myōō* area with a *fudō myōō* (Acala). The experience is as if you are seeing a physical embodiment of the esoteric Shingon teachings.

The *kon-dō*, the grand main hall of Tō-ji, is larger than the *kō-dō*, with plenty of room for the halo of the primary religious image of the temple, the *yakushi nyorai* (healing Buddha). The fade vermilion color of the interior conveys the solemn atmosphere of the Buddha hall to visitors.

十二神将　薬師如来を信仰して薬師経をもつ行者を護る12の神将。

本尊薬師如来像の台座の周囲には十二神将が配され、また日光、月光の両脇侍菩薩はこころもち顔を傾けて、拝む私たちの顔をみつめるようで、このわずかな傾きが、まこと慈しみにあふれていてこの仏像の前から立ちさりがたい思いをいだく。

五重塔の内部

五重塔の内部は春と秋に特別公開され、初層の内陣に入場することができる（別料金）。空海が講堂とともに五重塔造営に着手して以来、この塔は4度の火災で焼失しており、現在の5代目の塔は1644年（寛永21）に徳川家光の寄進で再建したもので、高さ約55mと国内の古塔では最も高く、京都の象徴として聳えている。

五重塔の初層内陣は中央に心柱が立ち、これを大日如来とみたて、南に宝生如来、北に不空成就如来、東に阿閦如来、西に阿弥陀如来の各坐像を安置している。壁面には真言八祖像が、また周囲には金剛界曼荼羅の諸仏が精密画のごとく描かれている。

優美な檜皮葺の屋根をもつ大師堂と、東寺のなかでは最も古い建造物である宝蔵もみておきたい。

The statue of the *yakushi nyorai* is surrounded by twelve deities and the *nikkō* and *gekkō bosatsu* (Sunlight and Moonlight Boddhisattvas), who incline their heads as if they are peering at visiting worshippers. This subtle incline shows a real affection so it is hard to walk away.

The Interior of the Five-story Pagoda

The interior of the five-story pagoda is opened only in the spring and the autumn, when you can visit the first-floor sanctuary (extra fee). Since Kūkai built the pagoda and the *kō-dō*, the pagoda has burned down four times. The current fifth incarnation of the pagoda was built in 1644, with the support of Tokugawa Iemitsu. It is about 55 meters high, the tallest of its kind in Japan, and stands as a symbol of Kyoto.

In the center of the sanctuary stands a pillar depicting *dainichi nyorai*, surrounded by *hōshō nyorai* to the south, *fukūjōju nyorai* to the north, *aka nyorai* to the east, and *amida-nyorai* (Amitabha) to the west. On the walls are portraits of the eight Shingon saints surrounded by a *kongōkai* mandala of Buddhas.

The Taishi-dō, with its beautiful cypress shingle (*hiwada-buki*) roof, and Tō-ji's oldest building, the *hōzō* treasure house, are also worth visiting.

2

桃山から江戸の建築美の宝庫

西本願寺（にしほんがんじ） 東本願寺（ひがしほんがんじ）

京都市下京区堀川通花屋町下ル
075(371)5181
5時30分～17時30分(5月～8月は18時、11月～2月は5時30分～17時)
境内参拝自由(飛雲閣・書院は通常非公開・特別拝観日がある)
www.hongwanji.or.jp
京都駅より市バス9・28・75系統 西本願寺前下車1分

京都駅近くの東西ふたつの本願寺もぜひ訪れておきたい。仏教寺院の大建築の典型をこの両寺にみることができよう。

親鸞（しんらん）を宗祖とする浄土真宗（じょうどしんしゅう）は、現在、10派の本山、2万2000を超える寺院、約1300万人の信者をもつ日本最大の宗派である。西本願寺は本願寺派の本山、東本願寺は大谷（おおたに）派の本山である。

東本願寺　下京区烏丸通七条上ル
075(371)9181
境内参拝自由

本願寺と東西の分断

本願寺の歴史は、親鸞の没後、末娘覚信尼（かくしんに）が1272年（文永9）に、現在の知恩院（ちおんいん）三門の北付近に廟堂を建てたことにはじまり、その堂宇を覚信尼の孫、3世覚如（かくにょ）が本願寺と称し、8世蓮如（れんにょ）が大教団に発展させた。

蓮如　1415～99。室町時代の浄土真宗中興の祖。

この民衆教団の飛躍的な発展と組織力は、旧仏教界との衝突、時の権力者からの圧迫を

2. Treasure houses of architectural beauty from the Momoyama to Edo periods

Nishi Hongan-ji and Higashi Hongan-ji

Address: Horikawa-dōri Hanaya-chō-sagaru, Shimogyō-ku, Kyoto-shi
Tel: 075 (371) 5181
Hours: 5:30AM–5:30PM (May–August: 5:30AM–6:00PM; November–February: 5:30AM–5:00PM.
(Hiunkaku and shoin open only on special days.)
Admission: Free www.hongwanji.or.jp/english/
1 min walk from Nishihongan-ji-mae bus stop, bus 9,28 or 75 from Kyoto Sta.

The two Hongan-ji temples, Higashi (East) and Nishi (West), are the other two temples near Kyoto Station that should not be missed. In these temples, one can observe the architectural models for many Buddhist temples.

The Jōdo Shinshū sect of Buddhism founded by Shinran now boasts ten schools, more than 22,000 temples, and approximately thirteen million believers, making it Japan's largest sect. Nishi Hongan-ji is the head temple for the Hongan-ji sect, and Higashi Hongan-ji is the head temple for the Ōtani sect.

Hongan-ji: Split Between East and West

The history of Hongan-ji began after Shinran's death, in 1272, when his youngest daughter, nun Kakushin-ni, built the *byō-dō* (mausoleum) honoring her father north of the site where the *san-mon* gate of Chion-in stands today. Kakushin-ni's grandson, the priest Kakunyo, later named the *byō-dō* Hongan-ji, and a later descendant, the eighth head priest Rennyo, further cultivated the movement.

The vigorous growth of this popular movement fostered conflict with the old Buddhist regime, and under pressure of authorities,

生み、蓮如は近江、越前、山科と転々とする。しかし、山科本願寺も焼討にあい、大坂の石山本願寺に移る。織田信長が将軍足利義昭と対立するようになると、11世顕如は1570年(元亀元)義昭に味方して信長の陣営に攻撃をかけて、11年間にわたる石山戦争が勃発した。これは信長が正親町天皇に調停を依頼し、和議が成立、顕如が石山本願寺から退出することで終結した。

そののち紀伊、和泉貝塚を経て大坂天満へ本願寺は移っていくが、1591年(天正19)に豊臣秀吉の寄進をうけて現在の場所に寺域が定まった。

顕如には教如と准如というふたりの息子がいた。内部抗争があって、次男の准如が12世を継ぎ、教如は隠退させられた。そこに目をつけたのが徳川家康で、これまでいくたの為政者を悩ませた一大宗教王国の勢力を分断させるべく、教如に六条烏丸の土地を与え、1602年(慶長7)に東本願寺を建立させたのである。

西本願寺の伽藍

現在の御影堂は1636年(寛永13)、阿弥陀堂は1760年(宝暦10)の再建である。御影堂は東西48m、南北62m、高さ29mの偉容を誇り、内陣中央に親鸞の木像を祀る。外陣がきわめて大きく、734畳敷の大広間は全国からの信者を収容する。阿弥陀堂は、東西42m、

Rennyo was forced to move from one location to another, from Ōmi to Echizen to Yamashina. When the Yamashina Hongan-ji was burned, he moved to the Ishiyama Hongan-ji in Osaka. Oda Nobunaga had come into conflict with the shogun, Ashikaga Yoshiaki, and the eleventh head priest of Hongan-ji, Kennyo, made an alliance with Yoshiaki in 1570 and attacked the camp of Nobunaga, sparking the eleven-year-long Ishiyama War. Nobunaga requested the mediation of Emperor Ōgimachi, and peace was restored when Kennyo retired from the Ishiyama Hongan-ji.

Subsequently Hongan-ji moved several more times, from Kii to Izumikaizuka to Tenma in Osaka. Finally, in 1591, with the support of Toyotomi Hideyoshi, the temple was established in its current location.

Kennyo had two sons, Kyōnyo and Junnyo. Due to an internecine conflict, Junnyo, the second son, was named the twelfth successor to the leadership of Hongan-ji, and Kyōnyo went into seclusion. However, Tokugawa Ieyasu realized that it would be politic to divide the power of this "religious kingdom" that had troubled so many political leaders and awarded land in Rokujō-karasuma to Kyōnyo. In 1602, Higashi Hongan-ji was built on this land.

The Grand Temple at Nishi Hongan-ji

The present-day *goei-dō* was rebuilt in 1636 and the *amida-dō* in 1760. The *goei-dō* is an astonishing 48 meters from east to west, 62 meters from south to north, and 29 meters in height, with a **wooden statue** of Shinran in the center of the inner sanctum. The massive worship hall, covering an area of 734 *tatami* mats, welcomes worshippers from all over the country. The *amida-dō*

南北45m、高さ25mで、阿弥陀如来像を中心に、インド、中国、日本の六師を祀っている。このように本堂の阿弥陀堂より宗祖を祀る御影堂のほうが大きいのが真宗伽藍の特長といえる。

伏見城　桃山城とも。豊臣秀吉が1594年に築いた城。関ヶ原の戦で西軍の攻撃により落城。

聚楽第　豊臣秀吉が1587年に築いた絢爛豪華な城郭風の邸宅。

西本願寺の唐門は伏見城の遺構で、桃山時代の装飾彫刻の粋で、その美しさに日暮れまで見とれてしまうことから「日暮門」ともよばれている。また秀吉の聚楽第から移されたといわれる三層柿葺の楼閣建築である飛雲閣、渡辺了慶とその一門が描いた障壁画にかこまれる本願寺書院、現存する日本最古の北能舞台など、西本願寺の諸堂は桃山時代から江戸時代初期の装飾美を極めた建築物の宝庫である。

なお、東本願寺は約9万3000㎡（約2万8000坪）の広大な寺域のなかに、南北76m、東西58m、高さ38m、927畳の大広間をもち、木造建築では世界最大級の御影堂、その南側に南北52m、東西47m、高さ29mの本尊阿弥陀如来像を祀る阿弥陀堂が建つ。また寺宝として、親鸞自筆の『教行信証』6巻を所蔵している。

教行信証　浄土真宗の教義に関する根本教典。

rebuilt is 42 meters from east to west, 45 meters from south to north, and 25 meters in height, with a statue of the Amitabha in the center, honoring the six masters of India, China, and Japan. Making the *goei-dō*, which honors ancestors, larger than the *amida-dō* is a characteristic feature of a Jōdo Shinshū sect.

Nishi Hongan-ji's Chinese style *kara-mon* gate is a relic of Fushimi castle. Its nickname, "Higurashi-mon," comes from the habit of onlookers of staring at the Momoyama period decorative engravings until sundown ends their reverie. Nishi Hongan-ji is a veritable treasure house of architectural achievement from the Momoyama to the Edo period, also boasting the Hiunkaku, a three-story tower with a shake-shingled (*kokera-buki*) roof said to have been moved from the Jurakudai palace of Hideyoshi; the *shoin*, a study-cum-living room decorated with screen paintings by Watanabe Ryōkei and his disciples; and Japan's oldest existing Kita (North) Noh stage.

Higashi Hongan-ji's approximately 93,000m^2 of grounds contain the *goei-dō*, said to be the world's largest wooden structure at 76 meters (north-south) by 58 meters (east-west) and 38 meters in height, with a floor area of 927 *tatami* mats. To the south of the *goei-dō* stands the *amida-dō*, large itself at 52 meters north-south by 47 meters east-west and 29 meters in height, which shelters the temple's principal image of the Amitabha (*amida-nyorai*). Here also is contained another of the **temple's treasures**, a manuscript of "*Shinran's Kyōgyō Shinshō*" in six volumes, in his own hand.

3

宏大な禅宗伽藍と渓谷美

東福寺

とうふくじ

京都市東山区本町15-778
075(561)0087
9時〜16時
境内参拝自由(通天橋・開山堂は400円、方丈庭園は400円)
www.tofukuji.jp
京都駅よりJR奈良線　東福寺駅下車徒歩10分

京都駅からJR奈良線に乗ると一駅で東福寺駅となり、京阪電鉄にも同名の駅がある。両東福寺駅から本町通(ほんまちどおり)をわずかに南下すれば東福寺に行けるのだが、東山三十六峰のひとつ月輪山(つきのわさん)の山麓に展開する宏大な寺域は、あまりに広すぎて、どこをどのような順路で歩いていいのか判然としない。

そのため、本町通をさらに南下して、東福寺の南西に位置する南大門から境内に向かうことをおすすめする。

この南大門から先はゆるやかな上り坂になり、いかにも大寺の参道といった風景で、勅使門(ちょくしもん)に向かっているため正統なアプローチといえよう。

最古の三門と東福寺の歴史

勅使門は一般人には閉じられており、脇の六波羅門(ろくはらもん)から境内に足を踏み入れる。すると目前に禅宗寺院では日本最古、最大の三門が聳えているのがみえる。やはり、寺は三門か

3. A grand Zen temple and beautiful ravine

Tōfuku-ji

Address: 15-778 Honmachi, Higashiyama-ku, Kyoto-shi
Tel: 075 (561) 0087
Hours: 9:00AM–4:00PM
Admission: Free (Entry to Tsūten-kyō bridge and the kaizan-dō: ¥400; entry to the hōjō garden: ¥400)
www.tofukuji.jp/english/
10 min walk from JR Nara Line Tōfuku-ji Sta.

Tōfuku-ji Station is one stop from Kyoto Station on the JR Nara line, and is also on the Keihan Dentetsu line. Tōfuku-ji is a short walk south from either station along Honmachi St., but the broad precincts of the temple spreading out at the foot of Mt. Tsukinowasan, part of the Higashiyama mountain chain, are so extensive that it is hard to know what to approach first.

Therefore, my recommendation is to begin from the *nandai-mon* gate, at the southwest side of the temple.

The gentle incline of the path from *nandai-mon* gate is a typical scene of the approach to a great temple, and since it faces the *chokushi-mon* gate (imperial messenger's gate), it can be said that this is the official approach to Tōfuku-ji.

The Oldest *San-mon* Gate, and the History of Tōfuku-ji

The *chokushi-mon* gate is closed to the public, so one must enter the temple grounds through the *rokuhara-mon* gate next to it. When you do, you will see before you the oldest and biggest *san-mon* gate among Zen temples in Japan, making it clear why visitors

ら参拝するのが順序である。

東福寺は、1236年（嘉禎2）摂政九条道家が祖先を弔う寺として建立をはじめ、当時高僧として名の高い円爾弁円を開山として招き、1255年（建長7）息子の実経の代でようやく諸堂が完成、天台、真言、禅の三宗兼学の寺として、また九条家の菩提寺として宏大な地に寺観を整えたのである。東福寺という寺名は、奈良の東大寺の伽藍の偉容さと興福寺のすぐれた教学から一字ずつをとって命名された。

東福寺の山内と通天橋

境内の南に建つ三門は、応永年間（1394～1428）の再建で、応仁の乱の兵火やその後の火災からも焼失をまぬがれている。高さ約22m、正面約25m、側面約10mという入母屋造、本瓦葺、二階二重門の豪壮さで、左右には山廊をつけて楼上への階段を設けている。楼上内部の天井や梁には彩色画がほどこされ、宝冠釈迦如来像と十六羅漢像を安置する。

山廊　禅宗の三門の両側にある建物で、楼門の上に上がる階段がつけられている。

三門の北に巨大な法堂（本堂）が建つ。1881年（明治14）に方丈から出火して本堂や法堂、庫裏などを焼失したため、この法堂は1934年（昭和9）の再建である。仏殿をかねた法堂では毎年3月14日から16日まで釈迦念仏会が催され、日本最大級の涅槃図が掲げられることもあって多くの参拝客が訪れる。

涅槃図　釈迦入滅の状況を描いた図。入滅の場面だけのものと、その前後の8場面を描いたものがある。

法堂の北に1890年（明治23）に再建された

should enter the temple through the *san-mon* gate.

Tōfuku-ji was founded in 1236 by the imperial regent Kujō Michiie to mourn his ancestors. He invited the famous priest Enni Ben'en to open the temple, and in 1255, Michiie's son Sanetsune finally completed the buildings of the temple complex. The temple was established as a place where the teachings of the three sect of Japanese Buddhism, Tendai, Shingon, and Zen, would all be studied, and where the ancestors of the Kujō clan would be enshrined. The name "Tōfuku-ji" was coined by combining one character each from the names of Tōdai-ji in Nara, for its splendor, and Kōfuku-ji, for its great learning.

Tōfuku-ji's ground and Tsūten-kyō Bridge

The *san-mon* gate that stands on the south side of the grounds was rebuilt during the Ōei era (1394–1428) and escaped from the fires of the Ōnin War and subsequent disturbances. It stands 22 meters high, 25 meters wide, and 10 meters deep. It is built in the gable and hip roof (*irimoya-zukuri*) style, with a tiled roof and a two-story gate. On either side are *sanrō* structures forming a staircase to the top of the gate. The gate boasts decorated ceilings and beams and enshrine statues of the crowned Buddha and the sixteen Arhat.

To the north of the *san-mon* gate stands the massive *hattō*. In 1881, a fire started in the *hōjō* that consumed the *hondō*, the *hattō*, the *kuri*, and other buildings. The current *hattō* was rebuilt in 1934. In this building, which also serves as the *butsu-den* (Buddha hall), the Shaka Nenbutsue Service is celebrated every year on March 14–16, when Japan's largest Nehan-zu (portrayal of Nirvana) is displayed, attracting many worshippers.

The north of the *hattō* stands the *hōjō* rebuilt in 1890.

方丈が建つ。

東福寺の山内の景色で特筆すべきは、洗玉澗(せんぎょくかん)とよぶ渓谷に架けられた三つの橋廊(きょうろう)で、上から偃月橋(えんげつきょう)、通天橋(つうてんきょう)、臥雲橋(がうんきょう)が南北に渡る。よく知られているのが、方丈の西に架かる通天橋で紅葉の時期に多くの観光客が訪れる。橋の途中につくられた舞台からみる渓谷のあざやかな紅葉に人気がある。また、楓(かえで)の若葉が芽吹くころもすがすがしい景色で、秋の雑踏を避けて新緑を楽しむ人も多い。

通天橋を北に渡ると楼閣を屋上にのせた開山堂にいたる。その隣に開山の円爾弁円が住んでいた普門院(ふもんいん)が建つ。この一画は宏大な東福寺のなかにあって、それらの建物と山の緑に囲まれた静かな空間となり、室町期に作庭されたという庭園のたたずまいも落ちついている。通天橋の西には臥雲橋が通天橋とその橋廊下をやや見上げるような位置にある。ここからも渓谷を覆う美しい樹姿を眺めることができる。

One of the most notable features of Tōfuku-ji's ground setting is the system of bridges spanning the *sengyokukan* ravine, consisting of the *engetsu-kyō* bridge, the *tsūten-kyō* bridge, and the *gaun-kyō* bridge. Many tourists come to view the spectacular autumn leaves from the *tsūten-kyō* bridge, to the west of the *hōjō*. It is particularly popular to enjoy the bright foliage in the ravine from the deck constructed halfway across the bridge. The setting is also popular in the spring, when the young leaves of the maple are budding, so many people avoid the crowds of autumn to enjoy the new greenery.

Cross *tsūten-kyō* to the north, and you come to the *kaizan-dō* on the roof of the tower. Next to this is the *fumon-in*, where Enni Ben'en lived. In the middle of the broad grounds of the temple, these buildings and the quiet space encircled by the mountains help recreate the way the gardens must first have appeared when they were created in the Muromachi period. To the west of *tsūten-kyō* is *gaun-kyō*, from which you can look up at *tsūten-kyō*. There is also a beautiful view of the ravine below.

4

「御寺」と称する皇室の菩提寺

泉涌寺（せんにゅうじ）

京都市東山区泉涌寺山内町27
075(561)1551
9時〜16時30分（12月〜2月は9時〜16時）
500円（特別拝観は別料金）
mitera.org
京都駅より市バス208系統　泉涌寺道下車徒歩10分

東大路通（ひがしおおじ）を南に、JRの線路を跨ぐように越えると右手に巨大な楠（くすのき）がみえてくる。その背後の社が後白河上皇が熊野三山から勧請した新熊野（いまくまの）神社である。

熊野三山　熊野本宮大社・熊野速玉（はやたま）大社・熊野那智大社の総称。

さらに南へ歩くと泉涌寺道との交差点で、この東に入る道が泉涌寺の山内へ私たちを誘う。泉涌寺道を250mほど進むと泉涌寺の総門をくぐる。ここからはじまる参道は道の左右を石積（いしづみ）で区切って、高い樹木が緑陰をつくる気持ちのいい道で、ゆるやかな上り坂の両脇に泉涌寺の子院（しいん）が点在する。

那須与一（なすのよいち）の墓という石塔があり、10月第3日曜日におこなわれる「二十五菩薩練供養」で知られる即成院（そくじょういん）、鎌倉期の作で丈六（じょうろく）の木像釈迦如来立像を本尊とする戒光寺（かいこうじ）、また境内から市街を一望できる宿坊の悲田院（ひでんいん）などが樹林のなかに建っている。

丈六　釈迦の身長は1丈6尺（約4.8m）あったとされ、その大きさに造られた仏像。

泉涌寺の歴史

やがて参道はやや爪先上がりになって、泉

4. The ancestral temple of the imperial family

Sennyū-ji

Address: 27 Sennyū-ji Yamanouchi-chō, Higashiyama-ku, Kyoto-shi
Tel: 075 (561) 1551
Hours: 9:00AM–4:30PM (December–February: 9:00AM–4:00PM)
Admission: ¥500 (Additional charge for special worship)
mitera.org
10 min walk from Sennyū-ji-michi bus stop, bus 208 from Kyoto Sta.

If you follow Higashiōji St. south along the JR tracks, on the right you will see a large camphor tree, and just behind it the Imakumano-jinja, founded by the former Emperor Goshirakawa with deities reenshrined from the three great shrines of Kumano.

A little farther south, at the intersection with Sennyū-ji Rd., the road leading to Sennyū-ji beckons us to the east, where a stroll of 250 meters brings us through the main gate of the temple. The approach to the temple is defined by **piles of stones** on either side and high trees providing shady cover. The **sub-temple** of Sennyū-ji border the gently ascending entry path.

These sub-temples include the stone stupa marking the grave of Nasu-no-Yoichi; the Sokujō-in where the "25 Bosatsu nerikuyō" Service is held on the third Sunday of October; Kaikō-ji, with its principal treasure—the 4.8m wooden standing statue of the Buddha (*shaka nyorai*); and the Hiden-in, providing a broad view of the city.

The History of Sennyū-ji

At last the approach brings you under the Great gate of

涌寺の大門にたどりつく。そこは山深い静寂な雰囲気に満ちる。泉涌寺は、平安時代の初め、左大臣藤原緒嗣が**山荘**を営み、のちにその場所に法輪寺という寺を建てたことが草創といい、そののち寺勢は衰えていたが、1218年（建保6）に月輪大師俊芿が再興を志して、十万檀越の喜捨をあおぐため「泉涌寺勧縁疏」を著し、後鳥羽上皇に献上した。それにより、皇室や公家などから援助を得て、伽藍が完成した。

檀越　寺に布施をする人のこと。

寺名は境内の泉から清水がわき出たことから、泉涌寺と改めた。1242年（仁治3）に四条天皇が没すると山内に月輪陵が営まれ、以降、歴代の御陵が造営された。そのため泉涌寺は皇室の菩提寺となって「御寺」と尊称されるようになったのである。

泉涌寺の山内を歩く

泉涌寺の特徴は、参道をのぼりつめた大門から眺める境内の景色である。大門から仏殿など諸堂を坂の下に見下ろし、すり鉢の底に伽藍が位置して幅広い砂利道をゆっくり下って仏殿に近づいていく。この仏殿の鏡天井には狩野探幽筆の龍図や堂裏の壁面にはどこからみても正面となる白衣観音像がある。

また、大門を入って左手に楊貴妃の等身坐像の聖観音像を祀る楊貴妃観音堂が建つ。

楊貴妃　719～56。中国唐の玄宗皇帝の寵愛を一身に受けた絶世の美女。安史の乱で殺された。

Sennyū-ji, and you find yourself filled with a sense of the deep solitude of the mountains. Sennyū-ji began as the **mountain villa** of the court minister Fujiwara-no-Otsugu, which he later converted into a temple called Hōrin-ji. The temple's influence declined, but in 1218, Shunjō worked to revive it by writing the Sennyū-ji Kan'enso in an attempt to obtain the alms of 100,000 worshippers and presenting it to the former emperor Gotoba. With the help of the imperial family and the court, the temple was completed.

The temple's name comes from the pure water that came from a spring on the temple's grounds. In 1242, Emperor Shijō died, and his tomb Tsukinowa-ryō was built in the forest on the temple grounds, followed by a number of other imperial tombs. Eventually, Sennyū-ji became the ancestral burial place of the **imperial family,** coming to be known as "*the mi-tera*," or the imperial temple.

Walking the Grounds of Sennyū-ji

One of the special charms of Sennyū-ji is the view of the temple grounds from the Great gate after climbing to the end of the approach. Looking down at the *butsu-den* (Buddha hall) and the other buildings from the gate, the temple appears to be situated at the base of a great bowl. You walk down a gravel path to approach the *butsu-den*, the ceiling of which features a dragon painting by Kanō Tan'yū and, at the back of the hall, a painting of a white-robed Kannon, a full-face from any direction, standing within a lotus by the same artist.

If you turn to your left as you enter the Great gate, you will see the Yōkihi Kannon-dō, where a life-size seated image of the *shō-kannon* modeled on the legendary Chinese beauty Yang Kwei-fei

仏殿の背後に舎利殿(しゃりでん)、その右奥に1884年(明治17)明治天皇によって再建された霊明殿(れいめいでん)、さらに奥には中央に唐破風(からはふ)の門を置いた月輪陵の長大な透塀がみえる。

月輪陵の正門
The front gate of Tsukinowa-ryō

(Yōkihi) is enshrined.

Behind the *butsu-den* is the *shari-den* hall, and to the right is the *reimei-den*, rebuilt at the order of Emperor Meiji in 1884. Further on is the long transparent fence surrounding the Tsukinowa-ryō—the tomb of Emperor Shijō—with its distinctive Chinese gables (*karahafu*) Gate.

5

全国各地の「お稲荷さん」の総本社

伏見稲荷大社

京都市伏見区深草藪之内町68
075(641)7331
境内参拝自由
inari.jp
JR奈良線　稲荷下車徒歩１分

日本全国に四万社あるという稲荷神社の総本社がここ伏見稲荷大社である。初詣や祭礼日にかかわらず、ふだんの日でも商売繁盛や家内安全を願う多くの参拝者で賑わっている。

稲荷社の創建は平安京遷都（794年）以前の711年（和銅4）2月初午の日といい、この地に居住していた秦氏のひとり秦伊呂具が稲荷山の三カ峰に上・中・下社を建て大宮能売大神（上社）、佐田彦大神（中社）、宇迦之御魂大神（下社）の三神を祀ったことにはじまるとされる。

秦伊呂具は、傲慢にも餅を的にして弓矢に興じていたところ、その餅が白い鳥になって飛び去り、**家運**は衰えた。そのため、その鳥の降りた三つの峰に社を造営したのである。

ただ、もともと稲荷山は神南備山として信仰されて、秦氏の田の神であったと思われ、田の神は、春の農耕のさいに山から下り、秋の収穫後に山へ帰るという古くからの言い伝

神南備山　神が鎮座すると信じられた山。人里に近い形のよい円錐形の山で、豊かな森に覆われる。

5. The nation's head shrine for honoring the harvest deity

Fushimi-Inari-taisha

Address: 68 Fukakusa Yabunouchi-chō, Fushimi-ku, Kyoto-shi
Tel: 075 (641) 7331
Admission: Free
inari.jp/en/
1 min walk from JR Nara Line Inari Sta.

Fushimi-Inari-taisha is the head shrine of the reportedly 40,000 Inari-jinja through Japan. Unlike other shrines that are most crowded on New Year's Day and festival days, this shrine is lively with worshippers praying for commercial success and household safety every day of the year.

Fushimi-Inari-taisha is said to have been established in 711, even before the establishment of the capital itself in 794. A powerful clan named Hata-no-Irogu is said to have built shrines on each of the three peaks of Mt. Inariyama. The upper shrine was dedicated to Ōmiyanome-no-Ōkami, the middle shrine to Satahiko-no-Ōkami, and the lower shrine to Ukanomitama-no-Ōkami.

Legend has it that Hata-no-Irogu was using *mochi* (rice cakes) as a target for archery practice, an arrogant act. Suddenly the mochi turned into a white bird and flew away, and subsequently the **family fortunes** declined. Therefore he established shrines on each of the three peaks where the bird alighted.

However, a more likely explanation is that Mt. Inariyama was worshipped as a mountain where gods resided, including the god of the Hata clan's fields. The god of the fields was believed to come down from the mountain at the time of spring planting and return after the

えがあり、稲荷山を神域としてとらえたのであろう。稲荷はイネナリ(稲生)からの名である。

農業神、商売の守護神

平安京の官寺である東寺に入った空海は、827年（天長4）に東寺の鎮守として稲荷神を祀ったことで稲荷大社は広く人々から崇敬を集め、神階は正一位、『延喜式』の名神大社となった。さらに1072年（延久4）には後三条天皇の行幸から、歴代の天皇もそれにならった。

『延喜式』 延喜5年（905）から編纂が始められた律令施行の細則。全50巻。

応仁の乱で山上の社殿が焼失したため、いまの山麓の地へ移され、本殿は1499年（明応8）に五間社流造として建立。のちに豊臣秀吉によって修理され、また、楼門と社領百石余の寄進を受けている。いまも拝殿、本殿の檜皮葺の大屋根の美しさは比類がなく、社域の朱色も鮮やかである。

伏見稲荷大社といえば、朱の鳥居が林立してトンネルとなり、それは「**千本鳥居**」としてよく知られる。本殿の裏手からはじまり、途中二筋に分かれて奥社にいたる小さな朱の鳥居には奉納者の名が記されて、立錐の余地もなくここにも当社の人気のほどがうかがえる。

また、稲荷山中には小祠や小塚が無数にあって、それをめぐることを「お山めぐり」といい、稲荷大社発祥の峰へ登る篤信者も多い。この「お山めぐり」は奥社奉拝所からはじまり、稲荷山の山腹から標高233mの頂上までの約4kmを2時間で一巡する。

autumn harvest, so Mt. Inariyama was considered a divine place. The name 'Inari' probably comes from a phrase meaning rice cultivation.

Guardian Deity of Agriculture and Business

In 827, Kūkai, the head priest of Tō-ji, the chief administrative temple of Heian-kyō, designated Inari God as a guardian deity of Tō-ji. This resulted in a great increase in popularity and worship at the Inari-taisha. Its court rank was raised to the highest level and it was designated as the excellent shrine of the '*Engishiki*,' an important legal compendium. Then, in 1072, the shrine received an official visit from Emperor Gosanjō, setting a precedent that many subsequent emperors would follow.

During the Ōnin War, the building on the mountain was burned, and a new main sanctuary (*hon-den*) was built in its current location at the foot of the mountain in 1499, in the *gokensha-nagare* style structure. It was subsequently repaired by Toyotomi Hideyoshi, and the two-story gate and other contributions were added. Today the cypress shingle (*hiwada-buki*) roofs of the worship hall (*hai-den*) and the *hon-den* are particularly admired for their beauty. A vermilion color of the building is still clear and bright.

The signature vermilion "**thousand *torii* gate**" of the Fushimi-Inari-taisha are so numerous that they seem to form tunnels for visitors to walk through. Beginning from behind the *hon-den*, the lines of small *torii* gate have the names of their donors written on them. The dense forest of *torii* gate attests to the popularity of this shrine.

Around the area of Mt. Inariyama, small shrines and mounds are sprinkled through the forest, and strolling through them is known as "*Oyama-meguri*." The 4-kilometer route takes about two hours to complete, including the climb from the shrine to the 233-meter summit.

中国明様式の伽藍をめぐる

萬福寺

宇治市五ケ庄三番割34
0774(32)3900
9時〜16時30分
500円
www.obakusan.or.jp
JR奈良線　黄檗駅下車徒歩５分

日本三禅宗のひとつ黄檗宗の総本山が萬福寺である。中国福建省の黄檗山萬福寺の住持であった隠元隆琦は、明末期の混乱で長崎にのがれていた中国僧らに招かれ、日本に渡ってきた。それが1654年（承応3）のこと。その数年後、隠元は徳川4代将軍家綱の帰依を得て、宇治のこの地に故国と同名の萬福寺を創建（1661年）、明朝様式をそのままに踏襲した伽藍を造営した。

隠元は仏教儀礼も中国のままに従わせ、そのため、読経も黄檗唐音で発声して、僧も日本語を使うことを禁じられていた。さらに代々の住持も14、17世をのぞき21世まで中国からの渡来僧であった。

日本の禅寺とは異なる境内

それは、萬福寺を語るとき、よく例に出される菊舎尼の句「山門を出れば日本ぞ茶摘唄」にあらわされているように、萬福寺の山内はまったく中国風であり、寺を出れば茶どころ

6. A Ming dynasty-style temple

Manpuku-ji

Address: 34 Gokashō Sanbanwari, Uji-shi
Tel: 077 (432) 3900
Hours: 9:00AM–4:30PM
Admission: ¥500
www.obakusan.or.jp/en/
5 min walk from JR Nara Line Ōbaku Sta.

Manpuku-ji is the head temple of the Ōbaku Zen sect, one of the three Zen sect. In 1654, Ingen Ryūki, who was the head priest of the Ōbaku Manpuku-ji in Fujian, China, was invited to Japan by some Chinese monks who had fled to Nagasaki to escape the chaos of the end of the Ming dynasty. A few years later, Ingen succeeded in converting the fourth Tokugawa shogun, Ietsuna, and with his support built a replica of the Ming dynasty-style Manpuku-ji at Uji in 1661. The name Manpuku-ji was followed by the same one at his hometown.

Ingen followed the Chinese practice in his Buddhist teachings, including the Ōbaku pronunciation of the sutras, so he forbid his monks to use Japanese. Furthermore, all the head priests at the temple up to the twenty-first successor were, except the forteenth and seventeenth, all from China.

Temple Grounds Different from Those of a Japanese Zen Temple

The poet nun Kikusha wrote of the exotic atmosphere of Manpuku-ji, "I pass out of the *san-mon* gate / and find Japan again / in the song of the tea-pickers." Even today, within the grounds of the temple, the atmosphere feels completely Chinese,

宇治の日本的風景に一変するというわけで、それは今日でも同じような景色である。

萬福寺の総門を入ると右手は放生池で、池の正面に重層で山廊を左右に付設した楼門（山門）が建つ。扁額は隠元の筆になる。

この寺の特徴のひとつが、境内の諸堂をつなぐ道の意匠である。砂地の道の中央に菱形石の角をつないで縦一列に並べ、左右を細長い葛石でおさえた形式で、修行僧らは、その葛石のうえを歩き、決して中央に足を踏み入れてはならないといわれている。また、殿舎の廊下が**敷瓦**であることもほかの寺と趣を異にしており、靴をはいたまま諸堂をめぐることのできる感覚が新鮮である。

萬福寺の見どころ

明朝様式の伽藍配置は三門から直線上に、天王殿、大雄宝殿、法堂といった配置に並び、左右には対称的に諸堂が建って、それらを結ぶ回廊のようすもどこか中国風で、しかも禅房にふさわしく毅然としている。とくに私たちを驚かすのが、天王殿に祀られている金色の布袋尊で、豊満な躯と笑顔が奇態である。

布袋尊　?〜917。中国後梁の禅僧。大きな腹と福々しい顔で布の袋をもって托鉢した。日本では七福神のひとり。

さらに萬福寺の見どころを述べれば、

・総門の屋根に飾られている鯱に似たインドの想像上の動物「摩伽羅」の姿

and only when one leaves is one reminded that one is in Uji, the heartland of Japanese tea.

Enter the main gate, and on the right is the *hōjō* pond, with the two-story *san-mon* gate standing before it, flanked by its *sanrō* structures. The framed plaques with the names on the gate are in Ingen's hand.

One of the distinctive features of this temple is the design of the path that connects the various temple buildings, with diamond-shaped stones in the center and Kazura stone on both sides. It is said that petitioning monks could walk only on the Kazura stone and were not allowed to set foot in the center section. The **tiled floors** of the hallways are also unusual, allowing visitors to walk from one temple building to another without taking off their shoes.

Highlights of Manpuku-ji

The typical layout of a temple in the Ming dynasty-style places the Tennō-den, the *daiōhō-den*, and the *hattō* in a straight line originating at the *san-mon* gate, with other buildings arrayed symmetrically to the left and right. The corridors connecting the buildings are also in the Chinese style, yet somehow also suited to the life of the Zen monk in their austerity. A particularly notable feature of the temple is the golden statue of Hotei God enshrined in the Tennō-den, a somewhat comical figure with his chunky body and smiling face.

Other unusual features of Manpuku-ji include:

- The carving of a makara, an imaginary Indian creature that somewhat resembles a killer whale, on the roof of the main gate

・斎堂（食堂）の前につるされている大魚を模した開版
・大雄宝殿内の十八羅漢像の異相
・諸堂の正面左右に掛けられている対聯（細長い書軸）

といったもので、広い境内は三門から拝観順路の番号が示されていて親切である。

萬福寺の法堂
Hattō of Manpuku-ji

- The wooden carving of a large fish that hangs in front of the *sai-dō* dining hall on which the passing hours are sounded
- The strange visages of the eighteen Arhat statues in the *daiō-hōden*
- The *tsuiren*, or hanging scrolls, to the left and right of the entrances of several buildings.

All these are numbered, making it easy for visitors to follow the route through the temple grounds.

7

現存する日本最古の神社建築

宇治上神社

宇治市宇治山田59
0774(21)4634
境内参拝自由
京阪宇治線　宇治駅下車徒歩10分

宇治橋の東詰から宇治川の右岸に沿う道をさかのぼると、すぐ左手の石段上に宇治橋の守り寺といわれる橋寺放生院が建つ。646年（大化2）にはじめて橋が架けられたとき、同時に創建されたというが詳らかではない。さらに川上に向かって歩くと、はるか昔、応神天皇の皇子稚郎子の離宮跡といわれる地に宇治神社が、同皇子を祭神として鎮座している。山側の宇治上神社とあわせて、宇治離宮明神と称されていた。

橋寺放生院　聖徳太子の発願とか僧道登が宇治橋とともに646年に創建とかいわれる。

応神天皇　記紀に記された５世紀前後の第15代天皇。百済王朝と密な関係を築いたといわれる。

宇治上神社は、背後に山麓の緑林が迫る社域に拝殿と本殿だけが白砂敷の境内にひっそりと残る古社であるが、そのふたつの殿舎こそが、宇治上神社を世界遺産に登録させた建築物なのである。

平安朝をしのぶ優美な本殿

石橋を渡り、小さな門をくぐると檜皮葺の屋根が低い拝殿が正面に建つ。ふつう神社の拝殿というと高床式で四方が開け放たれたも

7. The oldest shrine buildings in Japan

Ujigami-jinja

Address: 59 Uji Yamada, Uji-shi
Tel: 077 (421) 4634
Admission: Free
10 min walk from Keihan Uji Line Uji Sta.

Heading east from Uji Bridge along the right side of the Uji River, you will shortly see on your left, at the top of a stone staircase, the Hashidera Hōjō-in, the guardian temple of the Uji Bridge. It is said to have been built at the same time as the first bridge, in 646. Proceeding farther up the river, the Uji-jinja stands on the site of a Imperial villa built for Prince Wakiiratsuko, son of Emperor Ōjin. Together with the Ujigami-jinja on the mountain above, the shrines are known as the Uji Rikyū Myōjin.

Within the white-sand grounds of the Ujigami-jinja, backed by the lush forest of the mountain, only the worship hall (*hai-den*) and the main sanctuary (*hon-den*) remain of the old buildings. These two structures are registered as world heritages.

The Sublime *Hon-den*, Recalling the Heian Court

Cross the stone bridge and pass under the small gate, and you stand before the *hai-den* front hall, with its low cypress shingle (*hiwada-buki*) roof. The typical *hai-den* is built in the *takayukashiki*

のであるが、ここ宇治上神社の拝殿は平安時代の寝殿造の様式をとり入れて、典雅な宮廷貴人の住宅のようである。屋根の左右に軒先から張り出された庇をもち、また中央に板扉を開き、両脇の面は蔀戸と白壁で構成され、床は低く、四周にはこれまた低い勾欄をもつ外縁をめぐらせている。

なんといっても、宇治上神社の白眉はこの優美な拝殿奥の本殿である。その外観は覆屋で、この覆屋も鎌倉期のものといわれ、切妻造の檜皮葺は端正な姿をみせる。前面に近寄って細かな格子戸から内部を拝すると、一間社流造の社殿が三棟並んでいるのがみえるはずだ。中央に応神天皇、右に仁徳天皇、左に稚郎子を祀る。

仁徳天皇　記紀に記された５世紀前半の第16代天皇。租税を３年間免除して民衆を助けたという伝承がある。

これが平安中期とも鎌倉初期のものといわれる日本最古の神社建築で、とくに階の左右に設けられた勾欄の美しい曲線、それは内陣にもくり返され、まことに繊細な造形である。また、境内には京の名水のひとつ桐原水が湧く。稚郎子の桐原日桁宮による名である。

ふたたび宇治川沿いの道に戻って、東に歩くと、道元を開祖とする曹洞宗の興聖寺への参道「琴坂」が川に向かって端緒を開いている。新緑や紅葉の時期、この琴を置いたように細長い参道はまるで**日本画**の美の世界になって私たちを魅了する。

興聖寺　江戸時代淀藩主永井尚政が再建した。

style structure in which the floor is raised off the ground on pillars, open on all four sides, but this shrine's *hai-den* is built in the *shinden-zukuri* style structure of the Heian period like the residence of a court noble. On the right and left sides of the roof, the *hisashi* awnings are suspended from the eaves. The handrail railing runs around the outer edge.

The pride of Ujigami-jinja is the *hon-den*, standing beyond this elegant *hai-den*. The exterior is said to date back to the Kamakura period, with a serene gable side of the gable (*kirizuma-zukuri*) and the shake-shingled (*hiwada-buki*) roof. When one approaches the fine latticed door of the *hon-den* closely, one can see the three shrine buildings in the *ichigensha-nagare* style structure. The center enshrines Emperor Ōjin, the building on the right Emperor Nintoku, and the one on the left is the shrine of Wakiitsurako.

These buildings, dating back to the mid-Heian or early Kamakura periods, are believed to be Japan's oldest shrine buildings. The beautiful curving handrail on either side of the staircase, which is repeated inside the *hon-den*, is particularly exquisite work. The shrine grounds also boast one of Kyoto's famous springs, the Kirihara-mizu spring. The name '*Kirihara*' comes from a palace of Wakiitsurako.

Return to the road along the Uji River and walk east, and you will see the opening of the Koto-zaka, the long, slender approach leading up to Kōshō-ji, a temple of the Sōtō Zen sect founded by Dōgen. Its name, meaning "*koto-zaka*," comes from its resemblance to a traditional, long, harp-like instrument (*koto*) placed on the ground. During the seasons of the spring buds and autumn colors, this approach seems to be part of the picturesque world of a classical **Japanese paintings**.

8

極楽浄土の世界をあらわす鳳凰堂

平等院（びょうどういん）

宇治市宇治蓮華116
0774(21)2861
8時30分～17時30分　600円(鳳翔館を含む)、
鳳凰堂は別途300円
www.byodoin.or.jp
JR奈良線　宇治駅下車徒歩10分

平等院は寺というよりも、その境内は鳳凰堂（ほうおうどう）を中心にした遺跡公園といったほうがいいだろう。そして、2001年に平等院ミュージアム「鳳翔館（ほうしょうかん）」が開館して、平等院の遺宝を詳細にみることができるようになった。

宇治橋の西詰から宇治茶を商う店に挟まれた石畳の道をゆくと、平等院の表門にでる。そこで拝観料をおさめ、園内に入ると、すぐに阿字池（あじいけ）がみえ、まことにあっけなく鳳凰堂があらわれる。

鳳凰堂と極楽浄土

鳳凰堂の主体である中堂（ちゅうどう）は、正面全長14.2m、側面11.8m、単層の入母屋造（いりもやづくり）で、正面部分だけ高くなった裳階（もこし）をまわし、本瓦屋根の頂辺に一対の鳳凰をとりつける。この中堂の屋根の四隅がピンと反って、堂全体に躍動感をもたらしている。そして南北に翼廊（よくろう）をのばし、その端部分に隅楼をのせて阿字池側につき出している。この翼廊の下部は柱だけで二

8. The Hōōdō hall that shows us paradise

Byōdō-in

Address: 116 Uji Renge, Uji-shi
Tel: 077 (421) 2861
Hours: 8:30AM–5:30PM
Admission: ¥600 (including Hōshō-kan, ¥300: Hōō-dō)
www.byodoin.or.jp/en/
10 min walk from JR Nara Line Uji Sta.

Rather than a temple, it is more accurate to call Byōdō-in a historic park featuring the Hōō-dō, or phoenix hall. In 2001, the Byōdō-in Museum, called the Hōshō-kan, was opened, allowing a closer view of the treasures of Byōdō-in.

If you walk from the west side of Uji bridge along the stone-paved street squeezed between the shops selling Uji tea, you will come to the front gate of Byōdō-in. Pay your entry fee here and enter the ground, and soon you will see Aji pond and the incomparable the Hōō-dō.

The Hōō-dō and the land of Perfect Bliss

The central hall that is the focus of the Hōō-dō is 14.2 meters across its face and 11.8 meters along the side, built in the gable and hip roof (*irimoya-zukuri*) style with a raised type of pent roof (*mokoshi*) in the front. On the top of the tile roof a pair of phoenixes is affixed. The four corners of the roof of the central hall curve up sharply, giving the structure as a whole an air of imminent motion. A pair of **transepts** extends to the north and south with small *sumirō* towers at the ends projecting out toward the pond.

階部分が板張りになり、中堂と行き来はできない。ということは、様式美のための建物なのである。

鳳凰堂東面には砂利を敷いた洲浜が阿字池になめらかに沈み、阿字池の水面に鳳凰堂が映る。そして中堂の中心には、ちょうどお顔のところだけ丸く刳った格子越しに阿弥陀如来像を拝することができ、阿字池という彼岸を越えて西方の極楽浄土をのぞむ形になっている。

中堂の須弥壇上に、平安中期の名仏師定朝の大傑作である阿弥陀如来像が**金箔**もあざやかに坐っておられる。像高約2.5m、定印をきっちりと結び、伏し目がちで頬は丸く豊かで柔和なお顔である。**光背**は掌を丸めた大きな手が像を守るようにあり、さらに天蓋は円蓋をなかにおさめた巨大なもので、透彫の細かい装飾がほどこされている。

また、中堂の壁面には「雲中供養菩薩」とよばれる52体の小仏像がさまざまな姿態をあらわして懸けられている。座像は約40cm、立像で90cmほどの大きさで、琵琶、琴、鼓などの楽器を演奏するもの、合掌し舞踏するものなどじつに多彩で、いまはその多くが「鳳翔館」に展示されている。

源融　822～95。六条河原に美しい邸宅を造営したり、各地に豪邸を築いた。

平等院の歴史

嵯峨天皇の皇子源融は、平安初期、この地に別荘を営んだ。のちに藤原道長の所有となり、さらに道長の子頼通によって、世が末法

藤原道長　966～1027。娘を天皇に嫁がせ外戚として権勢を誇る。藤原氏の栄華を確立。

The bottom portion of the transepts is built of open columns, with the second story covered. They do not open into the central portion of the building and are only for aesthetic appearance.

On the east face of the Hōō-dō a small graveled beach extends to Aji pond, and the building is reflected on the water's surface. In the center of the middle portion of the hall, just the face of the statue of the Amitabha is visible over a cutout portion of the lattice, as if we are looking the land of Perfect Bliss in the west.

The statue, sitting on its pedestal in the middle building, is the masterpiece of the middle of Heian period sculptor Jōchō. It is covered with **gold foil** and is approximately 2.5 meters high. The Amitabha sits with his hands in the mudra position, his eyes directed downward and his cheeks round and gentle. His **halo** is reminiscent of a large palm protecting the image, and the canopy above it is quite large, decorated with fine openwork carvings.

On the walls of the room are paintings of fifty-two small statue of Buddha known as the '*Unchū-kuyō Bosatsu*' striking various poses. The seated figures are approximately 40 cm tall, and the standing ones are approximately 90 cm tall. They play instruments and dance in a lively manner. Currently most of the images are displayed in the 'Hōshōkan.'

History of Byōdō-in

Minamoto-no-Tōru, the son of Emperor Saga, built a villa on this place in the early Heian period. Subsequently it came into the possession of Fujiwara-no-Michinaga, and was subsequently

藤原頼通 922～1074。道長の長子。後一条から三代の天皇の摂政・関白を務める。

末法 釈迦入滅後の仏教普及の期間を三区分した最後の時期で、仏の教えが廃れるという。

に入ったとされる1052年（永承7）に寺院に改め、天台宗平等院とした。その後、数度の兵火により山内の伽藍は焼失し、また応仁の乱で寺勢は衰退した。ただ阿弥陀堂は兵火を無事にくぐりぬけ、往時の華麗さをいまに伝えてくれる。阿弥陀堂を鳳凰堂とよんだのは江戸時代以降のことで、屋根の鳳凰、また中堂と翼廊が鳳凰（古来中国で尊ばれた空想上の瑞鳥（ずいちょう））が翼を広げた姿に似ていることからの呼称である。

いま平等院の境内には、ほかに鎌倉初期の建築になる観音堂と鐘楼があるだけで、この鐘楼の鐘は天下三名鐘のひとつとして名高い。天下三名鐘とは、勢いの東大寺、形の平等院、声の園城寺（三井寺）の鐘をいい、平等院の鐘は名鐘に数えられている（いまは「鳳翔館」に展示）。

turned into a temple of the Tendai sect by Fujiwara-no-Yorimichi in 1052, when the world seemed to have entered an age of disorder. Various fires reduced the temple buildings to ashes, and at the time of the Ōnin War, the temple's activities had greatly declined. The *amida-dō*, fortunately, escaped the fires of war, preserving some of the splendor of the past for us to see. In the Edo period, the *amida-dō* began to be known as the Hōō-dō, due either to a pair of phoenix (*hōō*) on its roof or to the resemblance of the building to a phoenix taking flight.

Today the only other buildings remaining on the temple grounds are the *kannon-dō* and the bell tower, built in the early Kamakura period. The bell is famous as one of a group of "Three Great Bells," the bell of Tōdai-ji being famous for its vigor, the one of Byōdō-in for its form, and the one of Onjō-ji for its tone. The bells of some other temples have also been cited as belonging to this group, but the Byōdō-in bell certainly deserves to be counted among bells of distinction. (It currently is on display in the Hōshō-kan.)

9

武家の信仰を集めた山頂の神社

石清水八幡宮

八幡市八幡高坊30
075(981)3001
5時30分～18時30分(季節により変動)
境内参拝自由
www.iwashimizu.or.jp
京阪本線石清水八幡宮駅下車、石清水八幡宮参道ケーブル乗り換えケーブル八幡宮山上駅より徒歩7分

石清水八幡宮が山頂に鎮座する男山（標高142.5m）は木津川、宇治川、桂川が合流した淀川を見下ろし、西の天王山と向かいあい、麓に山間の道と河川を通すため、古来、西国との交通や軍事の要衝として重要視されてきた。

この男山に社殿が創建されたのは859年（貞観元）のこと。南都七大寺のひとつであった大安寺の僧行教が宇佐八幡に参籠して、その最後の日の夜、八幡神より「われを京に奉れ」という神託を受け、それを清和天皇（在位858～76）に奏上したことにより社殿を建立した、と社伝ではいう。

なお、社名は男山中腹に霊泉「石清水」が湧き、そこにかつて石清水寺があったことによる。この寺は雄徳山護国寺と改まり、神宮寺となって明治の神仏分離まで当社を管理していた。

天王山　京都の西にある標高270mの山。1582年の山崎の合戦の際、豊臣秀吉がこの山を占有したことが勝敗を分けたため、勝敗の分かれ目を「天王山」という。

南都七大寺　平城京周辺にある七つの大寺。東大寺、興福寺、元興寺、大安寺、薬師寺、西大寺、法隆寺の総称。

9. A mountaintop shrine bespeaks the devotion of a warrior clan

Iwashimizu Hachiman-gū

Address: 30 Yawata Takabō, Yawata-shi
Tel: 075 (981) 3001
Hours: 5:30AM–6:30PM (May vary depending on season)
Admission: Free
www.iwashimizu.or.jp
7 min walk from Iwashimizu Hachiman-gū-sandō Cable Line Hachiman-gū-sanjō Sta. from Keihan Line Iwashimizu Hachiman-gū Sta.

From the peak of Mt. Otokoyama (142.5 meters) where Iwashimizu Hachiman-gū is situated, one can look down on the Yodo River where the Kizu River, the Uji River, and the Katsura River converge on Mt. Tennōzan to the west, and on the roads and rivers that run between the mountains below. From old times, it was highly valued as a place to parley with western countries and a location of strategic value.

The shrine was built on top of Mt. Otokoyama in 859. The legend goes that a priest named Gyōkyō, of Daian-ji, one of the seven great temples in Nara, came on a pilgrimage to Usa Hachiman, and on the last night of his stay, he received a vision from the god of Hachiman saying, "Worship me in the capital." The priest carried this message to Emperor Seiwa (r. 858–76), and he was ordered to build a shrine in response.

The shrine's name 'Iwashimizu,' which means water that flows between rocks, came from the Iwashimizu-dera that had stood on Mt. Otokoyama. The temple's name was changed to Yūtokusan Gokoku-ji, and it was made into a temple that guards a Shinto oracle. The temple was responsible for the affairs of the shrine until the separation of Shinto and Buddhism in the Meiji era.

清浄な境内と社殿

この石清水八幡宮へ参拝するには京阪本線の中書島(ちゅうしょじま)駅から二つ目の石清水八幡宮(いわしみずはちまんぐう)駅が最寄駅である。以前は長く急な石段をのぼったが、いまは本殿近くまで石清水八幡宮駅から「石清水八幡宮参道ケーブル」が高低80mの差を数分で結び、足の便はいい。

新年の厄除大祭には楼門に2本の巨大な破魔矢(はまや)が高々と掲げられ、この神社が弓箭(ゆみや)の神で、武家の信仰を得た社であることがわかる。源頼信(みなもとのよりのぶ)・頼義(よりよし)父子が当社に武運長久を祈願したことから源氏一門の尊崇を集め、頼義の長男源義家(よしいえ)はここで元服したため、八幡太郎(はちまんたろう)と名のった。以来、源頼朝(よりとも)や足利将軍らもたびたび参詣し、社殿が戦禍や火災で焼失するたびに、織田信長や豊臣秀吉が再建した。徳川家康も多くの朱印地を与え、3代将軍家光は1634年（寛永11）に本殿、外殿、楼門、舞殿など今日みられる豪壮な社殿を造営した。

八幡太郎 1039～1106。前九年の役で功をあげ、後三年の役を平定。東国武士との関係を深め、源氏の勢力拠点を築いた。

延長180mにおよぶ廻廊が石段上の社殿をとり囲み、本殿の裏には数々の末摂社の小さな殿舎が神域にふさわしく清浄な佇まいで建ち並ぶ。また、境内の南西に「エジソン碑」がある。これは1879年（明治12）にエジソンが炭素白熱電球を発明したさい、石清水八幡宮の竹をフィラメントとして用いたことを記念するものである。

The Pure Shrine Grounds and Buildings

The most convenient station from which to visit the shrine is Iwashimizu Hachiman-gū Station on the Keihan Dentetsu Honsen line, two stops from Chūshojima Station. In the past one had to climb a long, steep, stone staircase, but the Mt. Otokoyama cable car has now opened from the train station up to near the *hon-den* 80 meters above, making the visit much more convenient.

At the New Year Yakuyoke Taisai Festival (a festival to ward off misfortune), two massive arrows are raised high above the two-story gate, reminding us that this shrine proved the devotion of a warrior clan. After Minamoto-no-Yorinobu and his son Yoriyoshi sought success in battle at this shrine, the whole clan pledged their devotion, and Yoriyoshi's oldest son Minamoto-no-Yoshiie performed a ceremony for attaining manhood here, taking the name Hachiman Tarō. Later Minamoto-no-Yoritomo and the Ashikaga shoguns sometimes came here for worship, and when the buildings were destroyed by war or fire, Oda Nobunaga and Toyotomi Hideyoshi had it rebuilt. Tokugawa Ieyasu also bestowed a large amount of land for building the shrine, and in 1634, the third shogun Iemitsu built the *hon-den*, the *gai-den*, the two-story gate, *mai-dono* and other grand buildings that we see today.

The 180-meter-long corridor encircles the main buildings at the top of the stone stairs. Behind the *hon-den* are several sub-shrines, serenely appropriate to the shrine environs. At the southwest side of the grounds stands the Edison Memorial, commemorating Thomas Edison's use of bamboo from Iwashimizu Hachiman-gū for the filament of his incandescent light bulb, invented in 1879.

エリア 3-1　Area 3-1

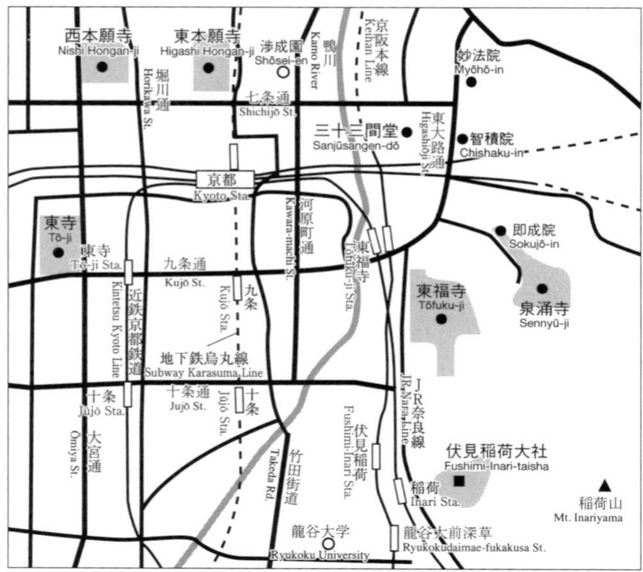

エリア 3-2　Area 3-2

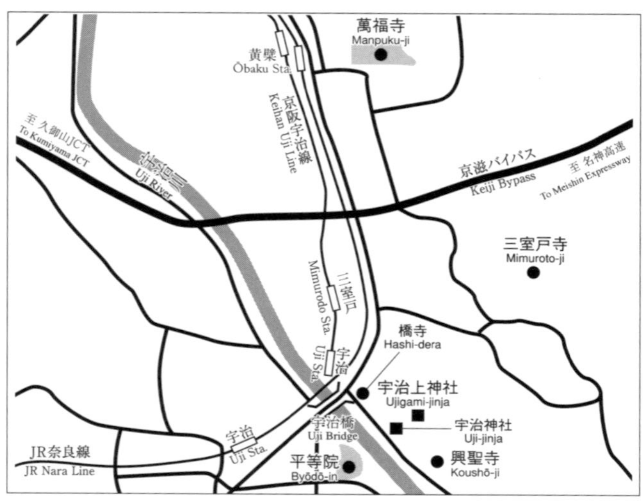

エリア４
Area 4

必見の建築、庭園、仏像が集中する地域
A Concentration of Must-See Buildings, Gardens, and Statues of Buddha

京都の北西域にあたるこのエリアは、観光的には最も贅沢でバラエティに富む寺社が点在して、本来なら1日2寺社程度をじっくり拝観するくらいの旅程の余裕をもちたいところだ。まず金閣寺には混雑を避けて朝早く出かけたほうが無難だ。日本の寺院建築のなかでもその特異さに燦然と輝く「金閣」に対面して、およそ1時間山内を歩けば、ここは済む。「きぬかけの路」を西に、約1.5kmを歩いて「石庭」の龍安寺。この庭はいっそ予備知識をもたないで眺めたほうがいい。観光タクシーの運転手が客に説明する声も耳をふさいで聞かないことだ。石だけの庭と向き合って、あなた個人がどのように感じるか——。

さらに西へ800mで仁和寺の二王門。この寺格の高い門跡寺院は諸堂塔それぞれに見どころが多く、京都の歴史を物語る。背後の「御室八十八ヶ所霊場」をめぐれば四国巡礼と同じご利益があるとか。

仁和寺から南へ下れば、臨済禅宗のなかで最大の末寺をもつ妙心寺で、山内の塔頭も40を越す数である。そして京都最古の寺、広隆寺を訪れる。金閣や石庭も必見のものだが、ここ広隆寺の「弥勒菩薩半跏思惟像」二体のうち「宝冠の弥勒」こそ、京都来訪の最高の眼福といっていい。

さらに重要な寺社のあるエリアは、紫野と北野、そして鷹峯である。紫野には、峻厳な禅寺として観光的拝観を拒む（一部塔頭は可）大徳寺があり、北野には菅原道真の怨霊を鎮め、いまは学問の神となった北野天満宮が親しげに建ち、鷹峯には壺中の天とでもいうべき光悦寺がひそんでいる。

This area, in the northwest of Kyoto, is filled with a rich variety of temples and shrines, allowing visitors to comfortably visit two sites per day. Be sure to set out early to visit Kinkaku-ji to avoid the crowds. To appreciate the brilliant Kinkaku (Golden Pavilion)—unique in Japanese temple architecture—and to stroll around the grounds should take about an hour. Then follow the Kinukake-no-Michi Rd. west about 1.5 kilometers to the Zen rock garden of Ryōan-ji. Try visiting this garden without any advance knowledge, or without listening to the explanations of your taxi driver. Simply come face to face with the rocks of the garden and experience your own individual reaction.

About 800 meters to the west stands the *niō-mon* gate of Ninna-ji. This high-ranking *monzeki* (indicating that members of an imperial family took orders here) temple boasts many famous buildings and tower that tell the history of Kyoto. Behind it is the Omuro Hachijūhachikasho Reijō (Omuro 88-Site Pilgrimage), a miniature version of a pilgrimage trail in Shikoku. It is said that walking this short path is equivalent in virtue to completing the entire route in Shikoku.

Heading south from Ninna-ji, you come to Myōshin-ji, the largest Zen branch temple, with more than forty sub-temples of its own in its ground. Here you can also visit Kyoto's oldest temple, Kōryū-ji. Of course the Golden Pavilion and the Zen rock garden are sights that should not be missed, but the crowned Maitreya statue at Kōryū-ji, one of the temple's two Maitreya Bodhisattva (*miroku bosatsu*) statues, may be Kyoto's most pleasing sight.

The Murasakino, Kitano, and Takagamine areas also contain important temples and shrines. In Murasakino is Daitoku-ji, a strict Zen temple where tourists are not welcome (except for at some of the sub-temples). In Kitano is Kitano Tenman-gū, where the vengeful ghost of Sugawara-no-Michizane is enshrined, and which is now the home of the god of learning. In Takagamine is Kōetsu-ji, a tiny, secluded bit of heaven that feels far from the vulgar world.

1

足利義満絶頂期の黄金の遺構

金閣寺（きんかくじ）

京都市北区金閣寺町１
075（461）0013
9時〜17時
400円
www.shokoku-ji.jp/kinkakuji/
京都駅より市バス101、205系統 金閣寺道下車徒歩７分

金閣寺の拝観入口では日本語、中国語、ハングル、英語併記の案内パンフレットが配られ、金閣寺がいかに外国人にも人気の寺院であることがわかる。中門をくぐるとすぐ鏡湖池（きょうこち）の畔にでて、そこから**金閣**を背景に記念写真を撮る観光客で雑踏している。

中世以降、日本の美は華やかな色を避けて、侘（わ）び、寂（さ）びというモノトーンの「艶消（つやけ）し」の世界に価値を認めるようになった。それが今日の日本人の美意識につながっている。その美意識は鎌倉時代より武家と結びついた**禅文化**が発祥した表現であるといってもいいわけで、だから、黄金に輝く「金閣」を禅寺にみるとき、私たちにとまどいが生じるのである。

侘び、寂び　もの閑かで、渋く古びた風趣。

金閣寺と通称するが、正式には北山鹿苑寺（きたやまろくおんじ）という臨済宗相国寺（りんざいしゅうしょうこくじ）派の禅寺である。禅刹と金箔に彩られた建物——この違和感は足利義満（あしかがよしみつ）の権勢にはじまる。

1. The golden remains of the peak of Ashikaga Yoshimitsu's career

Kinkaku-ji

Address: 1 Kinkaku-ji-chō, Kita-ku, Kyoto-shi
Tel: 075 (461) 0013
Hours: 9:00AM–5:00PM
Admission: ¥400
www.shokoku-ji.jp/en/kinkaku-ji/
7 min walk from Kinkaku-ji-michi bus stop, bus 101 or 205 from Kyoto Sta.

From the leaflet handed out at the gate of Kinkaku-ji, which are printed in Japanese, Chinese, Korean, and English, one can glean how popular a temple Kinkaku-ji is with foreign visitors. One passes through the middle gate near Kyōkochi pond to see a crowd of tourists taking photos with the **Golden Pavilion** (Kinkaku) in the background.

Since the Middle ages, Japanese beauty has avoided gaudy color and instead found value in the subtle monotones of the *wabi-sabi* aesthetic. This is a fundamental part of the aesthetic consciousness of modern Japanese, and has been linked to the **Zen culture** of warrior clan since the Kamakura period. Therefore it is a bit disorienting for us to look at the sparkling gold of Kinkaku as a Zen temple.

The formal name of the temple known as Kinkaku-ji is Kitayama Rokuon-ji, of the Rinzai Zen sect Syōkokuji school. The odd juxtaposition of a Zen temple and a building decorated in gold foil began due to the power of Ashikaga Yoshimitsu.

義満の公家意識が生んだ金閣寺

室町幕府第3代将軍として幕府の全盛期を築いた足利義満は1394年（応永元）将軍職を子の義持(よしもち)に譲り太政大臣になるが、幕府の実権は握ったまま翌年に出家する。そして、義満は自らを法皇に擬したものと考え、太上天皇の住まいである仙洞(せんとう)御所を欲した。その候補に上がったのが、衣笠山(きぬがさやま)東麓の地である。もともとこの地は平安貴族の遊楽の地で、とくに西園寺公経(さいおんじきんつね)が築いた山荘の北山第(きたやまだい)は苑池を中心に諸堂や邸宅を配して「天下の壮観」といわれた豪華なものであった。北山第の敷地を1397年（応永4）に手に入れた義満は、金閣（舎利殿(しゃりでん)）を中心に新たな殿楼の造営をはじめる。義満はここで政務をとり、公卿貴族を集めて和歌や管弦、猿楽(さるがく)を催し、後世、北山文化といわれる華やかな一時期を築いた。

太政大臣　国政を統轄する最高機関である太政官の最高位の位。

太上天皇　天皇の譲位後の称号。上皇とも。

仙洞御所　太上天皇（上皇）が住む御所。

西園寺公経　1171～1224。鎌倉幕府と強く結びついた公卿。承久の変では後鳥羽上皇の倒幕計画を密告、太政大臣になる。

北山文化　伝統的な公家文化と新興の武家文化が融合する時期に、禅僧による五山文化、水墨画、観阿弥・世阿弥の猿楽能が義満の庇護を受け発達。

金閣の浮遊感のある構造

義満が没すると、子の義持は義満の遺命により夢窓疎石(むそうそせき)を開山として禅寺に改め、義満の法号鹿苑院(ろくおんいん)から鹿苑寺と名づけた。そのため禅刹の中心に黄金の楼閣、金閣が残ることになった。鹿苑寺はその後、応仁の乱で多くの堂宇を失ったが、江戸時代初期に後水尾(ごみずのお)天皇の援助により再建されて、ほぼいまみる禅寺の伽藍というより**庭園寺院**という形に定まった。

「金閣」は義満が建立したままの形で残っていたが、1950年（昭和25）に鹿苑寺の若い僧

Kinkaku-ji Expresses Yoshimitsu's Aristocratic Consciousness

Yoshimitsu, the third Muromachi shogun, who brought the power of the Bakufu (government) to its peak, handed over the position of shogun to his son Yoshimochi in 1394 and took the position of Dajō Daijin (Supreme Minister of State), but the next year, still clutching the power of the Bakufu, he retired from the world to become a monk. Seeking to style himself as a tonsured emperor, Yoshimitsu envied Sentō Gosho, the mountain retreat of the former Emperor and ultimately found a location in the foothills of Mt. Kinugasayama, a pleasure area of the Heian period aristocracy. He acquired Kitayamadai, a famous villa of the nobleman Saionji Kintsune, in 1397 and began building new structures centered around the Golden Pavilion, his reliquary building. Yoshimitsu began conducting government affairs here and gathered the court aristocracy for poetry, music, and *sarugaku* play, creating the elegant tradition that would later be known as Kitayama culture.

The Golden Pavilion's Floating Structure

After Yoshimitsu died, his son Yoshimochi, following his orders, created a Zen temple on the site, headed by the priest Musō Soseki. It was called Rokuon-ji, after Yoshimitsu's posthumous Buddhist name, Rokuon'in. At the center of this Zen temple remained Kinkaku-ji built by Yoshimitsu. The temple suffered great damage during the Ōnin War, but in the early Edo period, Emperor Gomizunoo helped rebuild it to the form we see today, more a **garden temple** than a Zen temple.

The Golden Pavilion remained in the form built by Yoshimitsu, but in 1950 a young monk of Rokuon-ji set it on fire, burning it

によって放火され、全焼する。1955年（昭和30）に往時と同じ様式で復原され、さらに1986年から大規模修理がなされて、金箔がまぶしく輝く原初の姿が蘇ったのである。

金閣は三層の建物で、初層は「法水院（ほうすいいん）」といい寝殿造（しんでんづくり）風に公卿の邸宅として広縁をめぐらし、池側に柱を立て、その奥に蔀戸（しとみど）を設える。二層は「潮音洞（ちょうおんどう）」とよぶ鎌倉期の武家造の仏間で、三層は「究竟頂（くっきょうちょう）」といい禅宗仏殿風造で火頭窓（かとうまど）もみえる。二層、三層は全面に金箔をほどこして燦然と輝く。金閣は三層楼閣であるのに、どこか軽快感があるのは初層に屋根がなく二層につながっているところと、二層、三層の屋根が椹（さわら）の薄い板を重ねた柿葺（こけらぶき）で、しかも反りがゆるやかで平面的であることによる。

さらに鏡湖池の水面に映る金色の影によって浮き上がってみえることも金閣の超然とした存在をきわだたせている。もとは四方を池に囲まれていたから、その浮遊感はいっそう極楽浄土の楼閣のごとく思われたに違いない。

金閣放火事件
1950年（昭和25）7月2日未明の放火事件。この事件から文学的構想を得て、三島由紀夫『金閣寺』、事実に基づいた水上勉の『金閣炎上』が執筆された。

to the ground. In 1955 it was rebuilt in its original style, and it was substantially renovated again in 1986, rejuvenating its gold-foil brilliance.

The Golden Pavilion is a three-story building. The first floor, the 'Hōsui-in,' is a courtly residence in the *shinden-zukuri* style structure with a broad veranda and columns along the pond, with *shitomi* latticed doors on the inside. The second floor, 'Chōon-dō,' is a Buddhist altar room (*butsuma*) in the Kamakura-warrior-clan style structure, and the third floor, the 'Kukkyō-chō,' is a Zen Buddha hall with flame-shaped *katō* windows. The second and third floors are covered with gold foil, creating a brilliant radiance. Even the Golden Pavilion is a three-story building, it looks really light. This is from the facts that the first floor has no external roof, but the second and third floors have the shake-shingled (*kokera-buki*) roofs made of *sawara* cypress. Also the warp is subtle and flat.

One of the distinctive features of the Golden Pavilion is its image reflected, as if it is floating, in the Kyōkochi pond. Originally the pavilion was completely surrounded by the pond, and the floating image was thought to resemble a building in the land of Perfect Bliss.

2

禅境の極みという「石庭」は何を語る

龍安寺（りょうあんじ）

京都市右京区龍安寺御陵ノ下町13
075(463)2216
8時〜17時、(12月〜2月は8時30分〜16時30分)
500円
www.ryoanji.jp
京福北野線　龍安寺駅下車徒歩7分

油塀　もともとは城郭の補強用に油を混ぜて練った土で築いた塀。

臨済宗妙心寺派の龍安寺北側に庫裏と方丈が建ち、方丈の前庭がその著名な「石庭」である。東西25m、南北10m、油塀に囲まれたごく狭い空間に砂紋を描いた白砂を敷き、15個の石、立ったものもあれば、臥（ふ）したもの、周囲に杉苔を生じたもの、白砂にほとんど埋まったもの、それぞれの石が無造作に点々と配されて、ほかには一木一草とてない。この白砂に置かれた15の石を、虎が子を背負って川を渡るようすをあらわしたもの（「虎の子渡しの庭」という）、七五三の配置の妙、仏教の教えによるものなど、いろいろにいわれ、ともかく禅境の極みとされている。

石庭の禅味を教えたアメリカ人

禅とは何か、それを簡潔に答えられる日本人はどれほどいるのだろうか。「石庭こそ禅の心である」といわれても、凡人には、どこか

2. The zen rock garden called the extreme of Zen consciousness

Ryōan-ji

Address: 13 Ryōan-ji Goryōnoshita-chō, Ukyō-ku, Kyoto-shi
Tel: 075 (463) 2216
Hours: 8:00AM–5:00PM (December–February: 8:30AM–4:30PM)
Admission: ¥500
www.ryoanji.jp
7 min walk from Keifuku Kitano Railway Ryōanji Sta.

On the north side of Ryōan-ji a Zen temple of the Rinzai sect (Myōshin-ji school) stand the *kuri* and the *hōjō* (the main hall). In front of the *hōjō* is the famous *sekitei* (Zen rock garden). It is a rather small space, 25 meters east to west and 10 meters north to south, surrounded by an oiled dirt fence, containing fifteen stones, some standing vertically and others lying horizontally, some festooned with moss, others almost buried in the carefully patterned white sand that surrounds them. The rocks are simply arranged here and there, uninterrupted by tree or greenery. Some have said the stones are arranged to suggest a tiger carrying its cub on its back as it crosses a river, while others see an arrangement of numbers, and still others interpret the arrangement of the rocks as reflecting Buddhist teachings. In any case, they certainly reflect the artfulness of the Zen space.

The American Who Explained the Zen Meaning of the Rock Garden

How many Japanese people can give a simple answer to the question, "What is Zen?" Although it has been said that "The *sekitei* itself is the heart of Zen," the average person is not likely

釈然としない、解答のでないもどかしさが残るだけだ。

それに、この石庭を禅の芸術的表現の第一等と私たちに教えたのは、アメリカの彫刻家イサム・ノグチである。それも第二次世界大戦後のことで、古くから、今日のように騒がれていたわけではない。

室町幕府の管領細川勝元は妙心寺の義天玄承に深く帰依しており、徳大寺家がもっていた山荘を譲り受けて、1450年（宝徳2）に義天を住持に招いて龍安寺を創建した。しかし自身が東軍の主将となった応仁の乱で焼失、勝元も1473年（文明5）に没する。勝元の子細川政元が特芳禅傑をまねいて再建、塔頭も21院と数えるまでに隆盛したが、1797年（寛政9）の火災でほとんどの堂宇を焼失してしまう。

その後、塔頭西源院の方丈を移築し、庫裏も同時期に再建、また1981年（昭和56）に開山堂を建立した。現在、龍安寺の主だった建物はこの三堂だけである。

西側の樹林の道を歩き、境内を広さをたしかめながら、鏡容池の池畔をめぐる遊歩道をのんびりと散策するのも、景色が広く、狭く不可解な「石庭」を眺めたあとならなおさら心が晴れ晴れとしていいものである。

イサム・ノグチ 1904～88。詩人の父野口米次郎とアメリカ人作家の母との間に生まれる。彫刻家、画家、インテリアデザイナー、造園家、舞台芸術家として活躍。

徳大寺家 平安後期からはじまる藤原氏閑院流で清華家(摂家の次の位)。家名は衣笠の山荘に建てた徳大寺に因む。

to produce a clear explanation.

The person who taught us the true high level of the artistic expression of the rock garden was an American sculptor named Isamu Noguchi. This was after World War II, and the garden was not known worldwide as it is today.

The Muromachi Bakufu official Hosokawa Katsumoto, greatly impressed with the priest Giten Genshō of the Myōshin-ji, gave him a villa that had formerly belonged to the Tokudaiji family. Giten was to establish the temple Ryōan-ji with this villa in 1450, with himself as head priest. But the temple he had worked so hard for was destroyed in the Ōnin War, in which Katsumoto himself was killed in 1473. His son Masamoto rebuilt the temple with the priest Tokuhō Zenketsu at its head, and the temple prospered; its compound grew to some twenty-one sub-temples. In 1797, however, almost all the buildings were destroyed in a fire.

Currently the primary buildings of Ryōan-ji are the *hōjō* of the sub-temple Seigen-in, the *kuri*, and the *kaizan-dō*, the last of which was erected in 1981.

Walking along the path through the trees on the west side of the temple grounds and on the promenade on the edge of Kyōyōchi pond, one can appreciate the spaciousness of the grounds. After pondering the small mystery of the rock garden, the landscape seems all the more refreshing.

3

最高位の門跡寺院

仁和寺

京都市右京区御室大内33
075(461)1155
9時〜16時30分(3〜11月は9時〜17時)
御殿・桜まつり・霊宝館(春期・秋期のみ)各500円
www.ninnaji.jp
京都駅より市バス26系統　御室仁和寺下車徒歩1分

もしあなたが車を利用して、この章の寺々を巡るのならば、金閣寺参道前を起点として龍安寺、仁和寺、さらに福王子の交差点から広沢池の南辺を通り、大覚寺門前に至る観光道路「きぬかけの路」はとても便利な道路であると思うだろう。また健脚で自転車を駆る人もそう思うだろう。

広沢池　大覚寺の東にある周囲1.3kmの用水池。10世紀末に寛朝が開いたといわれ、観月と桜の名所。

もしあなたが徒歩でゆっくり寺々を訪れる人であれば、便利さゆえに交通量が多く、各寺の本来の参道を無惨に横切っているこの〝観光バス道路〟を苦々しく思うに違いない。

功罪半ばするこの「きぬかけの路」に面して仁和寺の豪壮な二王門が建つ。だから私たちはいきなり、この平安文化の香りが色濃く残る大寺に入ることになる。

二王門　1637〜44年にかけて建造。知恩院三門、南禅寺三門とともに京都の三大門。

仁和寺の歴史と建物

二王門をくぐると中門につづく幅広い参道が、道というより広大な空間として広がっている。この広さがまず仁和寺の特徴であり、

3. The highest-ranking *monzeki* temple

Ninna-ji

Address: 33 Omuro Ōuchi, Ukyō-ku, Kyoto-shi
Tel: 075 (461) 1155
Hours: 9:00AM–4:30PM (March–November: 9:00AM–17:00PM)
Admission: ¥500 each for Goten, Sakura Matsuri, Reihōkan (Spring and fall only)
www.ninnaji.jp/en/
1 min walk from Omuro-Ninna-ji bus stop, bus 26 from Kyoto Sta.

If you travel by car from one to another of the temples described in this chapter, the tourist road Kinukake-no-Michi Rd. is quite convenient. It begins in front of the approach to Kinkaku-ji, then proceeds to Ryōan-ji, Ninna-ji, and then Fukuōji crossing and then along the south side of Hirosawa pond, finishing at the gate of Daikaku-ji. It is also suitable for cyclists.

If you like to stroll in a relaxed manner from temple to temple, however, you may look with disdain on this "tourist bus road" that sticks to the heavily trafficked routes and ignores the traditional approaches to the temples.

It has its good and bad points, but the Kinukake-no-Michi Rd. does lead to the splendid *niō-mon* gate of Ninna-ji, so we shall quickly enter this grand temple, with its strong lingering scent of Heian period culture.

The History of Ninna-ji and Its Structure

Pass under the *niō-mon* gate, and the approach leading to the *chū-mon* gate of the temple is so broad it seems more like an open plaza than an approach. This feeling of openness is one of the

気持ちの余裕を生みだしてくれる。

886年（仁和2）光孝天皇の勅願によって、大内山の麓に伽藍の建立がはじめられるが、翌年光孝帝は没し、子の宇多天皇が888年（仁和4）に完成せた。仁和寺の寺名は年号による。

宇多天皇は退位後に出家して法皇となり、当寺に904年（延喜4）法務をおこなう僧坊がもうけられ、それは「御室」と尊称された。これが当地の地名となる。その後、次々に皇族が入寺して、仁和寺は門跡寺院として最高位にあった。しかし、武家政治とそれにともなう禅宗の勃興や応仁の乱で衰退、一時、寺域は双ケ丘に移り、17世紀初めになって第21世覚深法親王が徳川家光より支援を受け、旧地に伽藍を復興する。

紫宸殿　御所の正殿。仁和寺金堂は桃山時代の紫宸殿を江戸時代初期に移築。現存する最古の紫宸殿の遺構。

中門を入ると、正面に御所の紫宸殿を移した金堂が建つ。本瓦葺屋根の左右の反り返りが美しく、向拝と高欄を備えて寺の本堂というより、やはり御殿である。金堂に向かって右手前の高さ36mの五重塔は各層の屋根の大きさが同じという江戸期の建築様式を示す。

御室桜　現在の桜は寛永年間（1624～44）に植樹。土質により3mほどしか伸びない。

そして、境内の左手は遅咲きの桜として知られる「御室桜」の苑地が広がる。市中の桜がおおよそ散りはじめたころに、低い木に花を咲かせ、二度目の花見と京人に親しまれている。

本坊は二王門を入って左手の区域で東端に勅使門が建ち、旧御所の台所門であった表門の先に大玄関、つづいて白砂敷の前庭をもつ白書院、さらに門跡の対面所の黒書院がある。

signature features of Ninna-ji.

Construction of this temple at the foot of Mt. Ōuchisan began in 886, at the command of Emperor Kōkō. He died the next year, but his son, Emperor Uda, continued the work, completing it in 888 (Ninna 4). The temple's name comes from the era.

After he abdicated his throne, Emperor Uda became a monk, and in 904 completeed the monks' quarters, a room where legal affairs were seen to, and known as Omuro, giving the location its name. A number of princes later entered this same temple, making Ninna-ji the highest-ranking *monzeki* temple of this type. However, the rise of warrior-clan politics and their favored Zen practice, as well as the destruction of the Ōnin War, led to decline of the temple. It temporarily moved to Narabigaoka Hill, but in the early 17 century moved back to its original location with the support of Tokugawa Iemitsu, the third Tokugawa Shogun, and regained its former glory.

When you enter the *chū-mon* gate, you are greeted by the sight of the *kon-dō*, formerly the palace where state ceremonies were held. Its tiled roof, *gohai* (eaves), and *kōran* (handrail) recall a palace more than a temple's main hall (*hondō*). To the right stands the 36-meter-tall five-story pagoda, notable as an Edo period construction because all of its roofs are the same size.

On the left of the grounds is Omuro cherry tree, known for its late-blooming cherry blossoms. Kyoto residents enjoy coming here for cherry-blossom viewing when the flowers in the city are already scattered on the ground.

Remnants of the original temple include the *chokushi-mon* gate on the eastern edge (to the left when entering the *niō-mon* gate). Where the kitchen gate of the old palace stood is the main entrance, and the Shiro-shoin with its white-sand garden and Kuro-shoin (a room for greeting official visitors) are just beyond.

4

臨済宗のなかで最大の宗派

妙心寺

京都市右京区花園妙心寺町１
075(463)3121(代表)
境内参拝自由
(法堂天井の雲龍図、梵鐘、明智風呂９時10分～15時40分　700円)
www.myoshinji.or.jp
JR嵯峨野線　花園駅下車徒歩５分

　妙心寺の南門は下立売通に、北門は一条通に面している。寺域は東西約470m、南北約540mの広さを誇り、46の塔頭を数える。また日本全国に3400の末寺を擁し、臨済宗のなかでも妙心寺派は最大の宗派となっている。

　仁和寺から訪れるなら北門が近いが、禅宗伽藍は南に向くという原則に従って拝観するならば、丸太町通から北に歩いて（JR嵯峨野線花園駅が近い)、南門から山内を訪れたい。勅使門、山門、仏殿、法堂、寝堂、大方丈、庫裏と一直線に建ち並ぶ伽藍のようすはまことに堂々として訪れる私たちを圧倒する。

　花園天皇は退位すると、この地にあった離宮を禅寺に改めて、大徳寺開祖の宗峰妙超の弟子関山慧玄を招き、開山として創建した。1337年（建武41）のことといい、翌年、花園上皇は寺内に玉鳳院を建て参禅した。

　しかし、1399年（応永6）妙心寺と関係の深かった大内義弘が足利義満に反旗を翻して

4. The largest school of the Rinzai sect

Myōshin-ji

Address: 1 Hanazono Myōshin-ji-chō, Ukyō-ku, Kyoto-shi
Tel: 075 (463) 3121
Hours: Hattō ceiling paintings, temple bell, Akechi bath: 9:10AM–3:40PM
Admission: Free (Hattō ceiling paintings, temple bell, Akechi bath: ¥700)
www.myoshinji.or.jp/english/
5 min walk from JR Sagano Line Hanazono Sta.

Myōshin-ji's south gate is on Shimotachiuri St., and its north gate is on Ichijō St. The temple grounds are 470 meters across from east to west and 540 meters across from south to north, containing 46 sub-temples. Across Japan, the Myōshin-ji school boasts 3,400 branch temples, making it the largest school in the Rinzai sect.

If you are coming from Ninna-ji, the north gate is the closest, but since Zen temples are traditionally laid out to face south, we recommend coming from Marutamachi St. facing north (from Hanazono Station on the JR Sagano line), entering through the south gate. The layout of the temple is most impressive, with the *chokushi-mon* gate, the *san-mon* gate (main gate), the *butsu-den*, the *hattō*, the *shin-dō*, the *dai-hōjō*, and the *kuri* all laid out in a straight line.

When Emperor Hanazono abdicated his throne, he converted his villa at this site into a Zen temple under the direction of Kanzan Egen, the disciple of the priest Shūhō Myōchō, the founder of the Daitoku-ji. In 1337 the former emperor built the Gyokuhō-in for Zen meditation.

In 1399, however, Ōuchi Yoshihiro, who had close ties with Myōshin-ji, took up arms against Ashikaga Yoshimitsu and set

応永の乱を起こしたため、義満は寺地、寺領を没収し、妙心寺は南禅寺の支配下におかれる。1432年（永享4）尾張犬山の瑞泉寺から迎えられた日峰宗舜が中興して独立するが、応仁の乱により堂塔は焼失。1477年（文明9）土御門天皇が9世雪江宗深に再興の綸旨をくだして、伽藍を再建、その後、織田、豊臣、徳川ら各大名の支援も篤く、現在の大寺となった。

法堂の雲龍図と明智風呂

仏殿の北に、妙心寺最大の建造物である法堂が建ち、その北の寝堂とともに1656年（明暦2）の建築である。法堂の天井までの高さは13m、禅宗の法堂の鏡天井には、必ず丸龍が描かれる。これは、古来、仏法を保護する瑞獣である龍が法堂の空間を守るためだ。妙心寺の法堂の天井には直径12mのいまにも躍り出んばかりの狩野探幽筆の「雲龍図」が描かれている。また、大方丈は1654年（承応3）の建造で、阿弥陀三尊像を安置する。

山門の東側に位置する浴室は、明智光秀の叔父密宗和尚が、光秀の菩提を弔うために1587年（天正15）に創建し、1656年（明暦2）に改装されたもので「明智風呂」ともよばれる。風呂は東側面にある竈で火を焚き、板敷きの隙間から蒸気を出して温める蒸し風呂形式で、当時は僧侶だけでなく、ときには一般の民衆にも開放していたという。

狩野探幽 1602～74。狩野永徳の孫。幕府御用絵師として一族の繁栄を築いた。二条城の障壁画でも知られる。

明智光秀 1528?～82。織田信長に仕え、のちに本能寺の変を起こす。山崎の戦で豊臣秀吉に敗れた。

up Ouei War, and in retaliation Yoshimitsu claimed the temple land, placing it under the control of Nanzen-ji. In 1432, Nippō Sōshun, a priest from Zuisen-ji at Owariinuyama, resurrected the temple and reclaimed its independence, but in the Ōnin War the temple buildings were all burned. In 1477, Emperor Tsuchimikado commissioned the ninth head priest, Sekkō Sōshin to rebuilt the temple, and subsequently the temple flourished with the support of Oda, Toyotomi, and Tokugawa daimyo, becoming the great temple it is today.

The Dragon Paintings of the *Hattō* and the Akechi Bath

To the north of the *butsu-den* stands the *hattō*, Myōshin-ji's largest building. It and the *shin-dō* to its north were both built in 1656. The ceiling of the *hattō* is 13 meters high, and as with all ceiling in Zen *hattō*, it has a dragon painted on it, which was believed since ancient times to protect Buddhism. "*Unryūzu*," (dragon and clouds) the painting on Myvshin-ji's ceiling, 12 meters across, is by Kanō Tan'yū. Another of the temple's treasures is the three statues of Amitabha enshrined in the *dai-Hōjō*, built in 1654.

The bathhouse on the east side of the *san-mon* gate was built in 1587 by the monk Misshū, uncle of Akechi Mitsuhide, to mourn his nephew. Repaired in 1656, it is also known as Akechi bath. A steam bath heated through the cracks in the floors by the stove on its east side, at the time it was used not only by monks but also by local commoners.

5

日本一美しい仏像を収蔵

広隆寺

京都市右京区太秦蜂岡町32
075(861)1461
9時～17時(12月～2月は9時～16時30分)
境内参拝自由(霊宝殿700円)
京福嵐山本線　太秦広隆寺駅下車徒歩1分

広隆寺は京都で最も古い寺である。渡来人秦氏の長、秦河勝が聖徳太子より仏像を賜り、それを本尊として603年に寺を建立したことが、広隆寺の創建という。

秦氏　5世紀ころ渡来した弓月君が祖と伝わる氏族。京都の各地で土木や産業をおこす。

京福嵐山本線の太秦広隆寺駅をおりると目の前に1702年（元禄15）再建の雄大な南大門（楼門）がみえる。しかし行き交う車の交通量も多く、門前は雑然としている。ところが、一歩楼門をくぐると、境内には敷石の一本道が中央に通っていて落ちついた佇まいである。右手に赤堂とよばれる1165年（永万元）再建の講堂、敷石道の先に本堂である「上宮王院」が建つ。ここには毎年11月22日だけに開扉される現本尊の聖徳太子像が安置されている。上宮王院の西側に庫裡、その奥に檜皮葺屋根の八角円堂「桂宮院」が竹林にかこまれている。この桂宮院は法隆寺でいえば夢殿といった建物で、鎌倉期の瀟洒な建築である。そして境内の北奥に1982年に建てられた霊宝

5. Site of Japan's most beautiful Buddha statue

Kōryū-ji

Address: 32 Uzumasa Hachioka-chō, Ukyō-ku, Kyoto-shi
Tel: 075 (861) 1461
Hours: 9:00AM–5:00PM (December–February: 9:00AM–4:30PM)
Admission: Free (Reihō-den: ¥700)
1 min walk from Keifuku Arashiyama Line Uzumasa-Kōryū-ji Sta.

Kōryū-ji is the oldest temple in Kyoto. Hata-no-Kawakatsu, the head of the Hata clan (who came to Japan from Korea) is said to have bestowed a statue of the Buddha received from Prince Shōtoku and enshrined it as the principal image of the temple in 603.

If you alight from the Keifuku Arashiyama line at Uzumasa-Kōryū-ji Station, you will see the two-story, *nandai-mon* gate of the temple, rebuilt in 1702 before your eyes. This view is somewhat marred by the traffic passing in front of the gate. However, move on to pass under the gate, and you can enter a calmer world as you see the stone path through the temple grounds stretching out before you. On the right you can see the *kō-dō*, lecture hall, known as the "Red Hall," rebuilt in 1165, and at the end of the path is the main hall, the Jōgūō-in. It is here that the statue of Prince Shōtoku is enshrined, but it is available for viewing only once a year, on November 22. To the left of the Jōgūō-in is the *kuri*, and behind it is the Keikyū-in, an octagonal building with a cypress shingle (*hiwada-buki*) roof, in a grove of bamboo, styled upon the Yumedono at Horyū-ji. It is an excellent example of refined Kamakura period architecture. Further into the temple grounds

殿が、諸堂の高さにあわせるように配慮されて建設されている。

二体の美しい弥勒菩薩像

この霊宝殿に安置され、展覧される仏像群こそ京都最古の寺である広隆寺の永い歴史を物語るのである。飛鳥時代の仏像と伝わる二体の「弥勒菩薩半跏思惟像」がある。一体は「宝髻の弥勒」とよばれ、百済国からの貢献仏ともいわれる。右手の人差し指と中指がまるで頬に落ちる涙をそっとおさえているような位置にあるところから「泣き弥勒」と称される。楠の一木造で漆箔の金色がまだみてとれる。

半跏思惟像　片方の足を曲げ、もう片方の膝頭に乗せて座り、片手で頬杖をついて思いにふける仏像の姿。弥勒菩薩像に多い。

そして、もう一体の像が広隆寺を訪れる人びとのお目当てで、国宝の第一号に指定された「宝冠の弥勒」である。秦河勝が聖徳太子から賜った仏像だと伝えられるが、詳かではない。両眼を静かに伏せて口元にわずかな笑みをうかべている。右手の親指と薬指で軽く円をむすび、そのためほかの指が自然と丸みをつくる。中指はふくよかな頬に触れんばかりで、そのほんのわずかな距離に、永遠なる時間が感じられる。日本で一番美しい仏像だといってもいいだろう。

霊宝殿にはほかに天平時代や藤原時代の国宝の仏像が安置されて、各時代の仏像彫刻の多彩な表現形式を一覧することができる。

stands the *reihō-den* treasure house, built to conform to the other temple buildings in 1982.

Two Beautiful Maitreya Bodhisattva Statues

The Buddha statues on display in the *reihō-den* demonstrate the long history of Kōryū-ji as Kyoto's oldest temple. The statues, from the Asuka period, are of the Maitreya Bodhisattva (*miroku bosatsu*) with his right ring finger at his cheek as if he is deep in thought. One of the statues, known as "Hōkei no Miroku," is said to be a gift from Kudara, an ancient Korean kingdom. Since the index and middle fingers of his right hand appear to be tracing a tear rolling down his cheek, it is also known as the "Crying Miroku." It is carved from a camphor tree and traces of the original gold lacquer can still be seen.

The other Buddha statue of Kōryū-ji is Japan's first **national treasure**, "Hōkan no Miroku" (crowned Maitreya), said to have been received by Hata-no-Kawakatsu from Prince Shōtoku. Both eyes of the Buddha are cast downward, and a gentle smile plays at the mouth. The ring finger and thumb of the right hand are lightly touching, and the other fingers are curving naturally. The middle finger almost touches the cheek, and in that tiny distance, one can feel the infinite nature of time. The statue is often called Japan's most beautiful Buddha image.

The *reihō-den* also contains other national treasures from the Tenpyō and Fujiwara periods, allowing visitors to compare the different styles of carving used on Buddhas in different periods.

塔頭それぞれが超一級の美術品

大徳寺（だいとくじ）

京都市北区紫野大徳寺町53
075(491)0019
境内参拝自由(秋に方丈などの公開日あり)
京都駅より市バス205､206系統　大徳寺前下車徒歩5分

芳春院　前田利家の夫人（芳春院）が1608年（慶長13）に創建。通常非公開。

京都の市街は盆地の平坦地に広がっているため高低差がない。といっても京都も北へ向かって多少は高くなっている。それは大徳寺山内の北に位置する塔頭芳春院（ほうしゅんいん）の本堂の縁側が東寺の五重塔の天頂と同じ標高というから、55mほど高低差があることになる。

京都駅からおよそ6km北方、大徳寺の大伽藍が建つ周辺は、かつて「紫野（むらさきの）」とよばれ、大内裏（だいだいり）の北にあたり、天皇の遊猟地であり、紫野というから紫色の染材となる紫草（むらさきぐさ）が自生していたことが想像できる。

平安京を創設した桓武（かんむ）天皇の子淳和（じゅんな）天皇（在位823〜33）がこの地に雲林亭（うりんてい）（紫野院（むらさきのいん））という離宮を建て、その後、離宮を寺にかえて雲林院（うりんいん）とした。しかしその寺は衰退し、守護大名の赤松則村（あかまつのりむら）の帰依をうけた宗峰妙超（しゅうほうみょうちょう）が1315年（正和4）ころに一宇を建てた。これが大徳寺の最初の形であるといわれる。皇族たちの篤い信仰を得た大徳寺はおおいに栄えるが、

宗峰妙超　1282〜1337。鎌倉時代後期の臨済僧。大燈国師。

6. Sub-temples with exquisite artworks

Daitoku-ji

Address: 53 Murasakino Daitoku-ji-chō, Kita-ku, Kyoto-shi
Tel: 075 (491) 0019
Admission: Free (Hōjō and some other buildings open only in autumn)
5 min walk from Daitoku-ji-mae bus stop, bus 205 or 206 from Kyoto Sta.

Since the city of Kyoto spreads out across the flat land of the basin, there are few great differences in altitude from spot to spot. However, the northern end of the city is slightly higher. It is for this reason that when standing on the veranda of the *hondō* of Hōshun-in, one of the sub-temples of Daitoku-ji, one is at the same level as the top of the five-story pagoda of Tō-ji, at an altitude of 55 meters.

The vast grounds of Daitoku-ji lie about 6 kilometers north of Kyoto Station in an area formerly called Murasakino. Just north of the *daidairi* (the Court), the area was an imperial hunting ground. The name Murasakino may have come from the presence of plants used to produce a purple (*murasaki*) dye.

Emperor Junna (r. 823–33), the son of Emperor Kanmu, who built Heian-kyō, built an Imperial villa in this area called the Urin-tei. This villa was later converted to a temple, known as Urin-in, but this temple declined, and was replaced in 1315 by a small temple founded by the priest Shūhō Myōchō at the request of the *daimyō* Akamatsu Norimura. This would become Daitoku-ji. The temple prospered as the favored temple of many the imperial family, but in 1453, fire and the destruction of the Ōnin War saw

1453年（享徳2）の火災、応仁の乱の兵火で諸堂を焼失し、なお足利幕府は同じ臨済禅でも夢窓疎石の一流を支援していたこともあって、大徳寺は荒廃していく。

武門の尊崇を得て大禅刹となる

しかし、応仁の乱後、一休宗純が**住持**となり、一休に深く帰依していた堺の豪商たちが大徳寺の再興に尽した。さらに、茶道の祖といわれる村田珠光、画家の曾我蛇足、連歌師柴屋軒宗長、山崎宗鑑、また猿楽の金春禅竹といった当代一流の芸術家も一休を崇敬しており、それが大徳寺の在野禅刹としての隆盛をもたらした。

一休宗純　1394〜1481。室町時代中期の臨済僧。後小松天皇のご落胤と伝わる。晩年京田辺市の一休寺（酬恩庵）に隠棲。

1582年（天正10）、豊臣秀吉が織田信長の葬儀を営み、信長の菩提寺として塔頭総見院も建立、あわせて寺領を寄進して、それを契機にして戦国武将の塔頭建立が相次ぎ大徳寺は武家の信仰を受け、隆盛を極めた。

総見院　通常非公開。

そして秀吉の茶の師匠であった千利休をはじめ武門と茶道が結びつき、各塔頭にすぐれた茶室や茶庭が建築されていく。いま、大徳寺の塔頭は20余寺院あるが、いずれも建物を含め、庭、障壁画など超一級の美術品であるといっていい。

千利休　1522〜91。茶の湯の大成者。武野紹鷗に学び、侘茶を完成。豊臣秀吉に仕えたが、のち自刃。

山内をめぐり、「金毛閣」の史話を知る

大徳寺の東側を旧大宮通が南北に通っている。北大路通から北へその通りに入ると、駐

many of the temple buildings burned, and the temple was not favored during the Ashikaga Bakufu, even though it belonged to the Rinzai sect of Musō Soseki.

Becoming a Great Zen Temple with the Support of the Warrior Class

After the Ōnin War, Ikkyū Sōjun became the **head priest** of the temple and gained the support of many rich merchants in Sakai to restore the prosperity of Daitoku-ji. Many leading artists, such as the tea ceremony pioneer Murata Jukō, the painter Soga Jasoku, the *renga* poets Saiokuken Sōchō and Yamasaki Sōkan, and the *sarugaku* playwright and actor Konparu Zenchiku followed Ikkyū, making Daitoku-ji flourish as the Zen temple of the common people.

In 1582, Toyotomi Hideyoshi held a funeral for Oda Nobunaga and created a sub-temple, Sōken-in, at Daitoku-ji as a memorial temple for Nobunaga. This led many leading military figures to create sub-temples at Daitoku-ji, further extending its prosperity.

Hideyoshi studied the art of tea with Sen-no-Rikkyū, forging a strong bond between the warrior class and the way of tea. Many of the sub-temples at Daitoku-ji included exquisite tea-ceremony room and gardens. Today Daitoku-ji still has more than twenty of these sub-temples, many of which contain first-class works of art, including gardens, paintings on folding screens and walls, and the architecture of the buildings themselves.

Wandering Through the Woods to Learn the History of the Kinmōkaku Gate

Kyū-ōmiya St. runs along the eastern edge of Daitoku-ji. If you turn north onto this street from Kitaōji St., you will see the

車場があって、その先に大徳寺の総門が開いている。多くの人たちはこの総門から寺内に入るが、私は北大路通沿いの南門からのアプローチをおすすめしたい。まっすぐに大徳寺の諸堂に向かう道には松の並木と薄茶色の築地塀がほどよい高さでつづいて、塀ごしに塔頭の建物の屋根や木肌が近くにみえる景色が落ちついて好ましい。

築地塀　土塀のうえに屋根を葺いた塀のこと。

いっぽう総門を入ると、すぐに勅使門が南面して建つ。これは慶長年間（1596〜1615）に建てられた御所の南門を移したものといわれている。その北に朱塗りの三門（金毛閣）が柵に囲まれて建つ。大徳寺の三門は応仁の乱後に単層で再建されていた。織田信長の大葬儀の七年後、1589年（天正17）に千利休は大徳寺の三門を二重の楼閣に造替する。そして、自身の木像を楼上に安置した。この利休像は雪駄履きだった。これが問題になった。三門は寺へ参詣するだれもがくぐる。殿上貴人も通れば大名も通る。まして秀吉も通る。その上に利休が雪駄で立っている。これが利休の慢心であるとして秀吉から切腹を命じられたのである。

なお、大徳寺のなかで拝観料をおさめて見学できる塔頭は「龍源院」「瑞峯院」「大仙院」「高桐院」の4寺だけで、残念なことにそのほかは特別公開日を設ける以外は拝観を謝絶しているか、まったくの非公開である。

龍源院　本堂と表門は創建当時のもので、大徳寺山内で最古の建物。

瑞峯院　1535年、大友宗麟の創建。

大仙院　禅寺の方丈建築としては最古のもの。

高桐院　細川三斎が1590年に創建。参道が美しい。

main gate of Daitoku-ji just beyond the parking lot. Many visitors enter the temple through this gate, but I recommend the south gate on Kitaōji St. The approach to the temple buildings is lined with pine trees and pale-brown fence with roofing tile, over the top of which you can see the roofs of the sub-temples forming a pleasing landscape.

If you enter the main gate, you will come directly to the *chokushi-mon* gate, built during the Keichō era (1596–1615) and said to have been formerly used as the south gate of the imperial palace. Just to the north of this gate is the vermilion-lacquered *san-mon* gate, known as the Kinmōkaku gate, surrounded by a fence. The *san-mon* gate was rebuilt after the Ōnin War as a one-story structure, but seven years after the funeral of Oda Nobunaga, in 1589, Sen-no-Rikyū rebuilt it, adding a story and placing a wooden statue of himself on top of the tower. The statue depicts him wearing *setta* (leather-soled sandals), which turned out to be a problem. Everyone visiting the temple had to pass under the gate, however exalted their status. Even Hideyoshi, who took the placing of the statue at its top as a gesture of arrogance by Rikyū, and commanded him to commit *seppuku*, or ritual suicide.

Today, four of the sub-temples may be visited for an additional fee: Ryūgen-in, Zuihō-in, Daisen-in, and Kōtō-in. Unfortunately, the others are only open for visits on special days or not at all.

7

「天神さん」の名で親しまれる神社

北野天満宮

京都市上京区御前通今小路上ル馬喰町
075(461)1399
5時〜18時(冬期は5時30分〜17時30分)　境内参拝自由(宝物殿800円　毎月25日とほかに開館日あり　9時〜16時／梅苑1000円　2月初旬〜3月下旬　10時〜16時)
www.kitanotenmangu.or.jp
京都駅より市バス50、101系統　北野天満宮前下車徒歩1分

左京区の百万遍方向から鴨川を渡って、ほぼ直線で走ってきた今出川通は北野天満宮の手前、上七軒の交差点で曲折する。いかにも**学問の神**菅原道真公を祭神とする社域を大事にして道の方が遠慮したかたちだ。

菅原家は祖父から3代つづく文章博士の家で、道真公も877年(元慶元)に、その要職につき、藤原家の権力集中を嫌った醍醐天皇の親任を得て右大臣に登用される。しかし、そのことが藤原家に危機感を与え、時の左大臣藤原時平の陰謀によって道真公は太宰権帥に左遷させられてしまう。

御霊信仰と学問の神

九州の地で、道真公は望郷の念を抱きつつ903年(延喜3)2月25日に病死する。道真公没後、都では落雷や天変地異が頻発し、また藤原家に変死者が続出して、もちろん当事者

文章博士　728年に設置された大学寮の詩文と歴史の教授。平安後期から菅原・大江・藤原氏により独占。

左大臣・右大臣　太政大臣の下で、左大臣、右大臣の順位で政務を統轄した。

藤原時平　871〜909。宇多・醍醐天皇に仕え、左大臣になる。藤原氏の地位を確立。

太宰権帥　筑後国(九州)の太宰府長官である帥の権官。中央政治の左遷先といわれる。

7. The shrine affectionately known as "Tenjin-san"

Kitano Tenman-gū

Address: Bakuro-chō, Onmae-dōri Ima-kōji-agaru, Kamigyō-ku, Kyoto-shi
Tel: 075 (461) 1399
Hours: 5:00AM–6:00PM (Winter: 5:30AM–5:30PM)
Admission: Free (Treasure hall: ¥800, open on the 25th of the month and other indicated days, from 9:00AM–4:00PM; plum [ume] orchard: ¥1,000, early February–late-March, 10:00AM–4:00PM)
www.kitanotenmangu.or.jp
1 min walk from Kitano-tenman-gū-mae bus stop, bus 50 or 101 from Kyoto Sta.

Imadegawa St. crosses the Kamo River coming from Hyakumanben in Sakyō-ku and leads almost in a straight line to Kitano Tenman-gū, but it turns at the last minute at the Kamishichiken intersection—almost as if it is making way for the shrine while yielding to the sacred area where Sugawara-no-Michizane, **the god of learning**, is enshrined.

Three generations of the Sugawara family had held an academic position in the national academy, and Michizane received the same position in 877. Emperor Daigo, fearing the increasing political power of the Fujiwara clan, sought to limit it by naming Michizane Minister of the Right, the third position. However, this evoked a reaction from the Fujiwaras. The Minister of the Left, the second position, Fujiwara-no-Tokihira, plotted to have Michizane demoted to a much lower position, in Kyūshū far from Kyoto.

Worship of the Deceased, and the God of Learning

At his new post in remote Kyūshū, Michizane languished with homesickness and died on February 25, 903. After his death, the capital was plagued with lightning strikes and other natural disasters, and the Fujiwara clan suffered several accidental deaths.

の藤原時平も39歳という若さで死ぬ。世人たちは、道真公の悲劇を知っており、これらの出来事は道真公の**怨霊**の成せるわざと信じたのである。朝廷や藤原家は道真公の死後、右大臣に復任していたが、奇怪な現象はつづき、怨霊はまだ鎮まっていないと思われた。

そんなおり、942年（天慶5）多治比文子（たじひのあやこ）という巫女に「われを北野の地に社殿を建てて祀れ」という菅原道真公の託宣があった。さらに947年（天暦元）に近江比良宮（おうみひらぐう）の禰宜（ねぎ）であった神良種（みわのよしたね）の息子太郎丸（たろうまる）にも同様の託宣があり、良種は文子とともに、北野朝日寺（きたのあさひでら）の最鎮（さいちん）の協力をえて社殿を設けた。959年（天徳3）に右大臣藤原師輔（ふじわらのもろすけ）が邸宅の用材を移して神殿を造営したという。これが北野天満宮の創建である。

987年（永延元）には天満天神の名が勅号となり、祭礼が勅祭となった。そののち道真公の学識や文才から、北野天満宮は**学問の神**としてあがめられて、今日に至るのである。

北野天満宮の境内と梅

北野天満宮の大きな石鳥居を入ると、道真公の母を祀る伴氏社（ともうじしゃ）が建つ。左手には約5000坪の敷地をもつ梅苑があり、境内とあわせ約1500本という梅が、京都に早春を告げる。2月の梅花祭（ばいかさい）には大勢の人が梅見に訪れ、同時に催される上七軒の芸妓らによる**野点茶会**（のだてちゃかい）を楽しむ。

伴氏社　鳥居は京都三鳥居のひとつ。ほかに京都御苑厳島神社の唐破風鳥居、蚕の社の三柱鳥居。

上七軒　15世紀半ばにはじまった京都五花街のひとつ。春に「北野をどり」が開催される。

Fujiwara-no-Tokihira himself died at the young age of thirty-nine. The people of the time, knowing of Michizane's resentment, assumed that the events were due to his **vengeful ghost**. Although the position of Minister of the Right was restored to Michizane posthumously, the strange phenomena continued—his ghost seemed unpacified.

In 942, a shaman named Tajihi-no-Ayako reported a message from Michizane: "Build a shrine for me at Kitano." Five years later, in 947, Tarōmaru, the son of a Shinto priest named Miwa-no-Yoshitane, reported receiving a similar message. Yoshitane and Ayako worked together to acquire the cooperation of Saichin, a priest from Kitano Asahi-dera, to built a shrine to Michizane. In 959, the then–Minister of the Right, Fujiwara-no-Morosuke, gave his residence to be used as a shrine building. This was the inception of Kitano Tenman-gū.

In 987 the name Tenman Tenjin and the shrine's festival gained the official sanction of the court. Because of Michizane's academic and literary distinction, Kitano Tenman-gū became known as the **shrine for learning**, a status that continues to this day.

The Grounds and Plum Trees of Kitano Tenman-gū

After passing under the great stone *torii* gate (sacred gate) of Kitano Tenman-gū, you will see Tomouji-sha, a shrine honoring Michizane's mother, next to the approach. On the left side of the approach is a park of plum trees covering approximately 16,530m^2; the temple grounds as a whole contain some 1,500 plum trees to announce the coming of spring to Kyoto. Many visitors come to the shrine in February to the Baikasai Festival to view the plum

楼門を入ると、梅見のシーズン以外は比較的静かであって、京都人が「天神さん」と親しみを込めてよぶ庶民的な雰囲気にみちている。

三光門（中門）を中心にして回廊をめぐらした本殿の区域があり、**白砂**が敷かれて、やはりここは神厳な雰囲気に包まれている。北野天満宮の社殿は拝殿と本殿をつなぎ、棟を多くもつことから「八棟造」とよばれている。また、本殿区域以外にも見どころが多く、回廊の透塀の**欄間彫刻**とその外側に吊り下げられている金色の灯籠はとくに美しい。

本殿裏手の十二社や老松社、さらに文子天満宮の建つ一隅も静寂で落ちつく場所であり、また境内西には秀吉の築いた「御土居」が残り、深い緑に包まれている。

毎月25日の道真公の月命日には露店が並び、とくに1月25日の初天神、12月25日の終天神には大勢の人で雑踏する。

また、この神社では無病息災を願う「大茅の輪くぐり」が夏越の祓の神事として、6月25日におこなわれ、拝観者は直径約5mの茅の輪をくぐって境内に入る。

御土居　豊臣秀吉造営の南北約8.5km、東西約3.5kmの京都を囲む土塁。御土居の内部を洛中、外部を洛外とよぶ。

「天神さん」「弘法さん」　菅原道真の縁日で毎月25日に開催の「天神さん」、弘法大師空海の縁日で毎月21日に東寺で開催の「弘法さん」は賑やかに露店市がたつ。

blossoms, as well as the **open-air tea festival** where geisha from the nearby Kamishichiken area serve tea.

Pass through the two-story gate and, except during plum-blossom-viewing season, the grounds are relatively quiet. The local people affectionately call the shrine "Tenjin-san," and the shrine has an unpretentious, common feel to it.

By contrast, in the area of the main sanctuary (*hon-den*), surrounded by a walkway with the *sankō-mon* gate at its center, **white sand** covers the ground, giving the area an austere feel. The worship hall (*hai-den*) and the *hon-den* are connected in a building style known as *yatsumune* (many ridges) style structure. There are many items worth seeing outside the central *hon-den* area. The **transom carvings** on the fence around the walkway, and the gold lanterns hanging on its outer side, are particularly beautiful.

There are several serene spots behind the *hon-den*, including the Jūni-sha and the Oimatsu-sha, as well as the Ayako Tenman-gū. On the west side of the grounds is the Odoi, a remnant of the earthen walls built by Hideyoshi that encircled Kyoto, surrounded by a deep green mantle.

On the twenty-fifth of every month a memorial day is held for Michizane and flea market stalls fill the temple grounds. The celebrations in January (Hatsutenjin) and December (Shimaitenjin) are particularly popular.

Other annual events include the Ōchi-no-Wa kuguri Festival on June 25, where supplicants pray for good health by entering the temple grounds under a five-meter-wide thatch hoop.

8

本阿弥光悦の芸術村に建てた寺

光悦寺

京都市北区鷹峯光悦町29
075（491）1399
8時～17時（11月10～13日は閉門）
300円（紅葉時400円）
北大路バスターミナルより市バス北1系統　鷹峯源光庵前下車徒歩3分

千本通を北行すると、佛教大学をすぎたところから道は狭く、かなり急な上り坂になり、その坂道をのぼりつめた鷹峯に市中の寺院とは風趣を異にした閑寂な寺が点在している。そのうちのひとつ光悦寺を訪れる。

光悦寺という寺名はもちろん本阿弥光悦（1558～1637）による。本阿弥家は室町以来、刀剣鑑定の家系で、手入れから研磨をおこない、足利・豊臣・徳川の各政権に仕えた。光悦はそのほかに書、陶芸、蒔絵といった才能にもめぐまれて、とくに書は松花堂昭乗、近衛信尹とともに寛永の三筆といわれた。1615年（元和元）に徳川家康から鷹ヶ峰の地を与えられて、光悦は一族の工芸職人らを引きつれて、ここに芸術村を形成したのである。

また、熱心な法華経徒であった光悦は邸内に法華題目堂を建てた。それが光悦の死後、日慈上人を開山とする日蓮宗大虚山光悦寺のもとになった。

鷹峯の寺　天下の名妓吉野太夫(1606～43）ゆかりの常照寺、伏見城の遺構で「血天井」が伝わる源光庵などがある。

松花堂昭乗　1584～1639。真言宗の学僧。能書家で水墨画、彩色画にすぐれ、晩年八幡男山に茶室「松花堂」を建てる。

近衛信尹　1565～1614。後陽成天皇に仕え、左大臣、関白など。和様書道の三藐院流を興す。

8. The temple built in Hon'ami Kōetsu's artist village

Kōetsu-ji

Address: 29 Takagamine Kōetsu-chō, Kita-ku, Kyoto-shi
Tel: 075 (491) 1399
Hours: 8:00AM–5:00PM (Closed November 10–13)
Admission: ¥300 (During fall colors: ¥400)
3 min walk from Takagamine-genkō-an-mae bus stop, bus North 1 from Kitaōji Bus Terminal

If you walk north on Senbon St., the street narrows just after you pass Bukkyō University and starts slanting up quite steeply. In this area up this slope known as Takagamine are a number of quiet, unassuming temples unlike the elegant ones found elsewhere in the city. One of these is Kōetsu-ji.

The name Kōetsu-ji, of course, comes from Hon'ami Kōetsu (1558–1637). The Hon'ami clan had been sword connoisseur since the Muromachi period, serving the Ashikaga, Toyotomi, and Tokugawa dynasties. Kōetsu also showed talent in **calligraphy**, **ceramics**, and **lacquer**, although it was in the first of these that he was most excellent, being named along with Shōkadō Shōjō and Konoe Nobutada as the three great calligraphers of the Kan'ei era. In 1615, he was given a parcel of land by Tokugawa Ieyasu and gathered craftsmen and artisans into an artists' village.

An enthusiastic believer of the Hokke Sutra, Kōetsu erected the Hokke Daimoku-dō, which after his death was converted into Daikyosan Kōetsu-ji, a temple of the Nichiren Buddhist sect opening by Nichiji Shōnin.

山居の庵と光悦垣

光悦寺は寺というより山荘といった佇まいで、街道から山門へ向かう**石畳の参道**が幅といい、じつに長さといい歩を進めるに心地よく、静謐でまるで個人の別荘を訪れるといった感覚である。光悦寺は山門からわずかずつ境内に下ってゆく。ふつう山門から石段などをのぼって境内に入る寺が多いが、その点も山間の寺の趣があっていい。

光悦寺境内には、大正初期に再建された大虚庵（だいきょあん）をはじめ、光悦の木像をおさめる光悦堂をもつ三巴亭（みつどもえてい）、もと題目堂の了寂軒（りょうじゃくけん）、本阿弥庵などの茶室が、山気がただようなかに建っている。

もうひとつの眼福は、大虚庵前の光悦垣（こうえつがき）（臥牛垣（がぎゅうがき））である。ゆるやかな曲線をもってしつらえたその垣根は、竹を斜めに菱形をつくるように組み、さらに端にゆくほど垣の丈が低くなる。萩（はぎ）が絡まったり、紅葉（もみじ）が垣根にかぶさったりするようすが一幅の絵になっていて、日本画の佳品をみるようである。

京都の垣根　建仁寺垣、大徳寺垣、桂垣（桂離宮）、金閣寺垣、銀閣寺垣など。

A Mountain Villa and the Kōetsu-gaki

Kōetsu-ji is as much a mountain villa as a temple, and the **stone-paved approach** leading to it is long and serene, so that a visitor might have the feeling that she is visiting someone's villa. From the *san-mon* gate, one little by little finds oneself in the temple grounds. In most temples, one ascends from the *san-mon* gate on a stone staircase or the like into the temple grounds, but this is another distinction of a temple in the mountains.

This mountain air floats among the buildings of Kōetsu-ji, which include the Daikyo-an rebuilt in the early Taishō era; the Mitsudomoe-tei, containing the wooden statue of Kōetsu; the original Daimoku-dō (now called the Ryōjaku-ken); and the Hon'ami-an tea-ceremony house.

Another attractive feature is the so-called "Kōetsu-gaki" fence in front of the Daikyo-an. This gently curving hedge made of bamboo in a diamond pattern decreases in height along its length. The bush clover weaves around it and the autumn leaves cover the hedge like a scroll painting or a fine Japanese painting.

エリア 4　Area 4

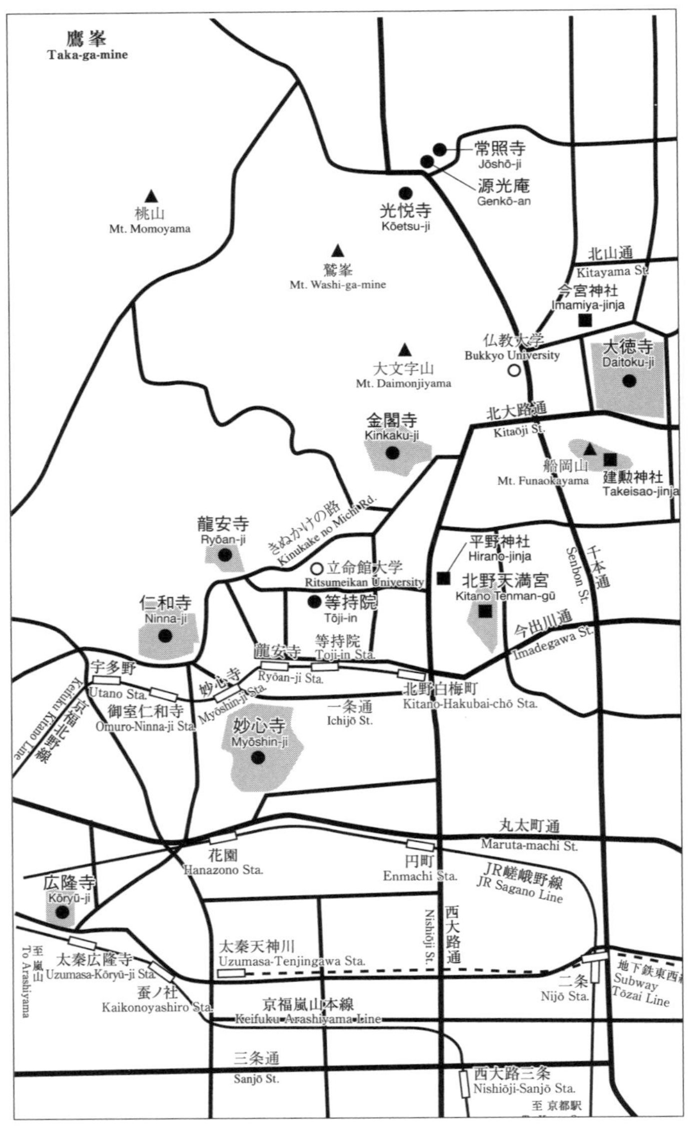

鷹峯
Taka-ga-mine
常照寺
Jōshō-ji
源光庵
Genkō-an
光悦寺
Kōetsu-ji
桃山
Mt. Momoyama
鷲峯
Mt. Washi-ga-mine
北山通
Kitayama St.
今宮神社
Imamiya-jinja
仏教大学
Bukkyo University
大徳寺
Daitoku-ji
大文字山
Mt. Daimonjiyama
北大路通
Kitaōji St.
金閣寺
Kinkaku-ji
船岡山
Mt. Funaokayama
建勲神社
Takeisao-jinja
きぬかけの路
Kinukake no Michi Rd.
龍安寺
Ryōan-ji
平野神社
Hirano-jinja
千本通
Senbon St.
立命館大学
Ritsumeikan University
北野天満宮
Kitano Tenman-gū
仁和寺
Ninna-ji
等持院
Tōji-in
今出川通
Imadegawa St.
等持院
Toji-in Sta.
龍安寺
Ryōan-ji Sta.
宇多野
Utano Sta.
妙心寺
Myōshin-ji Sta.
北野白梅町
Kitano-Hakubai-chō Sta.
京福北野線
Keifuku Kitano Line
御室仁和寺
Omuro-Ninna-ji Sta.
一条通
Ichijō St.
妙心寺
Myōshin-ji
丸太町通
Maruta-machi St.
花園
Hanazono Sta.
円町
Enmachi Sta.
JR嵯峨野線
JR Sagano Line
広隆寺
Kōryū-ji
西大路通
Nishiōji St.
太秦天神川
Uzumasa-Tenjingawa Sta.
至嵐山
To Arashiyama
太秦広隆寺
Uzumasa-Kōryū-ji Sta.
地下鉄東西線
Subway Tōzai Line
二条
Nijō Sta.
蚕ノ社
Kaikonoyashiro Sta.
京福嵐山本線
Keifuku Arashiyama Line
三条通
Sanjō St.
西大路三条
Nishiōji-Sanjō Sta.
至 京都駅

エリア５
Area 5

嵯峨野から粟生の光明寺まで巡る早足の旅
A Quick Trip from Sagano to Kōmyōji in Ao

この章で紹介する寺社はふつう同一のエリアに扱うことはない。しかし本書では、交通の便を考え、効率よく巡るため、あえて嵯峨野と松尾、さらには長岡京市の粟生まで含めた。

嵯峨野の大寺は天龍寺と清凉寺と大覚寺で、ほかは小規模な寺か、およそ庵とでもいう細微な寺である。だがそれら小寺が嵯峨の竹林にひそやかに建っていて、じつに風趣がある。人影のまばらな晩秋のそれも時雨どきにでも訪れたなら、いっそう身に浸む思いがするであろうが——。

しかし土、日や観光シーズンは、狭い境内ゆえに大勢の観光客にまぎれて観光することになる。嵯峨野への旅は、時期と時刻をよく吟味するべきである。

上記の三つの大寺も、天龍寺は夢窓疎石の庭、清凉寺は異国風な古貌の本尊、大覚寺は御殿風な諸堂と大沢池、と見どころがあって、急くことなく拝観したい寺である。

そして、嵐山の翠巒を背に、川面に近く直線で架かる渡月橋を渡ると、洛南へ走る阪急嵐山線の嵐山駅があって、ひと駅松尾駅まで乗れば、松尾大社は駅前である。古社月読神社を経て、苔寺（西芳寺）までわずかな距離で、事前に申し込んで拝観許可さえ得ておけば、名庭をゆっくり巡ることができるし、できなければ、竹の寺地蔵院へ赴いても、予想外と思われるほど閑寂な山寺の風情をみることができよう。

上桂駅から西向日駅に行けば、通常なら別建てで計画しなければならない光明寺への拝観も、その日の最後の寺として訪れることが可能である。

The temples and shrines introduced in this chapter are normally not grouped together. However, by paying attention to available transportation, this book allows you to effectively visit not only Sagano and Matsuo but even Ao, in Nagaokakyō City.

Sagano's great temples are Tenryū-ji, Seiryō-ji, and Daikaku-ji. The other temples described here are of smaller scale, even including tiny temples that are more like hermits' cottages. However, it is these small temples hidden in the bamboo groves that give Sagano its flavor. Visiting in the late autumn when few people are around or even in the rain may allow you some truly contemplative moments.

However, if you are visiting on a Saturday or Sunday or during the tourist season, the press of tourists in these small temples may be overwhelming, so it is very important to carefully consider the timing of your visit to Sagano.

The three temples mentioned above also have their famous sights and should be allowed ample time for visiting. These include the gardens of Musō Soseki at Tenryū-ji, the exotic face of the treasured statue at Seiryō-ji, and the palatial buildings and Ōsawa pond at Daikaku-ji.

With Mt. Arashiyama forming the backdrop, cross low-lying Togetsukyō bridge and you will come to Arashiyama Station, from where you can take the Hankyū Arashiyama Line one stop to Matsuo Station, which is right in front of Matsunoo-taisha. It is only a short walk past the old Tsukiyomi-jinja to Koke-dera (Saihō-ji), where, if you have made arrangements in advance, you can tour the famous gardens. If you have not already gotten a permit for Koke-dera, proceed to Jizō-in, among the bamboo, where you can enjoy the feeling of a mountain temple more tranquil than one could have expected.

Usually one needs to plan for another day to visit Kōmyō-ji, but if you go from Kamikatsura Station to Nishimukō Station, you should be able to fit a visit to Kōmyō-ji into the day as well.

1

名僧夢窓疎石が開創した禅刹

天龍寺

京都市右京区嵯峨天龍寺芒ノ馬場町68
075(881)1235
8時30分〜17時30分(10月21日〜3月20日は8時30分〜17時)
庭園500円(諸堂参拝は300円追加)
www.tenryuji.com
京福嵐山本線　嵐山駅下車徒歩2分

夢窓疎石と天龍寺船

嵯峨野の寺社めぐりは天龍寺からはじまる。京福嵐山本線の終着駅「嵐山」の目の前が天龍寺の境内である。

天龍寺は創建当初、いまの清涼寺あたりから嵐山までその範囲とするほど広大な寺域を誇り、京都五山の格付けで南禅寺を別格として天龍寺が第一位であった。それは足利尊氏が夢窓疎石の法統に末代まで帰依して天龍寺を加護する置文を残したように、尊氏以下、室町幕府の絶大な支援があったことによる。

天龍寺の開山夢窓疎石（1275〜1351）は肖像や頂相などをみればわかるが、柔和な顔と極端な撫で肩の弱々しい体躯で、どこに以下に述べる偉業をなしとげたエネルギーと政治的手腕がひそんでいるのかと思うほどである。

建武新政をおこない南朝を樹立した後醍醐天皇が1339年（暦応2）に崩ずると、夢窓疎石は、天皇と対立関係にあった足利尊氏や弟

頂相　禅宗の高僧の写実的肖像画のこと。

建武新政　後醍醐天皇による新政(1333〜35年)。足利尊氏と対立し、南北朝時代を招く。

1. The Zen temple founded by the famous priest Musō Soseki

Tenryū-ji

Address: 68 Saga Tenryū-ji Susukinobaba-chō, Ukyō-ku, Kyoto-shi
Tel: 075 (881) 1235
Hours: 8:30AM–5:30PM (October 21–March 20: 8:30AM–5:00PM)
Admission: Gardens only: ¥500 (Gardens and buildings: Additional ¥300)
www.tenryuji.com/en/
2 min walk from Keifuku Arashiyama Line Arashiyama Sta.

Musō Soseki and the Tenryū-ji Ship

A tour of the temples and shrines around Sagano begins from Tenryū-ji. When you alight from the Keifuku Arashiyama line at the last station, Arashiyama, the grounds of Tenryū-ji lie right in front of you.

At the time Tenryū-ji was built, it boasted extensive temple grounds from what today is Seiryō-ji to Arashiyama. Aside from Nanzen-ji, it ranks as the highest of Kyoto's five great Zen temples. This is largely due to the support of the Muromachi Bakufu, beginning with Ashikaga Takauji, who swore to protect Tenryū-ji for the sake of the holy teachings of Musō Soseki.

In his portraits, Soseki (1275–1351), the founder of Tenryū-ji, has a gentle face and sloping shoulders, but his amazing exploits and political acumen belied his weak appearance.

When Emperor Godaigo, who had formed the Southern Court, died in 1339, Soseki urged Ashikaga Takauji and his brother Tadayoshi, who had opposed the emperor, to built a temple

の直義に後醍醐帝の菩提を弔うため一寺の建立を勧める。尊氏もかつては信任を得ていた天皇を懐かしみ、かつ自責の念もあって、荘園を寄進して建築を支援するが、それでも十分な資金の調達ができず、夢窓疎石は、直義に計って中国の元との貿易船「天龍寺船」を計画する。

この天龍寺船は1342年（康永元）秋に渡航するのだが、疎石は、博多の商人に船の運営をゆだね、利益がどれほど多くても少なくても、5000貫文を寺におさめる約束をさせる。これにより伽藍の建築は進捗して、1345年（貞和元）8月、後醍醐天皇の七周忌法要とともに開堂大供養が催された。一禅僧が天皇の菩提寺を立案し、元との貿易を企画して資金を集めるという大事業を成しとげたのである。

しかし、豪壮な七堂伽藍を誇った天龍寺だが、660余年あまりの歴史のなかで8回も焼けている。1358年（延文3）の火災が最初で、以後1380年（康暦2）の4度目の焼失まで2世の春屋妙葩により再建、5度目は放火といわれ、堂宇のほか伝わっていた文書すべてが焼けてしまう。その次は応仁の乱により、そして江戸期に入り1815年（文化12）に焼失し、そして最後は幕末の蛤御門の変（1864年）に破れた長州軍の宿営地であったことから薩摩藩によって大砲が打ち込まれ焼かれてしまう。現在私たちがみる建物は明治以降の建築である。

蛤御門の変　長州藩が形勢挽回を図り、京都守護松平容保が指揮する諸藩の兵と御所蛤御門近辺で戦い敗れた事変。

to honor him. Takauji had once been loyal to the emperor and felt some personal responsibility for what had befallen him, so he donated a **manor** and supported the construction of a temple. However, there were not enough funds to complete the construction, so Soseki, with the help of Tadayoshi, organized ships to trade with China, the Tenryū-ji ship, in order to support the project.

The ship set sail in the autumn of 1342, and Soseki contracted with a Hakata, Kyūshū, merchant to operate the ship, obtaining a promise for a set amount of bullion regardless of the profit the ship made. This allowed construction of the temple to go forward, and in August 1345, on the seventh anniversary of Godaigo's death, a ceremony was held to mark the opening of the temple. For a single Zen priest to establish a temple venerating the emperor, and to gather funds for it by conducting trade with China, was a remarkable exploit.

Sadly, in its more than 660 years of history, the grand buildings of Tenryū-ji have been burned down eight times. The first fire was in 1358, and the second head priest, Shun'oku Myōha, rebuilt three more times by 1380. The fifth fire was said to be arson, and in addition to the buildings, all of the temple's carefully collected texts were destroyed. Fire struck again during the Ōnin War and again in the Edo period, in 1815, and once again in 1864 during the Hamaguri Gomon Rebellion, when rebel samurai from Chōshū (Yamaguchi) challenged the troops of the Bakufu. The buildings that we see today were all constructed since the Meiji era.

諸堂と借景の名庭園

天龍寺の参道に入ると、中央に放生池と広い樹木地、左右に甍（いらか）を連ねる塔頭の塀をみて、正面の法堂にいたる。この法堂は通常は非公開であるが、堂内に釈迦像と夢窓疎石、足利尊氏の木像を安置する。また、天井の龍の絵は、近年になって加山又造（かやままたぞう）の「雲龍図」が掲げられた。

拝観受付のある庫裏（くり）から本尊の木像釈迦如来坐像を安置する大方丈に入る。東庭は静かな白砂敷の庭、西は広縁の先に曹源池（そうげんち）を中心とする庭園、書院から廊下を渡って、1934年（昭和9）に完成した後醍醐帝聖廟の多宝殿（たほうでん）をめぐる。いったん庫裏に戻って、庭園入口から大方丈をぐるりと回ると、名庭として名高い池泉回遊式の天龍寺庭園が広がる。曹源池を中心に亀山（かめやま）や嵐山を借景にして、池の周囲をかこむ樹林が、春夏にはみずみずしい緑に、秋には黄赤の彩りをみせる。

作庭は夢窓疎石で疎石はほかに、等持院（とうじいん）、西芳寺（さいほうじ）（苔寺（こけでら））などの庭も手がけたといわれている。

等持院　歴代の足利将軍の廟所で臨済宗の禅寺。

北門から出て右へ行くと、黒木（くろき）の鳥居で知られる野宮（ののみや）神社で、いよいよ嵯峨野散策の佳境に入っていく。

The Buildings and the Famous Garden

When entering the grounds of Tenryū-ji along the approach, the *hōjō* pond and a broad expanse of woods are in the center, with sub-temples with tiled roofs joined by earthen walls to left and right, and the *hattō* just in front. The *hattō* is not normally open to the public, but inside are wooden statues of the Buddha, Soseki, and Ashikaga Takauji. "*Unryūzu*," the dragon painting on the ceiling, was done by Kayama Matazō recently.

From the entrance reception in the *kuri*, enter the *dai-hōjō* to see the seated wooden statue of the Buddha (*shaka nyorai*). The eastern garden is a peaceful space spread with white sand, and the western garden centers on Sōgen pond. You can exit the *shoin* (study-cum-living room) and use the walkway to examine the Tahō-den, completed in 1934 to honor Emperor Godaigo. Return to the *kuri* to enter the famous stroll pond Tenryū-ji garden. The garden, with Sōgen pond at its center, makes use of the surrounding landscape in the form of Mt. Kameyama and Mt. Arashiyama in its design. The trees that circle the pond are a clear green in spring and a gorgeous yellow in the fall.

In addition to the gardens here, Soseki also designed gardens at Tōji-in, Saihō-ji (Koke-dera), and other temples.

Leaving through the north gate and turning to the right, you will see the Nonomiya-jinja with its famous black-wood *torii* gate, and then we come at last to the high point of a stroll through Sagano.

2

清涼寺式釈迦像として知られる

清涼寺（せいりょうじ）

京都市右京区嵯峨釈迦堂藤ノ木町46
075（861）0343
9時～16時
400円
seiryoji.or.jp
京都駅より市バス28系統　嵯峨釈迦堂前下車徒歩3分

地元の人は清涼寺を「嵯峨の釈迦堂（さがのしゃかどう）」とよんで、篤い信仰をよせている。4月の第2土・日と第3日曜に催される「嵯峨大念仏狂言（さがだいねんぶつきょうげん）」、3月15日の夜におこなわれる「嵯峨のお松明（たいまつ）」（涅槃会（ねはんえ））は、地元の人以外にも大勢の見物客を集める。

鞍馬の火祭　由岐神社の祭礼で、10月22日の夜におこなわれる。

五山（ござん）の送り火、鞍馬（くらま）の火祭とともに京都三大火祭に数えられる嵯峨のお松明は、春の到来を知らせる行事である。高さ約7mの3本の松明には杉や竹の葉がつめられ、護摩木（ごまぎ）の火を移した藁束を投げ入れて点火する。古来、近隣の農家の人々はこの3本の松明の燃え具合で稲の豊凶を占ってきた。

清涼寺のある地には、かつて嵯峨天皇の皇子で『源氏物語』の光源氏（ひかるげんじ）のモデルという源融（みなもとのとおる）（822～95）の山荘「棲霞観（せいかかん）」があった。

『源氏物語』　平安時代中期、紫式部によって書かれた光源氏を主人公とする宮廷小説の傑作。54帖。

2. Known for its distinctive Buddha statue

Seiryō-ji

Address: 46 Saga Shaka-dō Fujinoki-chō, Ukyō-ku, Kyoto-shi
Tel: 075 (861) 0343
Hours: 9:00AM–4:00PM
Admission: ¥400
seiryoji.or.jp
3 min walk from Saga-Shaka-dō-mae bus stop, bus 28 from Kyoto Sta.

Local residents call Seiryō-ji "Saga-no-Shaka-dō," and it commands a deep religious loyalty. Its festivals and performances—the 'Saga Dainenbutsu Kyōgen' play on the second Saturday and Sunday and the third Sunday of April, and the 'Saga-no-O-taimatsu' (*nehan-e*) on the evening of March 15—attract both locals and visitors from other places.

The Saga-no-O-taimatsu is counted as one of Kyoto's three great fire festivals, along with the Gozan-no-Okuribi and the Kurama-no-Himatsuri, and is a harbinger of spring. Three torches, each 7 meters high, made of pine bound with cedar and bamboo leaves, are set alight. In the old days, nearby farmers forecast the prosperity of that year's rice crop by divining the flames of the torches.

The grounds of Seiryō-ji were the site of Seikakan, a mountain villa belonging to Minamoto-no-Tōru (822–95), a son of Emperor Saga, who is said to have been the model for the "chief character, Hikaru Genji," in Japan's classic novel *the Tale of Genji*.

異国的な釈迦如来立像と諸堂

945年（天慶8）醍醐天皇の皇子重明親王が寺内に新堂を建て等身大の釈迦像を安置したことで釈迦堂の名がついた。その後、宋より戻った東大寺の僧奝然が大寺の造営を志すがその途中で没し、弟子の盛算が勅許をえて、1016年（長和5）に棲霞寺の釈迦堂に現本尊の釈迦如来立像を安置して、華厳宗清凉寺と称した。

奝然 938～1016。平安時代中期の三輪宗の僧。983年入宋、989年東大寺別当となる。

この釈迦如来立像は釈迦の37歳の生き姿を刻んだもので、奝然が宋の太宗に謁見したおりに深く感動し、中国の仏師に頼み寸分違わず模刻させたという。この釈迦如来像は異国的な表情で「清凉寺式釈迦像」として知られる。

清凉寺は天台、真言、念仏宗を兼学する寺として隆盛したが、1190年（建久元）以降、たびたびの火災にみまわれ諸堂が焼失する。のちに徳川家康や綱吉の援助があり、本堂、多宝塔、仁王門など現在の伽藍が整う。いま、清凉寺は浄土宗知恩院派の寺である。

1776年（安永5）再建の仁王門は重層の楼門で内部に十六羅漢像を安置する。楼門をくぐると正面に1701年（元禄14）再建の単層入母屋造本瓦葺の本堂がみえる。その手前の右手に、空海が南都八宗の学僧を論破したという八宗論池があり、その奥に一切経堂、さらに棲霞寺の名残をとどめる阿弥陀堂が建つ。多宝塔の横には法然上人の大きな立像が立ち、本堂の本尊釈迦如来像と向かいあっている。

南都八宗　南都六宗（清水寺の項参照）に、平安時代の天台、真言を加えて称する。

A exotic Buddha Statue and the Temple Buildings

In 945, Prince Shigeakira, the son of Emperor Daigo, built a new building on the temple grounds to hold a life-size statue of the Buddha. The building was called the *shaka-dō*. In 1016, a priest named Seizan, a disciple of the Tōdai-ji priest Chōnen, received permission to install a standing statue of the Buddha (*shaka nyorai*) in the *shaka-dō* of Seika-ji, and renamed it Seiryō-ji, of the Kegon sect.

This statue portrayed the Buddha at the age of thirty-seven, and is a copy of the statue Chōnen was deeply moved by in China. It has an exotic expression that has caused this type of statue to be known as a "Seiryō-ji-style Buddha statue."

Seiryō-ji has prospered by welcoming Tendai, Shingon, and Nenbutsu sects, but since 1190, many of its buildings have been burned down by fires. With later help from Tokugawa Ieyasu and Tsunayoshi, the main hall (*hondō*), the *tahōtō*, and the *niō-mon* gate, among other structures, make up today's temple. Seiryō-ji is now a temple of the Jōdo sect, Chion-in school.

In 1776, the *niō-mon* gate was rebuilt as a multi-story structure that contains an image of the sixteen Arhats (*rakan*). Pass under the gate, and you will see the single-story *hondō*, in the gable and hip style (*irimoya-zukuri*) with a tiled roof, rebuilt in 1701. To the right is Hasshūron pond, where Kūkai is said to have refuted a famous philosophical argument with eight great temples in Nara of scholar monks. Further on is the *issaikyō-dō* and the *amida-dō*, the remnant of Seika-ji. Next to the *Tahōtō* is a large statue of saint Hōnen, standing as if he is facing the Buddha statue in the *hondō*.

3

日本最古の門跡寺院と大沢池

大覚寺

京都市右京区嵯峨大沢町４
075(871)0071
9時〜16時30分　500円
www.daikakuji.or.jp
京都駅より市バス28系統　大覚寺下車徒歩１分

嵯峨野には大きな池がふたつある。広沢池と大覚寺の寺域につづく大沢池である。この大沢池は嵯峨天皇が営まれた**離宮**「嵯峨院」の苑地で、池の周囲約1kmには桜や楓、松が植えられ、春の花見や秋の月見の時期がとくに美しい景色となって多くの人が訪れる。船を池に浮かべて催す「観月の夕べ」が知られている。

離宮嵯峨院を876年（貞観18）に嵯峨天皇の正子内親王（淳和天皇の皇后）が寺に改め、開山として出家した第二子の恒寂法親王を迎えた。

そののち、後嵯峨、亀山両天皇が譲位後に出家して、ここ大覚寺に入り、1308年（延慶元）に後宇多法皇が入寺して、大覚寺を仙洞御所としたことから南朝の大覚寺統がおこり、北朝の持明院統と皇位をめぐって対立した。この南北朝の対立は、1392年に合一の講和会議が当寺でおこなわれ、南朝の後亀山天皇が北朝の後小松天皇に**三種の神器**を引き渡し、い

大覚寺統　鎌倉後期〜南北朝時代に分裂した皇統のうち、亀山天皇（在位1259〜74）の皇統。

持明院統　大覚寺統に対し皇位を争った後深草天皇（在位1246〜59）の皇統。

三種の神器　皇位の象徴として歴代天皇が受け継いできた宝物。八咫鏡、天叢雲剣、八尺瓊曲玉。

3. Japan's oldest monzeki temple, and Ōsawa pond

Daikaku-ji

Address: 4 Saga Ōsawa-chō, Ukyō-ku, Kyoto-shi
Tel: 075 (871) 0071
Hours: 9:00AM–4:30PM
Admission: ¥500
www.daikakuji.or.jp
1 min walk from Daikaku-ji bus stop, bus 28 from Kyoto Sta.

There are two large ponds in the Sagano area: Hirosawa pond and Osawa pond, next to the temple grounds of Daikaku-ji. Osawa pond is part of the estate of Emperor Saga's **Imperial villa** Saga-in, and the pond is bordered by approximately a kilometer of cherry, maple, and pine trees. It is very popular in spring for cherry-blossom viewing and in autumn for moon viewing. The latter is particularly exquisite when done from a boat floating in the pond.

In 876, Empeor Saga's daughter Princess Seishi, later the Empress of Emperor Junna, converted Saga-in into a temple and commissioned her second son Kōjaku, who had taken his orders, to be its head priest.

Later, Emperors Gosaga and Kameyama both took up residence at the temple after entering the priesthood. Followed by Emperor Gouda, and the idea of a "Daikaku-ji line" of the Southern Court became known, in conflict with the "Jimyō-in line" of the Northern Court. At last in 1392 a conference to reconcile the Northern and Southern Courts was held at Daikaku-ji, and the Southern Court's Emperor Gokameyama relinquished his **three sacred treasures** to the Northern Court's Emperor Gokomatsu.

ちおうの終結をみた。

このように大覚寺は天皇や皇統の入寺がつづく、日本最古の門跡寺院(仁和寺は888年創建)としての格式を保つことになる。

寺というより御所というべき諸堂

当寺は嵯峨山と号し、「旧嵯峨御所大覚寺門跡」と称する真言宗大覚寺派の大本山である。といって、大覚寺は仰々しい山門を構えるわけではない。細流にかかる石橋を渡ると簡素な表門があって、その先に十六弁の**菊紋**を描いた白幕を下げる式台玄関がみえる。このようすも寺というより、まさに御所という佇まいである。

十六弁の菊紋　皇室の紋章。1869年に皇室以外にこの紋章の使用を禁止する令が出た。

この式台玄関(大玄関)の正面には狩野永徳筆の「松に山鳥図」が描かれている。大玄関のうしろが正寝殿(客殿)で十二室の小間をもち、上段の間は後宇多上皇が院政をおこなった「御冠の間」(再現)である。この正寝殿から宸殿、さらに御影堂や五大堂をむすぶ板敷の渡廊下は、柱を雨に、屈曲する廊下を稲妻に見たてて「村雨の廊下」とも「稲妻の廊下」ともよばれている。

狩野永徳　1543～90。狩野家4代目の画家。豪快な筆致で知られる。「洛中洛外図」など。

宸殿は延宝年間(1673~81)に後水尾天皇より下賜されたもので、皇后の東福門院和子が使用していた御所の建物という。襖絵は狩野山楽筆の「牡丹図」「紅葉図」で、桃山美術の代表的作品として名高い。

狩野山楽　1559～1635。永徳に学び、京狩野家の祖となる。永徳の画風を引き継ぎつつ装飾性を高めた。

本尊の秘仏五大明王を祀る五大堂は大覚寺の本堂で、大沢池のほとりに建つ。

The entry of these the emperors and imperial family members into Daikaku-ji (called *monzeki* temple) in this manner led to its formal recognition as Japan's oldest *monzeki* temple (Ninna-ji was founded in 888).

Temple Buildings That Seem More Like the Palace

Daikaku-ji is titled as "Saga-san," but its formal Shingon name is "old Saga Imperial Palace Daikaku-ji *monzeki*." Despite this grand monicker, Daikaku-ji does not have a grand *san-mon* gate. You cross a small stream over a stone bridge to the simple front gate, and a doorway covered by a white curtain with a sixteen-petaled **chrysanthemum crest** stands before you. This too seems more like the palace than a temple.

Before the main entrance is a painting by Kanō Eitoku, "*Mountain Birds on a Pine Tree*," and beyond the entrance is the *seishin-den* guesthouse, with twelve small rooms. The upper area is a reconstruction Gokan-no-Ma, the room where the former Emperor Gouda conducted a shadow government. The corridor connecting the *seishin-den* to the *shin-den* and other buildings such as *miei-dō* and *godai-dō* is called the Murasame (rain)-no-Rōka or the Inazuma (lightning)-no-Rōka, because its designs are intended to suggest rain and lightning.

The *shin-den* was bestowed during the Enpō era (1673–81) by Emperor Gomizunoo and is believed to have formerly been the palace used by Empress Tōfukumon'in Kazuko. It boasts paintings on *fusuma* by Kanō Sanraku of peonies and autumn leaves that are considered great representative works of the art style of Momoyama.

The *godai-dō* honoring the Five Great Vidyarajas is the *hondō* of the temple and stands next to Ōsawa pond.

4

嵯峨野の寺社めぐり

野宮(ののみや)神社から 愛宕念仏寺(おたぎねんぶつじ)

愛宕念仏寺 Otagi Nenbutsu-ji

野宮神社
京都市右京区嵯峨野宮町1　075(871)1972
9時～17時　境内参拝自由
www.nonomiya.com

常寂光寺 Jōjakkō-ji

常寂光寺
京都市右京区嵯峨小倉山小倉町3　075(861)0435
9時～17時　500円
www.jojakko-ji.or.jp

二尊院
京都市右京区嵯峨二尊院門前長神町27
075(861)0687
9時～17時　500円
nisonin.jp

野宮神社 黒木の鳥居
Nonomiya-jinja, the black *torii*

祇王寺
京都市右京区嵯峨鳥居本小坂町32　075(861)3574
9時～17時　300円(大覚寺との共通拝観券600円)
www.giouji.or.jp

滝口寺
京都市右京区嵯峨亀山町10-4　075(871)3929
9時～17時　300円

二尊院 Nison-in

化野念仏寺
京都市右京区嵯峨鳥居本化野町17　075(861)2221
9時～16時30分(12月～2月は9時～15時30分)
500円　www.nenbutsuji.jp

直指庵
京都市右京区北嵯峨北ノ段町3　075(871)1880
9時～16時
500円　www5e.biglobe.ne.jp/~jikisian/

直指庵 Jikishi-an

愛宕念仏寺
京都市右京区嵯峨鳥居本深谷町2-5　075(865)1231
8時～17時　300円　www.otagiji.com

4. A tour of the temples and shrines of Sagano

Nonomiya-jinja

Address: 1 Saganomiya-chō, Ukyō-ku, Kyoto-shi
Tel: 075 (871) 1972 Hours: 9:00AM–5:00PM
Admission: Free www.nonomiya.com/eng.html

Jōjakkō-ji

Address: 3 Saga Ogurayama Ogura-chō, Ukyō-ku, Kyoto-shi
Tel: 075 (861) 0435 Hours: 9:00AM–5:00PM
Admission: ¥500 www.jojakko-ji.or.jp

Nison-in

Address: 27 Saga Nison-in Monzen Chōjin-chō, Ukyō-ku, Kyoto-shi
Tel: 075 (861) 0687 Hours: 9:00AM–5:00PM
Admission: ¥500 nisonin.jp

Giō-ji

Address: 32 Saga Torii Motokozaka-chō, Ukyō-ku, Kyoto-shi
Tel: 075 (861) 3574 Hours: 9:00–5:00PM
Admission: ¥300 (Daikaku-ji shared pass: ¥600)
www.giouji.or.jp/en

Takiguchi-dera

Address: 10-4 Saga Kameyama-chō, Ukyō-ku, Kyoto-shi
Tel: 075 (871) 3929
Hours: 9:00AM–5:00PM Admission: ¥300

Adashino Nenbutsu-ji

Address: 17 Saga Torii Motoadashino-chō, Ukyō-ku, Kyoto-shi
Tel: 075 (861) 2221
Hours: 9:00AM–4:30PM (December–February: 9:00AM–3:30PM)
Admission: ¥500 www.nenbutsuji.jp/

Jikishi-an

Address: 3 Kita-saga Kitanodan-chō, Ukyō-ku, Kyoto-shi
Tel: 075 (871) 1880 Hours: 9:00AM–4:00PM
Admission: ¥500 www5e.biglobe.ne.jp/–jikisian/

Otagi Nenbutsu-ji

Address: 2-5 Saga Torii Motofukatani-chō, Ukyō-ku, Kyoto-shi
Tel: 075 (865) 1231 Hours: 8:00AM–5:00PM
Admission: ¥300 www.otagiji.com

天龍寺の北門を出て東に歩くと竹林に囲まれて「野宮神社」が建っている。「野宮」とは皇女が斎宮（伊勢神宮に奉仕）や斎院（賀茂社に奉仕）になる前に、一年間潔斎する宮のことで、斎宮は嵯峨野、斎院は紫野に社殿を造ることが通例であったという。ここ野宮神社がいつの時代の斎宮のものかは詳らかではないが、『源氏物語』の「賢木」の帖に描かれたものといわれている。樹皮のついたままの素朴な「黒木の鳥居」が再現されて、遺風を伝えている。

次に嵯峨野散策の人たちの足は「常寂光寺」に向かう。小倉山の深々とした樹林はこの寺の総門に迫って、それは仁王門をくぐって諸堂をめぐると、すでに山腹の濃い緑のただなかに身をおくことになる。常寂光寺の寺名は、この地が永遠の浄土であるような明媚な地だというところから命名された。

日蓮宗の僧日禛が寛永年間（1624〜44）に隠棲所として住まい、没後、日禛に帰依していた京都の商人たちが堂宇を整備した。本堂の脇を上ると小ぶりな多宝塔が嵯峨野の里をみおろすように建っている。

常寂光寺の北に、天台宗に属する「二尊院」が、これもまた小倉山の山腹に分け入るように諸堂を構えている。二尊院とは、釈迦如来像と阿弥陀如来像の二尊を本尊として祀ることからの寺名で、釈迦如来は、人間が誕生して人生の旅をはじめるときにあらわれる仏であり、阿弥陀如来は、人が寿命を閉じるとき

Leaving the north gate of Tenryū-ji and walking north, you come to Nonomiya-jinja within a bamboo grove. "Nonomiya" means a shrine where **imperial princesses** would live for a year of purification before becoming shrine attendants at Ise or Kamo Shrine. Those who were to serve at Ise would normally build a shrine in the Sagano area, while those bound for Kamo would build a shrine at Murasakino. Thus, the Nonomiya-jinja is apparently the shrine built by a princess preparing to serve at Ise, possibly the princess described in the "Sakaki" chapter of *the Tale of Genji*. The simple "black *torii* gate," with the bark still on, has been reconstructed to convey the feeling of that old time.

Walkers through the Sagano area come next to Jōjakkō-ji. The dense woods of Mt. Ogurayama bristle close to the main gate of this temple, so when you pass under the *niō-mon* gate to see the temple buildings, you still feel as if you are in the bosom of the deep woods. Jōjakkō-ji's name suggests that the site is so beautiful that it evokes the eternal pure land.

The Nichiren monk Nittei lived in seclusion here during the Kan'ei period (1624–44), and after his death, the Kyoto merchants who revered him erected the temple. If you walk up the path next to the *hondō*, the small *Tahōtō* tower overlooks Sagano village.

Just to the north of Jōjakkō-ji is Nison-in, affiliated with the Tendai sect. The buildings of this temple too seem to be hidden in Mt. Ogurayama's hillside. Its name comes from the fact that it venerates two statues, one of the Buddha (*shaka nyorai*) and one of the Amitabha (*amida-nyorai*). The Shaka Nyorai appears when a human being is born and begins the journey of life, and the Amitabha comes from the land of Perfect Bliss to meet a person

極楽浄土から迎えにくる仏とされている。

承和年間（834〜48）に嵯峨天皇の勅願により慈覚大師円仁が開創した二尊教院華台寺が当寺のはじまりといい、その寺が衰微したのち、法然が再興したという。

慈覚大師円仁 794〜864。平安初期の天台僧。密教法門を確立し、854年に天台座主。

総門を入ると、100mほどのゆるやかな上り坂の参道がつづく。左右から楓の枝が差し交して、「紅葉の馬場」と名づけられたように晩秋には美しいトンネルとなる。また本堂前の庭は白砂敷のなかに島状の植込がある簡素な造りであるが、本堂の屋根越しに山の深い緑を背景にして、静かで落ちついた景色をみせている。

二尊院からさらに北に歩くと、『平家物語』の悲話が伝わる「祇王寺」と「滝口寺」が細道の先に奥まって建つ。いずれも小さな寺であるが、山の緑林のなかにひっそりとあって、いかにも嵯峨野らしい佇まいにでとくに若い女性たちの人気を集め、観光シーズンは訪れる人で雑踏するほどだ。

『平家物語』 平家一門の栄華と滅亡を著した軍記物語。琵琶法師によって語られた。

8月23、24日におこなわれる幻想的な千灯供養で知られる「化野念仏寺」は、祇王寺から歩いて5分ほど北に位置して、ここも8000体をこえるという**石仏**、石塔群をみにくる人で季節を問わず混雑している。

嵐山から嵯峨野にかけての風光は京都のなかでも第一等のものだから、大勢の人の足が向くのはしかたがない。できれば春、秋の観光シーズンを避け、しかも早朝の時間を選ん

at life's end.

The temple is said to have begun during the Jōwa era (834–48), by edict of Emperor Saga. The noted Saint Ennin (known after his death as the Jikaku Daishi) founded the temple as the Nisonkyō-in Kedai-ji, but the temple declined until it was restored by Hōnen.

When you enter the main gate, you ascend a gently sloping approach for about 100 meters, with maple branches extending from both sides. In late autumn, the branches form a beautiful "tunnel" of autumn color. The garden in front of the *hondō* is laid with white sand with the greenery like islands in the middle. Above the roof of the *hondō*, the deep greenery of the mountain provides a serene backdrop.

Continuing north from Nison-in, one can follow a narrow path to two temples described in the tragedy of the *the Tale of the Heike*, Giō-ji and Takiguchi-dera. Both of the small temples are half-hidden among the forest and perfectly exemplifies the atmosphere of the Sagano region, which is particularly popular with young women. During tourist season they are both lively with visitors.

Adashino Nenbutsu-ji is well known for its fantastical Sentō Kuyō memorial ritual, performed on August 23–24. This temple is just five minutes' walk north of Giō-ji, and regardless of the season, is always filled with visitors to pay their respects to the 8,000 **stone Buddha statues** and small stone pagodas.

The landscape from Arashiyama to Sagano is one of Kyoto's finest and consequently most popular. If possible, I recommend that you try to avoid the high tourist seasons of spring and autumn and visit during the early morning. If you can manage to make it

で散策することをおすすめする。そして、北嵯峨のはずれに建つ「直指庵(じきしあん)」や清滝に近い「愛宕念仏寺(おたぎねんぶつじ)」といった少し遠隔地の寺まで足を伸ばせば静寂な嵯峨野の趣を堪能できよう。

to the slightly out-of-the-way Jikishi-an and Otagi Nenbutsu-ji, near Kiyotaki, you will be rewarded with a peaceful glimpse of Sagano.

5

京都の西の古社は酒の神

松尾大社（まつのおたいしゃ）

京都市西京区嵐山宮町３
075(871)5016
境内参拝自由(庭園９時〜16時は500円)
www.matsunoo.or.jp
京都駅より市バス28系統　松尾大社前下車徒歩１分

阪急嵐山線の松尾大社（まつおたいしゃ）駅を降りると西側に近年の造営になる朱色の大鳥居が高々とみえる。平安神宮の大鳥居（24m）につぐ14mの高さという。参道を進み脇勧請（わきかんじょう）という太縄の吊り下げられた朱の古い鳥居をくぐると、楼門の間から拝殿がみえる。そこで佇んで楼門のうえに覆い被さるような背後の山と諸堂との景観をまず目に焼きつけておきたい。なぜならば、社殿背後の松尾山（標高223m）が松尾大社の旧鎮座地で全山が神域であるからだ。

松尾大社の創建は701年（大宝元）、この地に蟠踞（ばんきょ）していた秦（はた）氏が、その松尾山の磐座（いわくら）の神霊を勧請して山麓に社殿を建てたことにはじまるという。730年（天平2）には朝廷から大社の称号が与えられている。祭神は大山咋神（おおやまくいのかみ）と市杵島姫命（いちきしまひめのみこと）で、大山咋神は上賀茂神社の祭神賀茂別雷命（かもわけいかずちのみこと）の父親になる。

磐座　神が宿るとされる石。その石のある山を神南備山とする。

平安京遷都後には王城鎮護の社として、東の賀茂社、西の松尾社と称されて尊崇された。

5. An old shrine to the west of Kyoto, the god of sake

Address: 3 Arashiyama Miyamachi, Saikyō-ku, Kyoto-shi
Tel: 075 (871) 5016
Admission: Free (Gardens: 9:00AM–4:00PM ¥500)
www.matsunoo.or.jp/en/
1 min walk from Matsuo-taisha-mae bus stop, bus 28 from Kyoto Sta.

Get off at Matsuo-taisha Station on the Hankyu Arashiyama line, and on the west side you will see a large vermilion *torii* gate, some 14 meters tall, surpassed in height only by the one at the Heian-jingū, which is 24 meters tall. Proceed on the approach and pass under the old vermilion *torii* gate with a thick straw rope suspended from it, known as the *wakikanjō*. From here, you can see the worship hall (*hai-den*) through the two-story gate. You may want to stop and let the view of mountains and shrine buildings beyond the gate soak in. The mountain in the background of the shrine, Mt. Matsuosan (223 meters), is the holy ground for the shrine.

Matsunoo-taisha was established in 701 by the ruling Hata clan, who sought to honor the divine spirit from the holy rock of Mt. Matsuosan. In 730, it was recognized as a taisha, or "great shrine," by the Court. The shrine deities were Ōyamakui-no-Kami and Ichikishimahime-no-Mikoto, the former being the father of Kamowakeikazuchi-no-Mikoto, the shrine deity of Kamigamo-jinja.

After the capital was moved at Heian-kyō, the shrine was named as the official guardian shrine of the capital, along with

清和天皇（在位858～76）は松尾社に正一位を贈り、また『延喜式』では名神大社となり「二十二社の制」（1039年に後朱雀天皇が制定）において上七社のひとつに数えられていた。

二十二社の制 11世紀中頃より朝廷の奉幣対象として尊崇を受けた二十二の社。伊勢・石清水・賀茂・春日など。

立派な社殿と奉納された酒樽

また松尾大社は、室町時代以降、酒の神として信仰されて、境内裏には霊泉「亀の井」が湧いている。この井戸の水を醸造のさいにまぜると酒が腐らないという伝説がある。そのため、境内の神輿庫の脇に各地の酒樽が百樽も積みあげられ、いかにもこの社が酒の神であることがみてとれる。

楼門をくぐり細流にかかる石橋を渡ると、堂々とした拝殿が建ち、その先に釣殿と本殿とつづく。松尾大社の本殿は「松尾造」とよばれる建築様式で檜皮葺、三間社両流造、1542年（天文11）の再造営である。

なお、京都の中心を東西に走る四条通は、東端が八坂神社で西端が松尾大社となる。いまは松尾大社の境外摂社となっている古社月読神社が南に5分ほどのところに古色蒼然とした佇まいで建っている。森閑とした神社である。

月読神社 5世紀末の古社で856年に現在地に移った。

the Kamo-jinja of east, and Matsuo-jinja of west. Emperor Seiwa (r. 858–76) named Matsuo-jinja as the highest ranking, and in the *Engishiki* it is termed a "Myōjin-taisha," or one of the top seven shrines in the system of twenty-two shrines established in 1039 by Emperor Gosuzaku.

Splendid buildings and Sacrificial Sake Barrels

Beginning in the Muromachi period, the Matsunoo-taisha was the place for worshipping the god of *sake* (Japanese spirits) because of the holy Kamenoi spring that flows on the shrine grounds. It was believed that the water of the spring could keep *sake* made with it from going bad. It is for this reason that more than one hundred of *sake* casks are piled on the shrine grounds as offerings.

Pass under the two-story gate and cross the stone bridge over a narrow stream, and the magnificent *hai-den* stands before you, connected to the *tsuri-dono* and the main sanctuary (*hon-den*). The shrine's *hon-den* has a distinct style of roof called *matsuo-zukuri* made from the bark of the Japanese cypress. It was rebuilt in 1542.

Shijō St. spans the center of Kyoto, running from Yasaka-jinja in the east to Matsunoo-taisha in the west. A sub-shrine located outside the compound of Matsunoo-taisha is Tsukiyomi-jinja, an old shrine of ancient appearance about five minutes south.

6

作庭の見本となった上下の庭

苔寺

京都市西京区松尾神ケ谷町56
075(391)3631
往復葉書に、希望日、人数、代表者の氏名住所を明記の上、2カ月前〜1週間前までに必着で参拝申し込み。時間は西芳寺より指定。
参拝冥加料3000円(庭園だけの拝観は不可)
saihoji-kokedera.com
京都駅より京都バス73、83系統　苔寺・すず虫寺下車徒歩3分

苔寺はいま残念ながらふらっと訪ねて拝観できる寺ではない。**苔庭**の保護と周辺環境への配慮から、事前の申し込み制になっている。

西芳寺(苔寺)の創建は、聖徳太子が別邸を建てたことによるとか、行基が天平年間(729〜49)に聖武天皇の勅願により開創した「西方寺」がそのはじまりとかいわれ、明らかではない。ただ、建久年間(1190〜99)中原師員が諸堂を再建して、西方寺、穢土寺の二寺に分けるとともに法然を招いて浄土宗に改宗したということは諸書に記されている。

行基 668〜749。奈良時代の僧。池の堤や橋梁架設などの社会事業をおこない「行基菩薩」と称された。

その後、兵火で荒廃するが、中原師員の子孫の摂津親秀が1339年(暦応2)夢窓疎石を招請して復興する。あわせて西方寺を西芳寺とし、浄土宗から臨済宗に改めた。

夢窓疎石は堂宇とともに庭園の大修復に着手、上下二段構えの名庭を造った。天龍寺の建立をはじめる少し前のことである。この造園はおおいに評判をよんで足利将軍らの参詣

6. A split-level garden that became a model for garden design

Koke-dera

Address: 56 Matsuo Jingatani-chō, Saikyō-ku, Kyoto-shi

Tel: 075 (391) 3631

Application one week–two months ahead of desired date of visit required. Send a return-paid postcard with desired date, number of visitors, and representative's name and address. Hours: Determined by Saihō-ji.

Admission: ¥3,000 (Entry to garden only not allowed)

saihoij-kokedera.com

1 min walk from Koke-dera/Suzumushi-dera bus stop, Kyoto bus 73 or 83 from Kyoto Sta.

Unfortunately, it is no longer possible to visit Koke-dera on the spur of the moment. To preserve the **moss garden** and in respect of the surrounding environment, advance reservations are required.

There are several versions of how Saihō-ji (Koke-dera) was established, one claiming that it was a palace of Prince Shōtoku, another that it was established by the priest Gyōki during the Tenpyō era (729–49) at the request of Emperor Shōmu. However, it is established in written documents that during the Kenkyū era (1190–99), Nakahara Morokazu rebuilt several of the buildings, dividing them among two temples, Saihō-ji and Edo-dera, invited priest Hōnen and converted to the Jōdo sect.

The temple suffered from the depredations of war, but Morokazu's descendant Settsu Chikahide revived the temple in 1339, inviting Musō Soseki to lead it, changing the temple from the Jōdo to the Rinzai sect.

Soseki undertook not only to rebuild the temple buildings, but also the gardens, creating a famous two-level garden. This was slightly before he established Tenryū-ji, and the acclaim he received for his work at Saihō-ji resulted in the Ashikaga shoguns

があいつぎ、また足利義政の東山山荘（銀閣寺）の庭づくりの規範になったという。しかし、応仁の乱や洪水の被害で庭園は荒れはて、本願寺の蓮如（れんにょ）によっていったんは再造園されるが、のちに兵火や水害で寺域は再び荒れ、現在の姿は明治初期の復興による。

名高い苔庭をめぐる

入寺を許可された拝観者は本堂で説法を受け写経をおさめたのちに順次、庭園を拝見することになる。庫裏の前を築地塀に向かい小さな門をくぐると、池泉回遊式の下の庭である苔庭が、池と老樹の景色のなかに、じつにふんわりと広がっている。苔地に踏み入らぬようにめぐらされた苑路に従って静かに歩む。

湘南亭茶室　苔寺創建から伝わる建築物。明るく開放的な茶室（再建）。

まず、湘南亭（しょうなんてい）茶室をみて、池に浮かぶ朝日ヶ島と夕日ヶ島の木洩れ陽に映える緑苔の光景、池畔が水面に沈み込むようすをじっくりとみておきたい。苔庭をほぼ一周すると、向上関（こうじょうかん）という小さな門があり、その先は上の段の枯山水石組の庭になる。

地蔵院　室町幕府の管領細川頼之（よりゆき）が1367年に創建。

浄住寺　隠元の弟子、僧鉄牛が1687年に再建した。

なお苔寺の南の丘にふたつの閑静な禅寺がある。ひとつが「竹の寺」とよばれる地蔵院（じぞういん）（臨済宗）で、もうひとつが黄檗宗（おうばくしゅう）の浄住寺（じょうじゅうじ）である。いずれも山懐に抱かれた緑の多い気持ちのいい寺として推奨したい。

attending the temple; Soseki's work later became the model for the garden at Ashikaga Yoshimasa's Higashiyama villa, later to become Ginkaku-ji (the Silver Pavilion). However, the gardens were destroyed by Ōnin War and floods. Rennyo of Hongan-ji reconstructed the gardens, but the temple was again devastated in later wars and natural disasters. It was restored to its present form in the early Meiji era.

Strolling Around the Famous Moss Garden

After listening to a sermon in the *hondō* and admiring the sutra manuscripts, visitors who have been able to enter the temple may visit the gardens. Passing through a small gate in front of the *kuri* you come upon the lower garden, a moss circuit-style garden surrounding a pond. The moss softly spreads out in the setting of ponds and trees. Walk gently along the path, taking care to avoid stepping into the moss.

Looking at the Shōnantei tea-ceremony house, you can admire the interplay of sunlight and greenery in the reflections of the two small islands in the pond and the mossy edge where the land meets the water. If you walk all the way around the moss garden you will see the small gate called the Kōjōkan, which leads to the upper *karesansui-ishigumi* garden (a dry landscape garden constructed only with rocks and sand).

On the small hill to the south of Koke-dera stand two peaceful little Zen temples. Jizō-in, called "Take-no-Tera" (bamboo temple), is the Rinzai sect, and Jōjū-ji belongs to the Ōbaku sect. Both are appealing little temples nestled in the deep greenery of the heart of the mountain.

7

劇的な感動を覚える美しい参道

光明寺

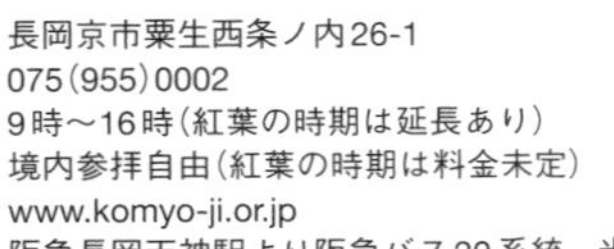

長岡京市粟生西条ノ内26-1
075（955）0002
9時～16時（紅葉の時期は延長あり）
境内参拝自由（紅葉の時期は料金未定）
www.komyo-ji.or.jp
阪急長岡天神駅より阪急バス20系統　光明寺下車1分

左京区黒谷に金戒光明寺があるため、ここ光明寺はこの地の地名を冠して「粟生光明寺」と通称することが多い。正しくは念仏三昧院光明寺、西山浄土宗の総本山である。

阪急京都線の西向日駅から西にゆくと、光明寺道が一直線に寺の総門に向かって伸びている。光明寺の美しさはこの総門をくぐったところからはじまる。幅が広く二、三歩で一段を上るほどのなだらかさで奥行きの深い石段がまっすぐに、しかもゆったりとして目前にあらわれる。不定形な割石を敷き、階の先端は切石で押さえているこの参道の整然とした美しさは比類のないもので、左右の木々が枝を低く重ねて石段上に垂れ、春夏の緑、秋の紅葉を愛でるには極上の場所である。ことに、前夜の風で隙間なく散り敷かれた黄赤の落葉を踏みしめてのぼる気分は、劇場の舞台に立つような感動さえ覚えるほどだ。

7. The beautiful approach that evokes strong emotions

Kōmyō-ji

Address: 26-1 Ao Saijōnai, Nagaokakyō-shi
Tel: 075 (955) 0002
Hours: 9:00AM–4:00PM (Closing time extendet during fall colors)
Admission: Free (During fall colors: depend)
www.komyo-ji.or.jp
3 min walk from Kōmyō-ji bus stop, Hankyu bus 20 from Hankyu Nagaoka-tenjin Sta.

There is a Konkai Kōmyō-ji in Kurodani, Sakyō-ku, so when specifying this Kōmyō-ji, local people add the local place name, calling it Ao-no-Kōmyō-ji. Its official name is Nenbutsuzanmai-in Kōmyō-ji, and it is the head temple of the Seizan school, Jōdo sect.

Walk west from Nishi-Mukō St. on the Hankyu Kyoto line, and Kōmyō-ji St. is a straight line to the main gate of the temple. The beauty of Kōmyō-ji is immediately apparent as soon as one passes through the gate. In front, you see the gentle sloped stone steps with its width of two or three strides. Uneven shape of stones are paved and the hewn stones are attached at the edge of each steps. Nothing can be compared with this distinctive stone staircase, with the trees trailing their branches low on either side, make walking up this gentle slope distinctive either in the green of spring and summer or the red of autumn. In particular, the feeling of stepping through the gold and red leaves scattered over the steps evokes the strong emotion of stepping onto the stage of a theater.

法然の遺志を継ぐ寺

熊谷直実 1141～1208。鎌倉初期の武士。一の谷の戦で、若年の平敦盛を討ち、人生の無常を感じて出家。法然に師事して蓮生と称す。

光明寺は法然に帰依した武将熊谷直実(蓮生)が、この地に念仏三昧堂を設け、法然を開山としたことにはじまる。1198年(建久9)のことである。

法然が入寂したのは1212年のことで、廟所ははじめ東山大谷にあったが、1227年(嘉禄3)叡山の僧徒にあばかれようとしたので、弟子たちは太秦の来迎院に移し、さらに当地で荼毘に付し、遺骨を納めた宗廟を建てた。そのとき石棺から光明が発したので光明寺としたという説のほか、来迎院に移した棺から光明があらわれ、この地を指したので、弟子たちはここで荼毘に付したところ、紫雲と香気がただよい、そのことを聞いた四条天皇が光明寺の勅額を与えた、という由来もある。

典雅な石段をのぼり終えて、境内の高台に入ると、目の先は宏壮な瓦屋根の御影堂(本堂)である。現在の建物は1753年(宝暦3)の再建で、法然の実母の手紙を貼り合わせて造った「張抜の御影」という法然像を安置する。北側に阿弥陀堂があり、本堂との渡り廊下の下をくぐると、法然本廟の石段の下に出る。境内は広く、自由にみて回れるが、この本廟には一般参拝客は立ち入れない。

薬医門 本柱の後方に二本の控柱を立て、切妻屋根をかけた門の形式。弓矢の攻撃を止める「矢喰い門」の転訛とも。

帰路は一段低くなっている方丈から薬医門にいたる道を歩く。表参道とは景色の異なる砂利敷きの小径であるが、ここも閑寂な趣があっていい。

The Temple Maintains Hōnen's Dying Wish

The military commander Kumagai Naozane, who became a follower of Hōnen and changed his name to Renjō upon becoming a Buddhist priest, built the Nenbutsuzanmai-dō on this spot and asked Hōnen to establish a temple in 1198.

Hōnen died in 1212, and his body was first laid to rest in Higashiyama Otani, but in 1227, the monk of Enryaku learned of this, and Hōnen's disciples moved his remains to Raigō-in, in Uzumasa, cremated there and interring his bones in a mausoleum. A light was seen beaming out of his sarcophagus, so the temple was called Kōmyō-ji (from the individual characters meaning "light" and "bright"). Another version of the legend was that when it was moved to Raigō-in, light was seen shining from the sarcophagus, indicating Kōmyō-ji, so the disciples cremated there, upon which a **purple cloud** and pleasant fragrance drifted around them. Hearing of this, Empeor Shijō bestowed an imperial scroll upon Kōmyō-ji.

At the top of the elegant staircase, you reach the high ground of the temple compound and are greeted with the sight of the magnificent tiled roof of the *miei-dō* (*hondō*), the main hall of the temple. The current structure was rebuilt in 1753 and contains a statue of Hōnen known as the Harinuki-no-Miei, which is a paper-mache sculpture said to have been made with a letter written by Hōnen's mother. On the north side of the temple grounds is the *amida-dō*. If you walk under the walkway between the *hondō* and the *amida-dō*, you come to the bottom of the stone staircase leading to Hōnen's mausoleum. The grounds are spacious and you are free to walk around as you like, but you are requested not to enter the mausoleum area.

On your way back down, you pass *hōjō* one level below and the *yakuimon* gate. Unlike the approach, the exit path is narrow, but it has its own peaceful charm.

エリア５　Area 5

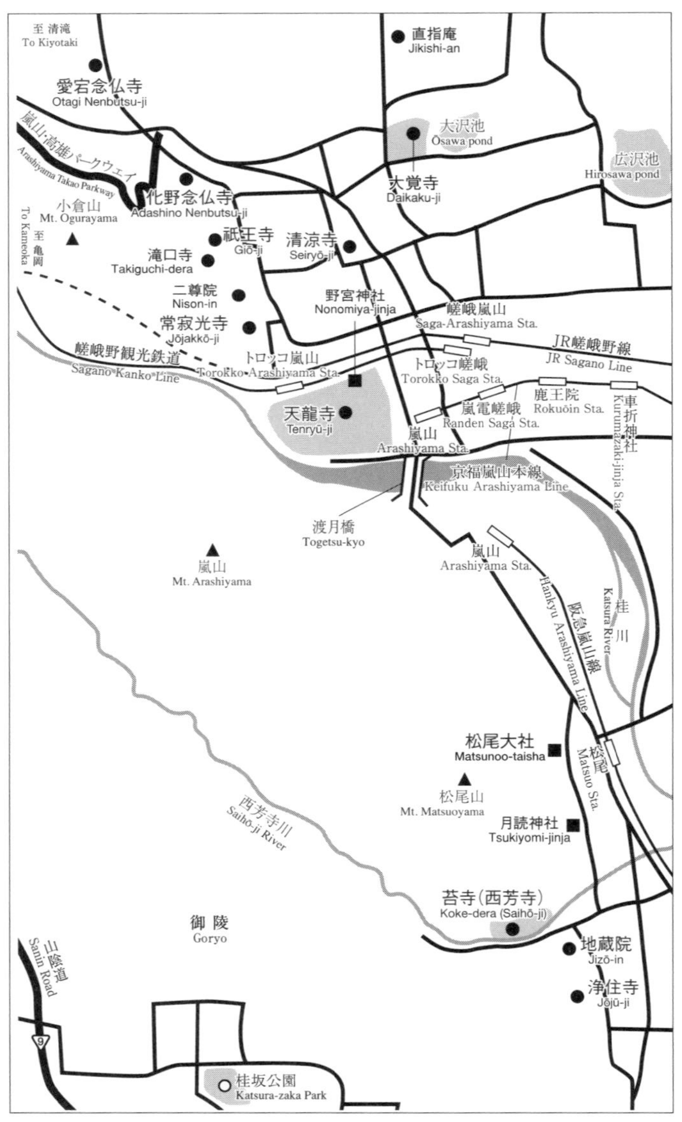

至 清滝
To Kiyotaki
愛宕念仏寺
Otagi Nenbutsu-ji
嵐山·高雄パークウェイ
Arashiyama Takao Parkway
化野念仏寺
Adashino Nenbutsu-ji
小倉山
Mt. Ogurayama
至亀岡
To Kameoka
祇王寺
Giō-ji
滝口寺
Takiguchi-dera
二尊院
Nison-in
常寂光寺
Jōjakkō-ji
嵯峨野観光鉄道
Sagano Kanko Line
トロッコ嵐山
Torokko Arashiyama Sta.
直指庵
Jikishi-an
大沢池
Ōsawa pond
大覚寺
Daikaku-ji
広沢池
Hirosawa pond
清涼寺
Seiryō-ji
野宮神社
Nonomiya-jinja
嵯峨嵐山
Saga-Arashiyama Sta.
JR嵯峨野線
JR Sagano Line
トロッコ嵯峨
Torokko Saga Sta.
天龍寺
Tenryū-ji
嵐電嵯峨
Randen Saga Sta.
鹿王院
Rokuōin Sta.
車折神社
Kurumazaki-jinja Sta.
嵐山
Arashiyama Sta.
京福嵐山本線
Keifuku Arashiyama Line
渡月橋
Togetsu-kyo
嵐山
Mt. Arashiyama
嵐山
Arashiyama Sta.
阪急嵐山線
Hankyu Arashiyama Line
桂川
Katsura River
松尾大社
Matsunoo-taisha
松尾
Matsuo Sta.
松尾山
Mt. Matsuoyama
月読神社
Tsukiyomi-jinja
西芳寺川
Saihō-ji River
苔寺（西芳寺）
Koke-dera (Saihō-ji)
地蔵院
Jizō-in
浄住寺
Jōjū-ji
御陵
Goryo
山陰道
Sanin Road
9
桂坂公園
Katsura-zaka Park

エリア６
Area 6

京都の各地に点在する忘れ得ぬ寺社
Unforgettable Temples and Shrines Scattered Around Kyoto

「**詩仙堂と曼殊院**」は白川通の東、山懐に位置して、近隣には金福寺、八大神社、さらに少しきつい登り坂を覚悟すれば狸谷山不動院、円光寺、鷺森神社といった寺があって、1日の寺社散歩コースとしては格好のエリアとなる。

「**三千院と寂光院**」は大原の里にあって、ここも市街から遠隔地となるから、来迎院や勝林院、さらに古知谷の山寺阿弥陀寺を巡るほぼ1日のコースである。秋の紅葉シーズンはたいへんな人出となるのでお勧めしないが、それ以外ならレンタカーなど車で訪ねると便利だ。

「**鞍馬寺と貴船神社**」は健脚向きである。叡山電鉄にそれぞれ最寄駅があるといっても、両寺社の本殿までは相当の坂道で、足ごしらえを確かにして出かけたい。

「**神護寺と高山寺**」は交通の便が悪い。車以外はバス便だから、もちろん丸1日を西明寺を含めたこの三尾の寺の拝観に当てるべきだ。しかし、その周辺の景観は市中の寺ではみることができない佳景であって、京都の奥深さを実感する絶好の地である。

「**毘沙門堂と勧修寺と醍醐寺**」は地下鉄東西線沿線に位置する。山科、醍醐というと、京都郊外というイメージが、とくに京都人に強い。そのため、わざわざそこまで行かなくても、いいお寺はほかにあります、といわれるが、いずれも市中にないおおらかな別天地であって、ぜひ訪れておきたい寺である。上醍醐はことにそうである。西の愛宕神社と同様、つらい山道行だが、いずれも京都寺社観光のフィナーレを飾るにふさわしい寺社であることは間違いない。

Shisen-dō and Manshu-in: These two temples are east of Shirakawa St. in the bosom of the mountains. Nearby are Konpuku-ji, Hachidai-jinja, and, if you are prepared for a bit of a climb, Tanukidaniyama-fudō-in, Enkō-ji, and Saginomori-jinja. All of these make for an excellent full day's course of temples and shrines.

Sanzen-in and Jakkō-in: These temples are near the village of Ōhara, at somewhat of a distance from the city center, but along with Raigō-in, Shōrin-in, and Amida-ji (the mountain temple of Kochitani), they make up a good one-day course. This area is extremely crowded in the autumn color season, so I do not recommend visiting at that time. You may want to rent a car to visit this area.

Kurama-dera and Kifune-jinja: These destinations are good for sturdy walkers. Although the Eizan Dentetsu line comes nearest, it is a steep slope up to the main buildings of both of these, so be prepared for exertion.

Jingo-ji and Kōzan-ji: These two temples are not easily accessible by public transportation. If you don't have your own car, buses are available, and along with Saimyō-ji, these three temples will make up a good full day of touring. The views in this area cannot be had from temples in the city; here is where you can have the true, deep Kyoto experience.

Bishamon-dō, Kajū-ji, and Daigo-ji: These temples are located on the Tozai subway line. Kyoto residents tend to think of Yamashina and Daigo as the suburbs, and may tell you not to bother going here. But in fact these are friendly, welcoming spots unlike any in the city and well worth visiting. In particular, Kami-Daigo in Daigo-ji should not be missed. Like the Atago-jinja to the west, it is located on a difficult mountain road, but either of these would be fully appropriate as a finale to one's exploration of the temples and shrines of Kyoto.

1

ある教養人の後半生を物語る

詩仙堂

京都市左京区一乗寺門口町27
075(781)2954
9時〜17時(5月23日は閉門)
500円
kyoto-shisendo.net
京都駅から市バス5系統　一乗寺下り松町下車徒歩10分

白川通北大路の交差点を東に入ると閑静な住宅地になり、その山麓の地に、規模は小さいながらも名刹といわれる寺が点在して、静けさを好む人たちの散策路になっている。

蕪村　与謝蕪村。1716〜83。江戸中期の俳人で画家。

芭蕉　松尾芭蕉。1644〜94。江戸前期の俳人。俳聖とよばれる。『奥の細道』は日本紀行文学の最高峰。

金福寺　芭蕉と親交があった鉄舟が貞享年間(1684〜88)に再興。裏山に蕪村の墓がある。

まず、蕪村が敬愛した芭蕉を偲んで再建した芭蕉庵が残る臨済宗の金福寺(こんぷくじ)。そのすぐ北に、小グループの観光客が必ず訪れるといっていい詩仙堂が**竹塀**の間に小さな表門を構えている。

詩仙堂を建てた石川丈山(いしかわじょうざん)(1583〜1672)はもともと三河(みかわ)武士で徳川家康の近侍として仕えていた。大坂夏の陣のおり、先駆けをしたことが軍規に反すると処罰されたため、禄を辞して京都に隠棲した。洛北の地に終の栖を求め、これまでの蓄えをもとにみずからの趣味をいかした山荘を造営したのである。それは1641年(寛永18)、丈山が59歳のときという。爾来、90歳で没するまでのおよそ30年間、悠々自適の生活をおくった。

1. The later life of a cultured man

Shisen-dō

Address: 27 Ichijō-ji Monguchi-chō, Sakyō-ku, Kyoto-shi
Tel: 075 (781) 2954
Hours: 9:00AM–5:00PM (Closed on May 23)
Admission: ¥500
kyoto-shisendo.net
10 min walk from Ichijō-ji Sagarimatsu-chō bus stop, bus 5 from Kyoto Sta.

If you walk east from the Shirakawa-dōri Kitaōji St. intersection, you will find yourself in a peaceful residential area at the foot of the mountains. The area is dotted with small but exquisite temples, making it a perfect strolling path for those who appreciate quietness.

The first temple you will see is the Rinzai sect Konpuku-ji, known for the Bashō-an, a hermitage associated with the haiku poet by an admirer who was also a famous poet, Buson. Just north of here is Shisen-dō, with a small front gate in its **bamboo fence**, a temple that is regularly visited by groups of tourists.

Ishikawa Jōzan (1583–1672), who built Shisen-dō, was a warrior in the noted Mikawa tradition and an attendant of Tokugawa Ieyasu. During the Summer Battle of Osaka, Jōzan charged ahead, an infraction of military rules, for which he was punished. As a result, he relinquished his position and went into seclusion in Kyoto. He found a refuge in the north side of Kyoto, and built a mountain villa. That was in 1641, when Jōzan was fifty-nine. He lived a happy peaceful life there until he was ninety, socializing with scholars and artists.

彼は一流の学者や文人と交流し、丈山自身も漢詩や書に優れ、学問と思索、創作にあけくれた。さらに丈山は作庭家としても一流で、詩仙堂はもちろんのこと、渉成園や修学院離宮などの設計もしたといわれている。この丈山の後半生は、まことに羨ましいもので、59歳で現役を引退して、清閑な住まいを得、好きな学問と芸術の道に生きた。

渉成園　徳川家光が寄進した東本願寺の別邸。周囲に枳殻が植えられ「枳殻邸」ともいう。

諸堂と庭に佇む

詩仙堂は近年曹洞宗永平寺の末寺となっている。建物は1748年（寛延元）と1967年（昭和42）の再興・改修をへて多少変更されているが、ほぼ往時の姿を伝えている。

表門を入り、石段をわずかにのぼると「凹凸窠」（山荘の当初の名称）の額を見上げて玄関に入る。そして、まずこの寺の名である詩仙の間（四畳半）になる。詩仙とは、漢・晋・唐・宋代の詩人36人のことで、彼らの画像を四方の長押に掲げた堂であるから詩仙堂という。つづく広い書院は二方が開け放たれ、前庭にはいくつもの植込が丸味をもって刈りそろえられ、紅葉時には、植込の緑色と庭に枝をのばす赤黄の紅葉色がなによりも美しい。

凹凸窠「凹凸な土地の住居」という意味からの名。

苑地には白砂が敷きつめられて、草花の色彩をいっそうひきたて、また山の斜面を利用した庭であるため、高低差があって、上・中・下に分かれた庭は実際の敷地より広くみせてみごたえがある。

He excelled at Chinese-style poetry and calligraphy, and he devoted himself to study and meditation. Also highly skilled at garden construction, in addition to Shisen-dō, Jōzan is credited with the design of the gardens at Shōseien and Shūgakuin Imperial villa, among others. Retireing from his title at fifty-nine, finding a peaceful place to live, and pursuing the study and art that he loved, Jōzan's life was truly enviable.

Standing at the Buildings and Gardens

In recent years, Shisen-dō has become a branch temple of Eihei-ji, a Sōtō sect temple. The buildings were rebuilt and repaired in 1748 and 1967, and some changes have been made, but generally their original character has been retained.

When you enter the front gate and ascend a small stone staircase, you will see the nameplate of the villa, "Ōtotsuka," (original name) before you go in the entrance of the temple. The first space you find yourself in is the room that gives the temple its name, the Shisen hall, which is quite small (four and a half *tatami* mats). The word *shisen* refers to the great classical Chinese poets from the Era of Han, Chin, Tang and Song, thirty-six of whom are pictured on the walls of the room. Next you enter the spacious *shoin* (study-cum-living room), which is open to the garden with round cutted green planting, allowing beautiful views of the gold and crimson leaves in the autumn.

The gardens are strewn with white sand, which sets off the colors of the grasses and flowers. The garden also uses the background of the mountain, creating top, middle, and bottom sections and making it feel much more spacious than it actually is.

2

ある法親王の美意識を物語る

曼殊院

京都市左京区一乗寺竹ノ内町42
075(781)5010
9時〜17時
600円
www.manshuinmonzeki.jp
京都駅から市バス5系統　一乗寺清水町下車徒歩20分

曼殊院を現在地に再興した良尚法親王は、桂離宮の造営をはじめた八条宮智仁親王（正親町天皇の孫）を父に、同離宮を完成させた智忠親王を兄に、また修学院離宮を造営した後水尾天皇の猶子となった人物で、周囲にそれぞれ風雅で趣向に富む建築および庭園の美を結実させた親兄弟をもつため、みずからの美意識を再建する曼殊院にあらわしたかったであろうことは想像にかたくない。

転々とした寺地

まず当院の歴史を記す。最澄が比叡山に阿弥陀仏を安置した堂を建立したことにはじまる（延暦年間＝782〜806）というが、その寺名は不詳。のちに是算国師が叡山西塔北谷に移し、東尾坊と称したという。天仁年間（1108〜10）に、東尾坊から曼殊院に名を改めた。曼はながながと跡をひく意、殊は普通とはまったく違うという意である。

永久年間（1113〜18）に是算国師が北野天

2. The aesthetic sense of a monk-prince

Manshu-in

Address: 42 Ichijō-ji Takenouchi-chō, Sakyō-ku, Kyoto-shi
Tel: 075 (781) 5010
Hours: 9:00AM–5:00PM
Admission: ¥600
www.manshuinmonzeki.jp
20 min walk from Ichijō-ji-Shimizu-chō bus stop, bus 5 from Kyoto Sta.

Ryōshō, the monk-prince who restored Manshu-in, was the son of Prince Hachijōnomiya Toshihito, the grandson of Emperor Ōgimachi. Hachijōnomiya began the building of the Katsura Imperial villa, which was completed by Prince Toshitada, the brother of Ryōshō. Finally, Ryōshō was the adopted son of Emperor Gomizunoo, who built the Shūgakuin Imperial villa. I can imagine that among so many relatives who exhibited their exquisite taste in buildings and gardens, he saw Manshu-in as an opportunity to demonstrate his own aesthetic sense.

A Moveable Temple

First, some history: The temple is considered to have started when Saichō built the hall where the Amitabha is enshrined at Hieizan during Enryaku era (782–806), but the name of the temple at that time is not known. Later, Saint Zesan Kokushi moved to Enryaku-ji's Saitō Kitadani and changed the name of the temple to Tōbi-bō. During the Tennin era (1108–10), the name was changed again to Manshu-in. The "man" means possessing a long history, and the "shu" means unusual.

During the Eikyū era (1113–18), Saint Zesan was also affiliated

満宮と兼務をするため建てた北山の別院を本院にして移転した。ところが、足利義満が金閣寺を建立することになり、北山から御所近く、やはり義満が創建した相国寺の寺域にふたたび寺地を移した。

文明年間（1469~87）に伏見宮貞常親王の子慈運法親王が入寺して､門跡寺院となった。そして、天台座主となった良尚法親王の奏請によって、江戸初期の1656年（明暦2）に現在の地に再興されたのである。

天台座主　比叡山延暦寺の住職で一門を統轄する最高職。824年義真を初世とする。

美しい意匠の寺院

さて、曼殊院の良尚法親王による美の意匠をみてみよう。長い坂道をあがると正面に勅使門がまずみえる。門前に幅の広い石段を設け、左右には高々とした石垣と樹木を等間隔で配した緑の盛土、さらにそのうえに長い白壁の塀が、まるで外敵の攻撃から守る城壁のごとくつづく。この武張った構えは、大原の三千院にも東山の妙法院にもみられ、門跡寺院の威光を誇示する造りなのだろう。勅使門は閉ざされており、一般人は北側の通用門から入山する。

庫裡の内部は豪壮な梁と木組がみごとで、そこに竈が設えてあり、下台所として使われていたという。大玄関虎の間の「竹虎図」(伝狩野永徳)、孔雀の間の岸駒の襖絵、長い廊下を渡って、本尊阿弥陀如来を安置する大書院（本堂）とみていくうちに、私たちは曼殊院の

岸駒　1749（56?）～1838。江戸後期の画家で、岸派の祖。写実的な花鳥画・動物画に秀でる。

with the Kitano Tenman-gū, so he made the sub-temple at Kitayama his main temple, moving there. However, when Ashikaga Yoshimitsu built Kinkaku-ji, needing to be nearer the palace, the temple was moved again to the grounds of Shōkoku-ji, the temple built by Yoshimitsu.

During the Bunmei era (1469–87), Jiun, who was the son of Prince Fushiminomiya Sadatsune, entered the temple as a monk, making it one of the *monzeki* temples. At the request of Ryōshō, the Tendai monk who had become the temple's head priest, in 1656—in the early Edo period—the temple was restored to its current location.

A Beautifully Styled Temple

Ryōshō gave Manshu-in some beautiful design elements. Coming up the long slope to the front, the first thing one sees is the *chokushi-mon* gate. Before the gate is a broad stone staircase with a tall stone fence and an evenly spaced line of trees on either side. Outside of that a long white earthen wall stands as if to protect a castle wall from invaders. This military mien is an ostentatious display of power characteristic of the *monzeki* temples and can also be seen at Sanzen-in in Ōhara or Myōhō-in in Higashiyama. The *chokushi-mon* gate is kept closed, so regular visitors need to enter through the gate on the north side.

The interior of the *kuri* boasts splendid beams and wood construction. It contained an oven and was used as the lower kitchen. From the "Bamboo and Tiger" painting in the Tora-no-Ma entrance room, said to be painted by Kanō Eitoku, to the screen paintings in the Kujaku-no-Ma (peacocks room) painted by Gan Ku, to the *dai-shoin* (the main hall) where the temple's

美の意匠に魅せられていくことになるだろう。

長押の釘隠（富士山をかたどる）、襖の引手（瓢箪形など）、手摺の木工、それぞれに細緻な意匠が凝らされて、圧巻は小書院の欄間にみられる菊花をあつかった大胆なデザインである。また、その黄昏の間の奥には「曼殊院棚」とよばれる違い棚があって、それらひとつひとつに良尚法親王の創造性と美意識が伝わってくる。

遠州好み 小堀遠州だとこのように制作するだろうというのを、別の人が想像して制作したもの。

さらに、小書院の前庭は遠州好みの枯山水の庭園で、そのみごとな空間に拝観者の目が集まる。白砂を海原にみたて、鶴島には五葉の松（鶴）、亀島には這松（亀）を植えて、小書院の縁側を屋形船の船端に模しているという。

小書院に付属する三畳台目の遠州好みといわれる八窓軒茶室も端正である。曼殊院はそれほど広くはないが、堂内すべてに美の集約がなされている。

修学院離宮 左京区比叡山雲母坂の西麓にある1659年に後水尾上皇の別荘として造営された離宮。

なお、音羽川の北に修学院離宮の広大な苑地があって、その先に紅葉の美しい赤山禅院がひっそりと建つ。

赤山禅院 泰山府君（赤山明神）を祀る天台宗の寺。延暦寺の別院。

venerated statue of the Amitabha (*amida-nyorai*) stands, one can appreciate the attention to style and beauty that characterizes Manshu-in.

Further examples of craftsmanship include the hidden nails of the *nageshi* beams (modeled on Mt. Fuji), The handles (modeled on gourds) of the *fusuma* sliding screens, and the woodwork of the hand rails, all showing a great attention to detail. The masterpiece is the striking design of the transom in the *shō-shoin*, which is thick with chrysanthemum flowers. Also, be sure to note the splendid shelves in the Tasogare-no-Ma (twilight room), which are built in a style that has come to be known as "Manshu-in-dana" (Manshu-in style shelves). All of these elements show Ryōshō's creativity and aesthetic sensibility.

The garden outside the *shō-shoin* is built in the *karesansui* style (a dry landscape garden constructed only with rocks and sand), with the white sand representing the sea and two islands (*tsuru-shima* and *kame-shima*) with pine trees, respectively. The veranda of the *shō-shoin* is fashioned like the side of a pleasure boat looking out over this seascape.

There is also a fine small tea-ceremony room, Hassō-ken, next to the *shō-shoin*. Manshu-in is not large, but there is much beauty concentrated within its grounds.

Just north of the Otowa river from here lie the spacious grounds of the Shūgakuin Imperial villa, and beyond that, in autumn, the beautiful colors of Sekizanzen-in.

3

大原の地に美しい門跡寺院

三千院

京都市左京区大原来迎院町540
075(744)2531
9時～17時(11月は8時30分～17時、12月～2月は9時～16時30分)
700円
www.sanzenin.or.jp
京都駅より京都バス17、18系統　大原下車徒歩10分

京都駅からバスで約1時間、途中、白川通の花園橋から鯖街道とよばれる若狭街道を通って、大原の里に着く。大原は平安時代から貴人文人たちの**隠棲地**として、また都への薪炭の供給地として知られた地であった。いまも農村風景の広がるひなびた山里である。若狭街道の東側の山腹に、三千院、来迎院、勝林院、宝泉院といった天台宗の寺が建っている。

三千院は天台宗山門派の三門跡寺院のひとつで、梶井門跡と称する。もともと三千院は最澄が比叡山に根本中堂を造営するさい、東塔南谷の梨の大木のそばに一宇を建てたのがはじまりといい、それを承雲が貞観年間（859～77）に修造して円融房と名づけた。1086年（応徳3）白河天皇の中宮藤原賢子の菩提を弔うため東坂本梶井に円徳院が建てられると、これを円融房の里坊とし、堀河天皇の皇子である最雲法親王が門主となった。以来、梶井門

鯖街道　若狭で獲れた魚介類を京都に運んだ街道。とくに鯖が多かったため、この名でよばれる。

来迎院　仁寿年間(851～54)の創建。平安期の平安期の三尊坐像を有する。

勝林院　1186年の「大原問答」で知られる声明音律の声明音律の道場。

宝泉院　勝林院子院。「盤桓園」庭園が美しい。

3. A beautiful *monzeki* temple in Ōhara

Sanzen-in

Address: 540 Ōhara Raigō-in-chō, Sakyō-ku, Kyoto-shi
Tel: 075 (744) 2531
Hours: 9:00AM–5:00PM (November: 8:30AM–5:00PM, December–February: 9:00AM–4:30PM)
Admission: ¥700
www.sanzenin.or.jp
10 min walk from Ōhara bus stop, Kyoto bus 17 or 18 from Kyoto Sta.

The village of Ōhara is about one hour by bus from Kyoto Station, passing over the Hanazono Bridge and north on the Wakasakaidō Rd. commonly called the Sabakaidō Rd., or "Mackerel Road." Since the Heian period, Ōhara has been **a place of retreat** for nobles and artists, and it has also been known as a source of charcoal and firewood for the capital. It retains its agricultural landscape and feel of a country mountain village. In the heart of the mountain on the east side of the Wakasakaidō Rd. stand numerous Tendai sect, including Sanzen-in, Raigō-in, Shōrin-in, and Hōsen-in.

Sanzen-in is one of the three *monzeki* temples of the *san-mon* school of Tendai sect, known as the Kajii Monzeki. The temple originated with a single building built by Saichō next to a great pear tree at Tōtō Minamidani at Hieizan Enryaku-ji. During the Jōgan era (859–77), Shōun repaired it, calling it En'yū-bō. In 1086, the temple called Entoku-in was built to enshrine Fujiwara-no-Kenshi, the wife of Emperor Shirakawa, at Higashisakamoto Kajii. Later, this temple was attached to En'yū-bō, and Saiun, the son of Emperor Horikawa, became the head priest, and the temple was known as the Kajii Monzeki.

跡の称号をもつ。

しかし、円徳院は何度か焼失して、いまの大原に移った。その後、本坊も大原に移し魚山（ぎょざん）三千院と称した。魚山とは中国の天台山の西に位置し、円仁（えんにん）（慈覚大師（じかくだいし））が声明を学んだ地で、大原がかの地に似ていることから名をとられた。

往生極楽院と名庭

三千院の境内には、作家井上靖（いのうえやすし）が、まるで宝石箱だと賞賛した本堂の「往生極楽院（おうじょうごくらくいん）」が木立にかこまれ、深緑の苔の広がる庭園に浮かぶように建つ。往生極楽院は三間四面、単層の入母屋造、柿葺で、堂内には本尊の「阿弥陀如来坐像」と両脇侍（わきじ）の勢至（せいし）菩薩、観音菩薩が安置されている。いずれも藤原時代の作品で、とくに両脇侍の伏し目がちな慎ましやかな顔と「大和坐り（やまとずわり）」という正座に近い姿が慈愛にみちて、まことに好ましい。以前、この両脇仏には優美な瓔珞（ようらく）がかけられていたが、いまは外されている。

瓔珞　仏像を装飾するため頭や首にかける装身具。

また、三千院には、高低二面の庭園があり、上は「有清園（ゆうせいえん）」といい往生極楽院をとりかこむような池泉回遊式庭園で深々とした苔とそれに被さるように低く枝を広げた楓の緑が美しい。下の庭は「聚碧園（しゅうへきえん）」という**池庭**で池と植栽の刈込がみごとに調和する鑑賞庭園である。

However, Entoku-in was destroyed in a fire, several times, ultimately moving to Ōhara, and it was renamed Gyozan Sanzen-in. The name Gyozan came from its resemblance to a mountain in China and was bestowed by Ennin (the monk known posthumously as Jikaku Daishi), who had studied there.

The Ōjōgokuraku-in and a Prominent Garden

The author Inoue Yasushi has likened the *hondō* of Sanzen-in, the Ōjōgokuraku-in, to a jewel box. It stands surrounded by trees, seeming to float in a thick moss garden. It is a single-story building with a roof made from wooden planks, it contains the temple's venerated seated statue of the Amitabha (*amida-nyorai*) flanked by statues of *seishi bosatsu* and Avalokiteshware (Kannon). All of the statues were carved in the Fujiwara period, and the expressions on their faces and "*yamatozuwari*" style of sitting in a manner similar to the *seiza* position convey an attitude of love and modesty. Originally the two flanking statues wore beautiful ornaments, but this has been removed.

Sanzen-in has a two-level garden. The upper level is the Yūsei-en, a stroll pond garden that appears to encircle the Ojogokuraku-in, which is surrounded by thick moss and the drooping limbs of maple trees. The lower garden is the Shūheki-en, a **pond garden** with carefully combined plants harmonizing with the pond.

4

悲劇の女人が隠棲した寺

寂光院（じゃっこういん）

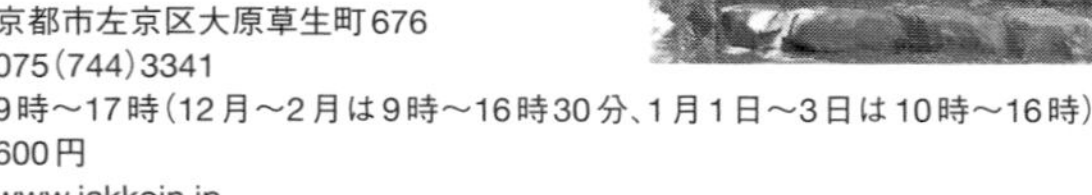

京都市左京区大原草生町676
075(744)3341
9時〜17時(12月〜2月は9時〜16時30分、1月1日〜3日は10時〜16時)
600円
www.jakkoin.jp
京都駅より京都バス17系統　大原下車徒歩15分

寂光院（天台宗尼寺）は若狭街道の西側、高野川に合流する草生川（くさおがわ）にそって細い道をのぼったところにある。三千院などの建つ東側とくらべて、いっそうのどかな農村地帯で、すれちがう地元の人が私たち観光客に道を譲るといったやさしさを示してくれる。

山道はしだいに爪先上がりになって、旅荘や茶店の軒をくぐるようにして緑陰のなかにたどりつく。閉ざされた門扉越しに建礼門院（けんれいもんいん）大原西陵（おおはらせいりょう）への長く細い石段がみえて、その少し先に大ぶりな平石をくみあわせた石段が山上の寂光院の境内へとつづく。

2000年（平成12）5月9日未明、放火とみられる火災により寂光院の本堂および本尊の地蔵菩薩立像が焼失した。これほど著名な寺院が火災にあったのは近年あまりないことで話題になった。しかし、2005年6月2日、寂光院本堂の再建を祝う落慶法要が営まれ、新本尊も4月に完成した。

4. The temple where a tragic lady secluded herself

Jakkō-in

Address: 676 Ōhara Kusao-chō, Sakyō-ku, Kyoto-shi
Tel: 075 (744) 3341
Hours: 9:00AM–5:00PM (December–February: 9:00AM–4:30PM; January 1–3: 10:00AM–4:00PM)
Admission: ¥600
www.jakkoin.jp/en/
15 min walk from Ōhara bus stop, Kyoto bus 17 from Kyoto Sta.

Jakkō-in, a Tendai sect convent, is on the west side of Wakasakaidō Rd., up a small path along the Kusao River, which flows into the Takano River. Unlike the east side of Takano River, where Sanzen-in and the other temples are, this is a peaceful rural area where the local people will courteously step out of your way on the path.

The mountain path weaves gently upward, passing inns and tea rooms as it winds into the green shade. Just past a closed gate, you will see a narrow stone staircase leading to the Kenreimon-in Ōhara west mausoleum, and just after that a broad stone staircase that leads to the mountaintop grounds of Jakkō-in.

In the early morning on May 9, 2000, a fire believed to be arson destroyed Jakkō-in's *hondō* and the temple's venerated statue of *jizō bosatsu*. It was the first time in recent years that such a noted temple had suffered a serious fire. However, on June 2, 2005, a memorial service was held to pray for the rebuilding of Jakkō-in, and a new statue of the principal image was completed in April.

建礼門院と寂光院

寂光院のはじまりは、寺伝では、594年に聖徳太子が父用明天皇の菩提を弔うために創建したというが、異説では空海の開基とし、また来迎院を再興した聖応大師良忍が創建したという説もあって、いずれも遠く歴史の霞がかかっている。

当寺がよく知られるのは、平氏滅亡の壇ノ浦の戦いで、子の安徳天皇とともに入水しながら助けられた建礼門院、すなわち平清盛の娘徳子がここに庵を結び隠棲したことで、それは『平家物語』などに詳らかで、1185年（文治元）徳子29歳のことである。翌年に舅である後白河法皇（高倉天皇の父）が建礼門院を見舞いに訪れる大原御幸は能の曲目や『平家物語』で知られるところである。

阿波内侍　藤原信西の娘。建礼門院に仕えた4人の女官のひとり。

なお、建礼門院の侍女である阿波内侍が柴刈にでたときの姿が真似られて、藍染め筒袖の着物、御所染めの前結びの帯、甲掛・脚絆の「大原女」のスタイルになったといわれる。

阿弥陀寺　弾誓上人が1609年に開いた念仏道場がはじまり。

なお、大原のバス停から高野川沿いに旧道を北上すると、浄土宗の阿弥陀寺が山深くに建っている。

Kenreimon-in and Jakkō-in

There are varying stories of the founding of Jakkō-in, all of them too far in the past to verify. The temple's official history has it that Prince Shōtoku built the first vestige of the temple in 594 to mourn his father, Emperor Yōmei. Other stories give credit for the founding of the temple to Kūkai or to Shōō Daishi Ryōnin, who rebuilt Raigō-in.

In any case, the temple became well known when Tokuko (Kenreimon-in), the daughter of Taira-no-Kiyomori, became a nun here in 1185, when she was twenty-nine. Tokuko and her son Emperor Antoku jumped into the sea, but only Tokuko was saved from drowning during the Battle of Dannoura, when her clan, the Taira, were defeated, as described in the Tale of the Heike. The visit of her father-in-law, Emperor Goshirakawa (the father of Emperor Takakura) to Kenreimon-in is portrayed in Noh drama and also in *the Tale of the Heike.*

In passing, the Ōhara-me style, an indigo *tsutsusode* kimono with a front-tied sash and gaiters, traces back to the costume worn by Awa-no-Naishi, the lady in waiting of the Kenreimon-in, when she went to collect firewood.

One more temple in the area is the Jōdo sect Amida-ji, which stands deep in the woods, north up the old road along the Takano River from the Ōhara bus stop.

5

天狗と義経ゆかりの寺

鞍馬寺（くらまでら）

京都市左京区鞍馬本町1074
075（741）2003
9時〜16時30分
愛山費300円
kuramadera.or.jp
叡山電鉄鞍馬線　鞍馬駅下車徒歩5分

叡山電鉄鞍馬線はしだいに登山電車の雰囲気になって、貴船口（きぶねぐち）駅、そして終着の鞍馬駅に、始発の出町柳（でまちやなぎ）駅から約30分で着く。そこは深い谷間の地である。山寺である鞍馬寺へは、鞍馬山ケーブルカーで昇ると楽だが、できれば九十九折（つづらおり）の参道を伝説の天狗が住むという霊気を感じながら境内にのぼってみたい。途中に鞍馬寺の鎮守社由岐（ゆき）神社が建つ。この神社の例祭が京都三大奇祭のひとつ「鞍馬の火祭」である。また同社の豪壮な割拝殿（わりはいでん）と巨木の「願かけ杉」も見ものである。

九十九折の参道は最後に石段となって本殿金堂にいたる。麓の仁王門から約30分の道のりである。

由岐神社　940年に朱雀天皇が御所に祀られていた由岐大祭神を移す。

割拝殿　拝殿の中央を通路にした形式のもの。豊臣秀頼によって再建された桃山時代の代表的建造物。

鞍馬寺の歴史と牛若丸の伝説

鞍馬寺は、770年（宝亀元）に奈良唐招提寺（とうしょうだいじ）を建立した鑑真和上（がんじんわじょう）の高弟鑑禎（がんてい）上人が霊夢に導かれ、毘沙門天（びしゃもんてん）をこの地に祀ったのがはじまりとされている。真言宗、天台宗と転じて

5. The temple of Tengu goblins and Yoshitsune
Kurama-dera

Address: 1074 Kurama Honmachi, Sakyō-ku, Kyoto-shi
Tel: 075 (741) 2003
Hours: 9:00AM–4:30PM
Admission: ¥300
kuramadera.or.jp
5 min walk from Eizan Railway Kurama Line Kurama Sta.

The Eizan Dentetsu Kurama-line train climbs the mountain from Demachiyanagi Station to Kurama Station in about thirty minutes. From there you can take the Kurama cable car to Kurama-dera, but if you're up to it, I recommend walking up the winding approach path called the *tsuzuraori* (zigzag path), which legend has it is populated by long-nosed Tengu goblins. On the way you will pass Yuki-jinja, the companion shrine to Kurama-dera. The shrine's festival, the Kurama-no-Himatsuri (Kurama fire festival), is one of the three wonder festivals of Kyoto. The shrine also boasts a particular *hai-den* and a and a giant cedar to which people pray that their wishes will be granted.

After about thirty minutes' walk from the *niō-mon* gate, the *tsuzuraori* culminates in a stone staircase, which brings you to the temple's main building, the *kon-dō* (*hon-den*).

The History of Kurama-dera and the Legend of Ushiwakamaru

Kurama-dera is said to have been established in 770 by Gantei, a disciple of the Chinese priest Ganjin who established Tōshōdai-ji in Nara. Gantei had a vision that led him to establish a temple in honor of Bishamonten, best known as the god of war.

きたが、1947年（昭和22）に鞍馬弘教を立教して、その総本山となった。千手観世音菩薩、毘沙門天王、護法魔王尊の三尊を三位一体として本尊とする。

この寺が鎮座する鞍馬山は「天狗さんがいはるお山」と古くから都人に畏怖されてきた。赤い顔で鼻の高い怪力の天狗は、**山岳信仰**と結びつき、修験者が**守護神**として祀ってきた。ことに鞍馬山の天狗は「僧正坊」とよばれ、日本各地の天狗の総元締めといわれる。

また源義経がまだ牛若丸とよばれていた7歳ころから十年間を鞍馬寺で過ごしたため、さまざまな伝説が残る。本殿金堂（標高410m）の背後に奥の院参道があって、牛若丸が修行中に水を飲んだ「息つぎの水」、地盤が固く地下に根が張れない杉の根が地上に露出した「木の根道」や「僧正ガ谷」では、天狗と兵法の稽古をしたといわれる。その荒々しい参道をゆくと、650万年前に人類救済のために金星からやってきたという超SF的な護法魔王尊を祀る奥の院に着く。

奥の院まできたら、元の道を戻るより、木の根の山道を西門まで下って貴船に出るほうが早い。20分ほどのハイキングである。

Subsequently, the temple was affiliated with the Shingon and then the Tendai sects, but in 1947, established its own sect, Kurama Kōkyō, with Kurama-dera as the head temple. A trinity of deities is venerated in the temple: Senju Kanzeon Bosatsu, Bishamon Tennō, and Gohōmaōson.

Mt. Kuramayama, the mountain where the temple is located, has been awed since ancient times by local residents as the home of the Tengu goblins. These red-faced, long-nosed goblins have a special connection to **mountain worship** and are venerated by mountain ascetics as **guardian deities**. The Tengu of Mt. Kuramayama are known as Sōjōbō, the overlords of all of Japan's Tengu.

There are also many legends about the ten years that Minamoto-no-Yoshitsune spent at Kurama-dera, when he was still called Ushiwakamaru. Behind the *kon-dō* (altitude 410 meters), there is a path to Oku-no-In. Along the path is a spring where Ushiwakamaru used to drink water when he was undergoing training, and he is said to have practiced military tactics with the Tengu in the Kino-nemichi ("Tree-root path," so called because the ground is so hard that the roots of trees have to stretch out above the ground) and Sōjōgadani areas there. If you continue along this rough path, you will come to the Oku-no-In temple where Gohōmaōson is worshipped. Although it sounds like science fiction, this deity is said to have come from Venus some 6.5 million years ago to save humanity.

Rather than returning by the main path, the easier descent is via the root-strewn mountain path to the west gate of the temple and down toward Kibune, a hike of about twenty minutes.

6

水の神、縁結びの神として知られる

貴船神社（きふね）

京都市左京区鞍馬貴船町180
075(741)2016
6時～20時(時期により変動)
境内参拝自由
kifunejinja.jp
叡山電鉄鞍馬線　貴船口下車徒歩25分

貴船口（きぶねぐち）駅から約2km、清流がときに急湍となり、白い飛沫をみせる貴船川沿いに歩くと二の鳥居が立っていて、その先の石段を80段ほどのぼると貴船神社の本社に着く。

貴船神社の創建時期は定かではないが、記紀神話の女神、玉依姫命（たまよりひめのみこと）が淀川、賀茂川を遡って、貴船川に入り、当地に小堂を建てたのが起源ともいう。また、1300年前の建て替えの記録が残っているというから、ともかく歴史は古い。

玉依姫命　記紀神話で神武天皇の母といわれる。

平安京遷都後は、貴船神社が御所の御用水である賀茂川の最上流にあたることから川上神（かわかみしん）として崇められ、日照りには黒馬が、長雨には白馬が朝廷より奉納された。やがて生きた馬に代えて板に馬の絵を描いた「板立馬（いたたてうま）」が奉納されることもあり、これが絵馬の起源となったといわれる。

6. Known for the god of water and the god of marriage

Kifune-jinja

Address: 180 Kurama Kibune-chō, Sakyō-ku, Kyoto-shi
Tel: 075 (741) 2016
Hours: 6:00AM–8:00PM (May vary depending on season)
Admission: Free
kifunejinja.jp
25 min walk from Eizan Railway Kurama Line Kibune Sta.

If you walk about 2 kilometers from Kibuneguchi Station, along the Kibune River, where the gentle stream sometimes turns into a rapid, you will see the second *torii* gate standing. Ascend the eighty or so steps of the stone staircase and you arrive at the main shurine of Kifune-jinja.

It is not known when the shrine was established, but it is said to have started with a small building built by Tamayorihime-no-Mikoto, a goddess mentioned in the ancient chronicles, who ascended the Yodo and Kamo Rivers to Kibune River. Whether or not this is true, a record exists of a renovation project on the building some thirteen hundred years ago, so it is certain that the history of the shrine is long.

After the capital was established at Kyoto, Kifune-jinja was recognized as the uppermost stream of the Kamo River, where the water used in palace rituals was obtained. Special envoys were sent from the court in supplication; a black horse was sent in dry weather, and a white horse on rainy days. In time, the actual horses were replaced by paintings of horses on a board known as the *itatateuma*, which is said to be the origin of the votive paintings known as *ema* (lit. "picture horse") used at shrines today.

本社、結社、奥宮を訪ねる

またこの地は、「気生根」「木生嶺」ともよばれ、気力が生じる根、嶺と信じられてきた。さらに水は命の源で、悪いものを流し、心を浄化するもので、こうして「気」と「水」に満ちた貴船神社は、心願成就の神として人々の信仰を集めてきた。

貴船神社は、以前700mほど上流のいまの「奥宮」の位置に本殿があったが、1055年（天喜3）貴船川の氾濫によって現在の位置に移された。また、2005年（平成17）に遷宮950年を期して、大修理がおこなわれた。

本宮から300mほどの川上にある「結社（中宮）」は縁結びの神社として知られ、その由来は平安時代の女流歌人和泉式部が心変わりした夫の愛を取り戻すために参詣して復縁したことによるといい、いまも「縁結びの宮」として、若い女性の参拝が多い。

和泉式部　生没年不詳。三十六歌仙のひとりで恋多き情熱の女流歌人。中京区新京極通の「誠心院」に墓所が残る。

さらに400mほど上流にある奥宮には、玉依姫命が乗ってきた船を人目にふれさせないように石で囲んだという船形石がある。航海や旅行にその小石をもっていくと安全に旅をすることができるという言い伝えがあり、山の中の神社ではあるが、船舶関係者の参拝も多い。さらには奥宮本殿の地下には**龍神**が住む龍穴があるといわれている。

Visiting the Main Shrine, the Middle Shrine, and the Inner Shrine

The name of this site has been assigned different characters (with the same pronunciation), so it has been worshipped as "the root of strength" and the "peak that gives strength." Since water is the source of life and is associated with washing away evil and cleansing the heart, Kifune-jinja, overflowing with "spirit" and "water," has been worshipped by many as enshrining the god of fulfilled wishes.

Originally, the main sanctuary (*hon-den*) was located where the Okunomiya now stands, 700 meters upstream from its current location, but in 1055 it was moved due to flooding of the Kibune River. In 2005, a major renovation was undertaken to mark the 950th anniversary of the shrine's founding.

300 meters upstream from the main shrine is the Yuinoyashiro, the middle shrine, which is known as the shrine of marriage. This is said to come from the success of the Heian-period poet Izumi Shikibu in reclaiming the love of her straying husband by praying at this shrine. Many young women still come to this shrine to express their prayers for love.

Continuing another 400 meters upstream, one finds the Okunomiya, the Inner Shrine, where there is a rock shaped like a ship, representing the legend that the ship used by Tamayorihime-no-Mikoto was placed here, surrounded by stones to keep out prying eyes. Because taking a stone from this shrine is believed to ensure a safe sea journey or other voyage, even though this is a mountain shrine, many worshippers here are linked to sea travel. It is also said that a **dragon god** lives beneath the Okunomiya *hon-den*.

7

真言密教の聖地

神護寺

京都市右京区梅ケ畑高雄町5
075(861)1769
9時〜16時
600円
jingoji.or.jp
京都駅よりJRバス高雄/京北線　山城高雄下車徒歩20分

同じように京都市街から離れ、北に位置する「大原」と「三尾」であるが、大原ののどけさに比べて三尾にはきびしさが漂う。「三尾」とは高尾（雄）、槇尾、栂尾をいい、「尾」には「すえ」とか「さき」「おわり」の意味があり、山が谷に落ち込む先端を示し、厳しい地形である。そして、それぞれに古刹をいただく。高雄山神護寺、槇尾山西明寺、栂尾高山寺である。いずれも清滝川の渓谷をのぞむ高台に建つ。

神護寺の創建と再建

神護寺は高雄山（標高428.6m）の山腹を平坦に切り開いたところに伽藍を構える真言宗の大寺である。和気清麻呂が出身地の河内に建てた「神願寺」と和気氏の氏寺とされる当地にあった「高雄山寺」が824年（天長元）に合併して「神護国祚真言寺」になり、やがて上の二字をとって神護寺と称された。唐から帰朝した空海は、809年（大同4）に高雄山寺に

和気清麻呂　733〜99。政僧道鏡を天皇にとの陰謀を阻止する。光仁・桓武天皇に仕えて平安遷都に尽力。

7. Holy site of the Esoteric shingon teachings

Jingo-ji

Address: 5 Umegahata Takao-chō, Ukyō-ku, Kyoto-shi
Tel: 075(861)1769
Hours: 9:00AM–4:00PM
Admission: ¥600
jingoji.or.jp
20 min walk from Yamashiro Takao bus stop, JR bus Takao-Keihoku Line from Kyoto Sta.

The Sanbi area is about as far from central Kyoto as Ōhara to the north, but unlike the tranquil scenes around Ōhara, Sanbi conveys a harsh, rigorous feeling. Sanbi means "three ridges," and refers to the forbidding landscape of Taka-o, Makino-o, and Togano-o at the edges of the mountains. All three of these areas are home to temples with illustrious histories that stand on mountain plateaus: Jingo-ji at Mt. Taka-o, Saimyō-ji at Mt. Makino-o, and Kōzan-ji at Mt. Togano-o.

The Founding and Rebuilding of Jingo-ji

Jingo-ji is a great Shingon sect temple built in a flat area carved out of the side of Mt. Taka-o (428.6 meters in altitude). In 824, Singan-ji, in Kawachi, the birthplace of Wake-no-Kiyomaro, and Takaosan-ji, the family temple of the Wake clan, merged to form Jingokokuso Shingon-ji. They compressed the characters of this long name to produce "Jingo-ji." Kūkai, returning from his time in China in 809, entered Takaosan-ji, attracting many followers and cementing its role as a central temple in the Shingon tradition.

入山、この寺を中心に活躍し、空海の弟子が伽藍を整え、真言宗寺院としての基礎をかためた。しかし1149年（久安5）の火災で金堂、真言堂など諸堂を失い衰微していく。

そのような神護寺を復興したのが文覚上人で、後白河上皇の勅許や源頼朝の援助をえて、神護寺は往時以上の盛観をみるまでになった。応仁の乱でいったん荒廃するが、豊臣秀吉や徳川家康の寺領寄進などにより、いま私たちが目の前にする諸堂の多くが再建される。

文覚 1139~1203。もとは北面の武士遠藤盛遠。袈裟御前との物語で知られる。

神護寺の境内をめぐる

街道からいったん清滝川の川べりに降りてさらにそこから長く急峻な石段をのぼりつめると、二天門ともいう豪壮な山門にいたる。山門をくぐると広大な空間が現出する。右手の山麓には書院、宝蔵、和気公霊廟が建つ。その裏手の石段上に鐘楼があり、875年（貞観17）鋳造の「三絶の鐘」とよばれる梵鐘がかかる。当時の著名な三文人が**銘文**にかかわったことによる。

中央の広々とした空間は五大堂と毘沙門堂の建つ場所に行きつき、右手には金堂への幅広い石段があらわれる。その石段の途中から五大堂と毘沙門堂をふり返るのも、じつに雄勝な景色である。両堂ともに1623年（元和9）の再建。

山内最大の建造物である1935年（昭和10）建立の金堂は大瓦屋根の流れも迫力があり、軒裏の木組柱に朱色をやや渋くしながらも鮮

However, in 1149, fire destroyed the *kon-dō*, the *shingon-dō*, and other temple buildings, leading to the temple's decline.

The priest Mongaku revived Jingo-ji, and with the support of former-emperor Goshirakawa and Minamoto-no-Yoritomo, it surpassed its former eminence. It suffered serious damage in the Ōnin War, but Toyotomi Hideyoshi and Tokugawa Ieyasu supported its rebuilding to the condition we see today.

Around the grounds at Jingo-ji

From the Road, head up the Kiyotaki River up a long, steep, stone staircase, and you will come to the grand *san-mon* gate (Main gate) of the temple, known as the *niten-mon*. Through the gate is a broad plaza. On the right side, in the shadow of the mountain, stand the *shoin* (study-cum-living room), the treasure house, and the Wake-kō Reibyō, the mausoleum. Beyond these buildings, at the top of the stone staircase, is the bell tower, containing a bell forged in the year 875 known as "Sanzetsu-no-Kane" with **inscriptions** by three noted literary men of the time.

Continue to the plaza, where the *godai-dō* and the *bishamon-dō* are located, and on the right you will see the broad stone staircase leading to the *kon-dō*. The view of the *godai-dō* and the *bishamon-dō* from halfway up the stairs is considered to be particularly affecting. Both buildings were reconstructed in 1623.

The largest building on the ground, the *kon-dō* was constructed in 1935. The flow of its tiled roof is forceful, and although the vermilion color of the wooden columns under the eaves has faded, it retains its vividness. As you ascend the staircase, the hall

明に残し、石段を一段上るごとに全貌があらわれてきて、その美しさは格別である。

金堂に安置される木造薬師如来立像、脇侍（わきじ）の日光・月光菩薩立像、さらに金堂の北に建つ多宝塔内の五大虚空蔵菩薩坐像（ごだいこくうぞうぼさつ）（五体）など、いずれも平安期の貴重な仏像である。

また毘沙門堂の西に建つ弘法大師住房跡の大師堂（納涼房（のうりょうぼう））は、正面三間、柿葺の入母屋造で屋根の低い瀟洒な建物で、山内で最古の建造物である。この大師堂から少し北にゆくと、地蔵院への道が一度浅い谷に降りて、次にさらに高い台上にあがるようにあって、錦雲渓（きんうんけい）と名づけられた清滝川の渓谷を一望する絶景地にいたる。

神護寺の境内
The grounds at Jingo-ji

gradually comes into view, revealing its remarkable beauty.

In the *kon-dō* can be seen a standing wooden statue of *yakushi nyorai* (Healing Buddha) flanked by statues of the *nikkō* and *gekkō bosatsu* (Daylight and Moonlight Bodhisattva). Just to the north is the treasure house, containing five seated statues of the Five Great *kokūzō* (Akasagarbha) *bosatsu*—very valuable Heian-period works.

Just west of the *bishamon-dō* is the *daishi-dō*, a memorial to Kōbō Daishi, an *irimoya-zukuri* building with the shake-shingled (*kokera-buki*) roof that is the oldest building on the temple. Just slightly north of the *daishi-dō*, the road to Jizō-in descends into a shallow valley and then back up to a high plateau with a breathtaking view of the Kin'unkei, a gorge of the Kiyotaki River.

8

老樹の茂る山中に建つ諸堂

高山寺(こうざんじ)

京都市右京区梅ケ畑栂尾町8
075(861)4204
8時30分〜17時
800円(秋期は別途500円)
kosanji.com
京都駅よりJRバス高雄/京北線　栂ノ尾下車徒歩5分

高山寺は三尾の寺のなかで最も北に位置する。清滝川に沿って走る周山(しゅうざん)街道の白雲橋(しらくもばし)の先に寺域への表参道が斜めに上っている。また、栂ノ尾(とがのお)バス停（広い駐車場がある）から急勾配のジグザグに屈曲した石段の裏参道からも境内に入ることができる。

境内といっても高山寺はうっそうとした老木が空を隠す山の中の寺だから、整然と諸堂が建ち並んでいるわけではない。表参道から立ち入れば、菱形の敷石が置かれた道の先に屹立する壁のような石段(金堂道(こんどうみち))があらわれ、その段上に金堂が一棟だけ建っている。ほかの堂宇は、金堂前を右方向にまわった斜面にひっそりと点在する。紅葉のシーズンをはずして訪れると、山内にはほとんど人影がない。

華厳宗　中国唐の法蔵(ほうぞう)が大成した。日本では奈良時代に東大寺を中心に研学され、鎌倉時代に明恵らが中興。総本山は奈良東大寺。

高山寺の創建と明恵上人

高山寺の創建は、774年（宝亀5）光仁天皇の勅願による華厳宗(けごんしゅう)の寺院、神願寺都賀尾坊(しんがんじとがのおぼう)にはじまるといわれ、平安初期には、天台宗

8. Temple buildings amid the thick trees

Kōzan-ji

Address: 8 Umegahata Toganoo-chō, Ukyō-ku, Kyoto-shi
Tel: 075 (861) 4204
Hours: 8:30AM–5:00PM
Admission: ¥800 (Additional ¥500 charge during autumn)
kosanji.com
5 min walk from Toganoo bus stop, JR bus Takao-Keihoku Line from Kyoto Sta.

Kōzan-ji is the most northerly of the Sanbi temples. Just beyond the Shirakumo-bashi bridge of the Shūzankaidō Rd., which runs along the Kiyotaki River, the approach to the temple rises up at a diagonal. The temple can also be approached by a back way up a steep, zigzag path from the Togano-o bus stop (with a large parking lot).

The temple grounds are nearly hidden by the dense trees that surround it so buildings are not in line. If you enter from the front approach path, you can follow the path of diamond-shaped stones to the stone staircase, the Kon-dō-michi, that looms up like a wall leading to where the *kon-dō* stands alone. The other temple buildings are scattered on the slope around the right side of the *kon-dō*. If you are not visiting during the autumn leaf-viewing season, the temple grounds may well be completely deserted.

The Establishment of Kōzan-ji and the Priest Myōe

Kōzan-ji was founded in 774 by order of Emperor Kōnin as a Kegon-sect temple with the name Shingan-ji Toganoo-bō. In the early Heian period, it changed to the Tendai sect and was renamed

に改宗して都賀尾寺（とがのおじ）と称した。その後、荒廃するが、神護寺を再興した文覚（もんがく）上人によって再興されて神護寺の別所となった。しかし文覚が佐渡に流罪となると、ふたたび寺域は荒れた。

文覚に師事していた明恵（みょうえ）は、1206年（建永元）に後鳥羽上皇の院宣をえて、華厳宗復興の道場として再興して、「日出先照高山之寺（ひいでてまずてらすこうざんのてら）」と勅額を賜り、高山寺とした。

明恵はほかの名僧のように宗祖や指導者とならず、ひたすら坐禅にあけくれ、高山寺にある石、木の根など明恵が坐らなかったものはないといわれた。その高潔な人柄は多くの人々から崇敬を得た。高山寺には「明恵上人樹上坐禅像」があり、木の枝に坐る上人が描かれている。

栄西 1141～1215。「ようさい」とも。四歳から比叡山に学び、入宋して臨済禅を虚庵懐敞（きあんえしょう）から受ける。日本の臨済宗の祖。

また、明恵上人は、入宋した栄西（えいさい）から茶の種を贈られ、茶園を営んだことでも知られている。いま高山寺の金堂道の右手に、わずかだが茶園が残っている。

渓谷の風が渡る「石水院」

金堂から明恵上人御廟、開山堂、茶室遺香庵（いこうあん）と、杉木立のなかに建つ諸堂をみて、石畳の坂道を下ってゆくと、国宝の「石水院（せきすいいん）」が建つ区域にでる。

「石水院」は五所堂（ごしょどう）ともいい、鎌倉時代初期の様式を伝える遺構で、住宅風（寝殿造）建築の傑作といわれる。石水院は1224年（貞応3）

Toganoo-ji. It later went into decline but was revived by the priest Mongaku, who had also revived Jingo-ji, and was named a subsidiary temple to Jingo-ji. However, when Mongaku was exiled to Sado, the temple again declined.

A disciple of Mongaku's named Myōe obtained the permission of the former Emperor Gotoba to resurrect the temple once again in the Kegon sect, and its name was changed to Kōzan-ji in honor of a rescript written by the emperor himself, describing the temple as "the mountain temple first illuminated by the sun."

Myōe did not seek to found a sect or to direct other priests, but only to sit in meditation (*zazen*). It is said that there is hardly a rock or tree around Kōzan-ji where Myōe did not sit to meditate. His purity attracted many admirers. There is a famous painting of him known as "Myōe Sitting Zazen on a Tree."

Myōe is also famous for his cultivation of tea from seeds received from Eisai to China. A small tea garden remains to the right of Kōzan-ji's *kon-dō*.

Sekisui-in, where the wind from the ravine blows

After visiting the *kon-dō*, Myōe's mausoleum, the *kaizan-dō*, the tea-ceremony house *ikōan*, and the various buildings among the cedars, follow the stone walkway down to the national treasure Sekisui-in.

Sekisui-in, also known as Gosho-dō, is built in the early Kamakura-period style, a masterpiece of residential (*shinden-zukuri*) building. Sekisui-in was moved from the former Emperor

に後鳥羽上皇の賀茂別院から移され、明恵上人の禅堂、庵室として使われており、1547年（天文16）の兵火でも焼失をまぬがれた。ただ今日みる石水院は、明治期に金堂の東にあった経蔵（きょうぞう）を移して改築したものである。

板間に置かれている善財童子（ぜんざいどうじ）像が外光によって影絵のようにみえ、明けはなたれた堂内は清滝川からの涼風が吹き抜ける。**縁側**に座って静かな時をすごす人も多い。

鳥獣人物戯画　4巻の白描の絵巻。12～13世紀の作。兎と蛙の相撲や猿の法会など動物を擬人化した風刺画。

また、寺宝の「**鳥獣人物戯画**（ちょうじゅうじんぶつぎが）」（複本、実物は東京と京都の国立博物館に寄託）や「明恵上人樹上坐禅像」もこの石水院内に展示されている。

高山寺は1966年（昭和41）まで真言宗御室（おむろ）派の別格本山であったが、いまは単立寺院である。

なお、高山寺から周山街道を下ると清滝川の流れの近くに西明寺（さいみょうじ）が建つ（9時～17時・400円）。空海の弟子智泉（ちせん）が神護寺の別院として創建し（天長年間 824～834）、その後徳川綱吉の実母桂昌院（けいしょういん）によって再興された。石段の下から見上げる当寺の薬医門（やくいもん）の佇まいは品格があって、とくに紅葉時はいちだんと美しい。

Gotoba's Kamo Remote palace Villa in 1224 for use as Myōe's *zen-dō* and retreat, and narrowly escaped being burned up in 1547. Sekisui-in we see today was rebuilt during the Meiji era from elements of the *kyō-zō*, which used to stand just east of the *kon-dō*.

The statue of *zenzai dōji* (the youth Sudhana) is cast into silhouette by the light from outside, and a cool breeze from the Kiyotaki River blows through the hall. Many people enjoy sitting on the **veranda** and passing some quiet moments.

Sekisui-in also contains another of the temple's treasures, a copy of the scroll, "**Scrolls of Frolicking Animals and Humans**," (the original is in the National Museum of Art in Tokyo and Kyoto), as well as the painting of Myōe in a tree.

Until 1966, Kōzan-ji was a primary temple of the Shingon sect Omuro school, but it is now an independent temple.

Descending from Kōzan-ji along the Shūzankaidō Rd., you will see Saimyō-ji near the Kiyotaki River (9:00AM–5:00PM, ¥400). Established by Kūkai's disciple Chisen as a subsidiary temple of Jingo-ji during the Tenchō era (824–34), the temple was later restored by Keishōin, the mother of Tokugawa Tsunayoshi. Looking up from the bottom of the stone stairway, you can see the elegance of the temple's Yakuimon gate of the temple. It is particularly beautiful in the autumn.

9

山科の高台に建つ桜と紅葉の名所

毘沙門堂(びしゃもんどう)

京都市山科区安朱稲荷山町18
075(581)0328
8時30分～17時(12月～3月15日は8時30分～16時30分)
境内参拝自由(諸堂拝観500円)
bishamon.or.jp
JR琵琶湖線または湖西線　山科駅下車徒歩20分

京都は三方を山に囲まれて、とよくいわれるが、実際は市街の東を限る東山連山を越えても、まだ京都市で、滋賀県との境の山並の間に山科(やましな)区の盆地が開けている。この山科地区も三方を山で囲まれているから、ミニ京都盆地といった風景である。

そんな山科地区において、まず第一に訪れたい寺が毘沙門堂である。JR山科駅の東に、北の山腹に一直線でのぼる道があって、その約900mの道はいかにも毘沙門堂への参道の趣だ。

毘沙門堂はもともとは、平親範(たいらのちかのり)が祖先の建てた三つの寺を合わせて、いまの上京区出雲路(かみぎょうくいずもじ)に毘沙門天を祀り再建した寺とも(1195年)、文武(もんむ)天皇の勅願により行基(ぎょうき)が開き、延暦年間(782～806)に最澄が下出雲路に自ら彫った毘沙門天を安置して毘沙門堂とよんだものともいう。

この出雲寺は兵火により焼失、慶長年間(1596～1615)に政僧といわれた天海(てんかい)僧正が、徳川家の支援を得て再興を志すが建築なかば

天海僧正　1536～1643。江戸初期の天台宗の僧。徳川家康の帰依を受け、2代秀忠、3代家光まで政僧として仕える。

9. High on the Yamashina plateau, famous for cherry blossoms and autumn colors

Bishamon-dō

Address: 18 Anshu Inariyama-chō, Yamashina-ku, Kyoto-shi
Tel: 075 (581) 0328
Hours: 8:30AM–5:00PM (December–March 15: 8:30AM–4:30PM)
Admission: Free (Entry to buildings: ¥500)
bishamon.or.jp
20 min walk from JR Biwako Line or Kosai Line Yamashina Sta.

It is often noted that Kyoto is surrounded on three sides by mountains, but in fact even beyond the Higashiyama mountain chain that forms the eastern boundary of the city lies Yamashina area. Still part of the city of Kyoto, this ward is situated in a basin that itself is surrounded on three sides by mountains, a sort of the mini-Kyoto Basin.

The most interesting temple to visit in Yamashina area is Bishamon-dō. Just to the east of JR Yamashina Station, a road rises straight north up the mountain for about 900 meters. It really looks like it could to be the approach to the temple.

There are two different versions of how Bishamon-dō came into being. In the first, it was formed in 1195 when Taira-no-Chikanori combined three temples founded by his family in what is today Izumoji in Kamigyō-ku. In the second version, it was opened by Gyōki at the order of Emperor Monmu. During the Enryaku era (782–806), Saichō named the temple Bishamon-dō, because he enshrined there a statue of Bishamonten that he had carved.

The temple was destroyed by fire, and during the Keichō era (1596–1615), Tenkai Sōjō, with the support of the Tokugawa clan worked to rebuild it, but his effort was interrupted by his death.

で没し、弟子の公海僧正が1665年（寛文5）に現在の地に諸堂を完成させた。そして後西天皇の第6皇子公弁法親王が入寺してより門跡寺院となった。

諸堂と襖絵

門前の極楽橋から急傾斜の石段を、金剛力士像を安置する仁王門までのぼると、境内は山腹の平坦地に広々として、唐門をへだて本堂の瓦屋根がみえる。本尊（秘仏）の毘沙門天は仏法守護四天王のひとつで北方世界を守護し、財宝・福徳の神で甲冑に身をかため宝棒を手にしている。

極楽橋　後西天皇（在位1654～63）が行幸のとき橋から上の景色が極楽浄土のようだと感嘆したことによる。

仏法守護四天王　ほかは持国天（東方）、増長天（南方）、広目天（西方）。

本堂の西回廊から板縁をふんで**霊殿**に入ると、阿弥陀如来を中心に歴代天皇や徳川将軍の位牌を安置、天井には四方にらみの龍が描かれている。建立は1693年（元禄6）という。

宸殿は後西天皇の御所内旧殿を皇子公弁法親王が拝領して移築した建物で、内部は障壁画116面で飾られる。この襖絵は狩野探幽の養子洞雲による。とくに「九老之図」に描かれた机は、みる位置を移動させてゆくと、机の向きが変わる不思議な逆遠近法という手法が用いられている。玄関脇の円山応挙筆「鯉の図」も同様の手法で描かれ、あたかも鯉がいきいきと泳いでいるかのようにみえる。

円山応挙　1733～95。江戸中期の画家で円山派の祖。写実性と装飾性が調和した画風を確立。

宸殿裏手には「晩翠園」という回遊式庭園があって、山の緑とあいまって静境をとどめている。

His disciple Kōkai completed some of the temple buildings in their current location in 1665. Later, the monk prince Kōben, the sixth son of Emperor Gosai took orders at the temple, making it a *monzeki* temple.

Temple Buildings and Screen Paintings

Climb up the steep stone stairway from the Gokuraku-bashi bridge to the *niō-mon* gate, where the statues of the *kongō rikishi* (Vajrapani) stand. The temple grounds stretch out on a level area on the mountainside, and through the Chinese style *kara-mon* gate, you can see the tiled roof of the *hondō*. The temple's venerated image of *bishamonten*, one of the Four Heavenly Kings and the god of treasure and prosperity, stands in his armor with his club in his hand.

From the western walkway of the *hondō*, you can enter the **mausoleum building** (*rei-den*), where mortuary tablets for many succesive emperors and Tokugawa shoguns surround the statue of the Amitabha (*amida-nyorai*). On the ceiling is a painting of a dragon glaring in all directions. The hall is believed to have been constructed in 1693.

The *shin-den* is a portion of Emperor Gosai's palace, transported by his son Kōben to this temple. The interior is decorated with 116 painted screens painted by Kanō Tōun, the adopted son of Kanō Tan'yū. One of particular interest is the "Painting of Nine Elders." The desk on the left side of the painting is said to be painted with an unusual reverse perspective that makes it appear to change orientation depending on where the viewer stands. Similarly, the painting of a carp that hangs next to the entryway by Maruyama Ōkyo uses a similar method, making the carp appear to be swimming.

Behind the *shin-den* is the Bansui-en stroll garden, which blends pleasingly with the greenery of the mountain.

10

池泉回遊式庭園をもつ真言の名刹

勧修寺(かじゅうじ)

京都市山科区勧修寺仁王堂町27-6
075(571)0048
9時〜16時
400円
地下鉄東西線　小野駅下車徒歩6分

山科区を南北に走る外環状線を南行して、名神高速道路の高架下をくぐったところに、ふたつの門跡寺院がある。いずれも真言宗に属する勧修寺と随心院(ずいしんいん)である。

勧修寺の創建は900年（昌泰3）で、醍醐天皇が生母藤原胤子(ふじわらのいんし)の菩提を弔うために建てられたという。905年（延喜5）に定額寺(じょうがくじ)となり、そののち法親王の入寺がつづいて、門跡寺院となり、勧修寺門跡とか山科門跡などとよばれ、第一級の寺格を誇ることになる。

定額寺　朝廷が保護した官寺。一定数に限られた。

しかし、醍醐寺との確執、応仁の乱による被害、秀吉の伏見城造営による寺地の縮小などで衰微するが、徳川幕府の寄進で寺観を整える。現在の建物はその当時のもので、とくに1697年（元禄10）明正(めいしょう)天皇の御殿を移した宸殿の端正な構えがいい。

さて、勧修寺でみるべきは名庭として知られる「勧修寺庭園」である。この庭園は書院南の平庭と氷室(ひむろ)池を中心にした池庭に分かれ

10. A Shingon temple with a "stroll pond garden"
Kajū-ji

Address: 27-6 Kanshū-ji Niōdō-chō, Yamashina-ku, Kyoto-shi
Tel: 075 (571) 0048
Hours: 9:00AM–4:00PM
Admission: ¥400
6 min walk from Subway Tozai Line Ono Sta.

Head south on the ring line that passes through Yamashina-ku, and after passing under the overpass of the Meishin Expressway, you will find two *monzeki* temples. Both affiliated with the Shingon sect, they are Kajū-ji and Zuishin-in.

Kajū-ji was established in 900 by Emperor Daigo as a memorial to his mother, Fujiwara-no-Inshi. In 905, it was chosen as an official temple and subsequently many monk-princes took orders there, establishing it as a *monzeki* temple. It was known by various names, including Kajū-ji Monzeki or Yamashina Monzeki, and was declared a first-class temple.

However, the temple declined due to antagonism with Daigo-ji, the depredations of the Ōnin War, and a reduction in its land because of the construction of Toyotomi Hideyoshi's Fushimi Castle, but with the support of the Tokugawa Bakufu, the temple was restored. The current buildings date from that era. Particularly notable is the *shin-den*, which was moved from the palace of Emperor Meishō in 1697.

The must-sees at Kajū-ji are its famous gardens, which are divided into the level-ground gardens to the south of the *shoin* and the pond gardens centered on Himuroike pond. The "stroll pond

る。池泉回遊式（かつては舟でめぐる舟遊式であった）の庭は、春から夏には、杜若、花菖蒲、睡蓮が咲き、とくに蓮は池を埋め尽くすほどで、深緑の葉と薄紅色の花が色あざやかである。中の島をへだてて、瀟洒な観音堂がみえ、山の常緑を背にして本堂や宸殿の屋根が陽に照るようすは、典雅な趣である。

平庭には白梅、八重桜、藤、泰山木など多種な花木が植えられて花の寺を演出し、紅葉の時期も多くの人を集める。

小野小町ゆかりの随心院

勧修寺から東へ600mほど歩くと真言宗小野派の大本山随心院の総門が五筋の築地にはさまれて開いている（9時〜16時30分･400円）。ほかの門跡寺院のように武張った構えでなく好ましい親しさである。ただ、境内に入ると、白壁と植込が整然と本坊の区域までつづき、やはり高貴な寺であることを示している。

もともとは991年（正暦2）仁海が建立した曼荼羅寺の子院といい、鎌倉時代に入り、門跡号が与えられ、随心院門跡と称した。

ここ随心院は小野小町の邸宅跡という話もあって、境内には小野小町化粧の井戸、小町文塚などがその由来を物語っている。

小野小町　平安前期の女流歌人。36歌仙のひとり。小野篁の娘とも。絶世の美人といわれた。

garden" (in the past, visitors viewed it from boats in the pond) is lively with *kakitsubata* irises, irises, and water lilies from spring to summer. The water lilies in particular fill the pond to overflowing, and the deep green leaves and pale red flowers are extremely picturesque. Across the pond is the elegant *kannon-dō*, and the roofs of the *hondō* and *shin-den* glow in the light against the backdrop of the mountain greenery.

The level-ground gardens are filled with white plum, double-blossomed cherry, wisteria, evergreen magnolia, and other plants and trees, and are an extremely popular destination for autumn leaf viewing.

Ono-no-Komachi's Zuishin-in

If you walk about 600 meters east from Kajū-ji, you will come upon the main gate of Zuishin-in, a Shingon sect temple of the Ono school (9:00AM–4:30PM, ¥400). The gate stands in the middle of a roofed mud wall, and unlike most *monzeki* temples, the atmosphere is not at all martial, but friendly. When one enters the grounds, however, the severe white walls and orderly plantings make it clear that this is indeed a temple of the noble.

Originally built as an sub-temple to Mandara-dera, built by Ninkai in 991, in the Kamakura period it was recognized as a *monzeki* temple and given the name Zuishin-in.

It is also said that Zuishin-in was once the palace of the poet Ono-no-Komachi, and some sites in the grounds, such as the well where she reportedly applied her makeup, and the reputed site of where she buried her love letters.

11

ひと山を寺域とする雄渾な大寺

醍醐寺（だいごじ）

京都市伏見区醍醐東大路町22
075（571）0002
9時〜17時（12月第1日曜の翌日〜2月は9時〜16時30分）
境内参拝自由（三宝院庭園・殿舎、霊宝館、伽藍拝観券800円　春期・秋期は1500円）
www.daigoji.or.jp
地下鉄東西線　醍醐駅下車徒歩10分

標高450mの醍醐山の山頂から西麓までの醍醐寺全域をいま山上の上醍醐（かみだいご）、山麓の下醍醐（しもだいご）と分けて、参詣客の多くは、金堂や五重塔、三宝院（さんぼういん）（子院）の建つ下醍醐だけをめぐることになる。というのは上醍醐への山道はかなりの急坂で、山頂の開山堂まで約2.6km、約1時間を歩き通さなければならず、気軽に拝観するといった気持ちでは行きつかないからだ。

醍醐寺はその山上にはじまった。貞観年間（859〜77）に聖宝（しょうぼう）（理源（りげん）大師）が草庵を設け、その後、山上に准胝堂（じゅんていどう）、如意輪堂（にょいりんどう）を建立、また聖宝に帰依した醍醐天皇により907年（延喜7）薬師堂（やくしどう）、五大堂（ごだいどう）が造営されて定額寺となった。

上醍醐にのぼる

醍醐の花見　1598年3月15日に豊臣秀吉が醍醐寺山内院で催した豪華絢爛な花見の宴。

旧奈良街道に面した総門を入ると「醍醐の花見」（再現行事＝4月第2日曜日）で華やぐ「桜の馬場」の広い参道が仁王門までつづく。仁王門の手前を右に、境内を囲む樹木に沿って南

11. The great temple that occupies a whole mountain
Daigo-ji

Address: 22 Daigo Higashi-ōji-chō, Fushimi-ku, Kyoto-shi
Tel: 075 (571) 0002
Hours: 9:00AM–5:00PM (First Monday after a Sunday in December–February: 9:00AM–4:30PM)
Admission: Free (Entry to Sanpō-in Garden, hai-den, Reihōkan, and temple: ¥800; spring and fall: ¥1,500)
www.daigoji.or.jp
10 min walk from Subway Tozai Line Daigo Sta.

The vast grounds of Daigo-ji, stretching from the 450-meter-high summit of Mt. Daigoyama down to the western foothills, are divided into two parts: Kami (Upper) Daigo and Shimo (Lower) Daigo. Most visitors only make it to the lower area, where they can see the *kon-dō*, the five-story pagoda, and Sanpō-in (an auxiliary temple). The road to Kami-Daigo is quite steep, and the 2.6-kilometer walk to the *kaizan-dō* at the summit takes a good hour, so it is not attempted lightly.

Daigo-ji began at the summit of the mountain. In the Jōgan era (859–77), Shōbō (later known as Rigen Daishi) built a hermitage there, later adding the *juntei-dō* and the *nyoirin-dō*. Emperor Daigo, who followed Shōbō's teachings, added the Yakushi-dō and the Godai-dō in 907. Then Daigo-ji became one of the officialy protected temples called *jōgaku-ji*.

Climbing Up to Kami-Daigo

Enter the main gate facing the Old Narakaidō Rd., and you find yourself in Sakura no Baba, a broad plaza where the annual Daigo Cherry blossoms viewing is held on the second Sunday in April each year. The plaza leads to the *niō-mon* gate. There is a

側の縁を回るように山道をのぼってゆくと成身院（女人堂）がみえてくる。やがて山道は槍山の「豊太閤花見跡」にいたる。1598年（慶長3）3月15日の「醍醐の花見」ではこの槍山の千畳敷の平地に花見御殿が建てられたという。

女人堂　かつては女性が社寺や霊場などへの立入りを禁じた「女人結界」があり、女性は女人堂で参拝した。

行程のほぼ中間点に不動の滝があって、ここからきつい坂道の上り坂となる。やがて坂道は終わり、上醍醐に入る。1434年（永享6）に再建された懸崖造の清龍宮拝殿、その横には、醍醐水の祠があり、この水こそ当寺の寺名の由来なのである。

聖宝が霊験により笠取山（醍醐山）に登ったとき、白髪の老翁に化身した地主神の横尾明神があらわれ、落葉の下から湧きでていた水を飲み「ああ醍醐味なるかな」といい、あわせて「よく密教を広めて衆生を利せよ」と告げ、忽然と姿を消した。聖宝はその水の湧くところに石を積み閼伽井とした。それが霊泉醍醐水で、このことにより山名とし寺名としたという話である。

醍醐味　醍醐は乳を発酵させて得られる五味の最上のものをいい、醍醐味は、醍醐のような味をほめていう。

閼伽井　閼伽は仏前に供えるもので、とくに水をいう。その閼伽を汲む井戸。

醍醐水の祠のさらに高台に上醍醐の本堂准胝堂が1968年（昭和43）の再建として建っていたが、2008年8月の落雷により全焼した。また、東にゆくと上醍醐最古の建造物である薬師堂（保安2年＝1121年の再建）、そして、少し急坂をあがると五大明王像を祀る五大堂があり「五大力さん」と通称される。つづいて懸崖造の如意輪堂と山上最大の建築物である開山堂がある。いずれも1606年（慶長11）

五大力さん　本尊の不動明王を中心に五大明王を祀る。2月23日に法要が営まれる。

temple approach to the right of this gate. If you take this path, which goes around the south side of the trees that encircle the temple grounds, Jōshin-in (*nyonin-dō*) will come into view. Finally the path comes to the "Hōtaikō (Toyotomi Hideyoshi) Hanami Ato," the remnants of a flower-viewing hall erected by order of Hideyoshi in a broad open area on March 15, 1598.

About halfway through your hike, you come to *fudō* Waterfall, and here the path turns steeply uphill for the rest of the clumb to Kami-Daigo. Next to Seiryūgū Hai-den, rebuilt in the *kengai-zukuri* style in 1434, is the Daigosui spring that gives the temple its name.

The story goes that Shōbō was climbing Mt. Kasatoriyama (byname Mt. Daigoyama), when a white-haired old man appeared before him and showed him the source of the spring beneath some fallen leaves. Revealing himself as Yoko-o Myōjin, the local deity, the deity urged Shōbō to disseminate the esoteric Buddhist teachings, and disappeared. Shōbō built a well at the spot where the water sprang up, and this miraculous spring gave the mountain and the temple their names.

The *hondō* of the temple, the Juntei-dō, was rebuilt in 1968, higher up the mountain, however it was burnt down by lightning in August 2008. Slightly east of here is the oldest building in Kami-Daigo, the Yakushi-dō, rebuilt in 1121, and a bit higher up the mountain is the Godai-dō, honoring the Five Myō-ō. The building is known as "Godairiki-san." Finally is the *nyoirin-dō*, built in the *Kengai-zukuri* style, and at the top of the mountain, the largest structure of the temple, the *kaizan-dō*. All of these buildings were rebuilt in 1606 with the support of Toyotomi

に豊臣秀頼によって再建されたものである。

下醍醐の伽藍と三宝院

三宝院 1115年、第十四世勝覚が創建し応仁の乱で焼失。1598年豊臣秀吉の援助で再興。

下醍醐の整備と造営も904年（延喜4）ころからはじめられ、926年（延長4）に釈迦堂（のちに金堂という）、951年（天暦5）に五重塔が完成した。そして、第14代座主勝覚が1115年（永久3）に三宝院を建立、つづいて理性院、金剛王院、報恩院、無量寿院の四院が創建され、三宝院とあわせて醍醐五門跡が成った。醍醐寺の座主は、五門跡から順次選ばれていたが、室町幕府の信任をえた座主満済（足利義満の養子）が三宝院門跡になり、幕政にも参加して権勢を誇ったため、その後三宝院門跡が醍醐寺座主を兼ねるようになった。この時期、醍醐寺は全盛期をむかえるのである。

しかし、応仁の乱で五重塔をのぞく伽藍のほとんどが灰燼に帰して、また膨大な寺領荘園も失った。第80代座主義演が豊臣秀吉の絶大な支援によって再興、1600年（慶長5）には紀州湯浅の満願寺の本堂を移して金堂を再建した。今日みる醍醐寺の伽藍配置は慶長年間（1596～1615）にほぼ復興したのである。

醍醐寺の五重塔は現存する京都最古の建造物といわれて、相輪の高さが塔の3分の1の約13m、五層の屋根は上にいくほど小さくなる様式とともに堂々とした安定感をみせている。

下醍醐の山内で最も重要な塔頭が三宝院である。醍醐寺の総門を入って広い参道（桜の

Hideyori.

The Temples of Shimo-Daigo and Sanpō-in

Construction at Shimo-Daigo area started around 904, with the *shaka-dō* (later called the *kon-dō*) in 926, and the five-story pagoda in 951. The fourteenth head priest, Shōgaku, built Sanpō-in in 1115, followed by Rishō-in, Kongōō-in, Hōon-in, and Muryōju-in. These, with Sanpō-in, make up the Daigo Five *monzeki*. The head priest of Daigo-ji was selected in turn from each of these five *monzeki* temples, until Mansai, an adopted son of Ashikaga Yoshimitsu, who was the head priest of Sanpō-in, maneuvered with the Bakufu authorities to give the position as head priest of Daigo-ji permanently to the person holding the high position at Sanpō-in. This led to Daigo-ji's period of greatest prosperity.

However, in the Ōnin War, almost all the temple buildings, except for the five-story pagoda, were destroyed, and the temple lost its expansive manor lands. With the support of Toyotomi Hideyoshi, the eightieth head priest, Gien, was able to restore the temple, and in 1600, the *hondō* from Mangan-ji, at Yuasa in Kishū (Wakayama), was moved to Daigo-ji and renamed the *kon-dō*. The layout of temple buildings we see today dates from this restoration during the Keichō era (1596–1615).

Daigo-ji's five-story pagoda is believed to be the oldest building in Kyoto. At 13 meters, its spire is one-third the height of the tower as a whole, and the roofs of the five levels are successively smaller as the tower ascends in an elegant style.

The most important sub-temple of Shimo-Daigo is Sanpō-in, which stands on the left when you enter the broad plaza (the

馬場）の左手に位置する。一般の出入口である表門を入ると、五七の桐文が染められた紫地の幕がかかる大玄関がみえ、そこから葵の間、秋草の間、勅使の間をへて、表書院、さらに秀吉が花見をおこなった純浄観にまわる。表書院からは南に秀吉が直接作庭を指示したという庭園が大きく開けて、この庭もじっくりとみておきたい。

また、奥宸殿には、修学院離宮の「霞棚」、桂離宮の「桂棚」とともに天下の三大名棚と称される「醍醐棚」がしつらえられている。

五七の桐文　三枚の桐の葉の上に桐花を中央に七つ、左右にそれぞれ五つつけた文。豊臣家の文でもあった。

上醍醐からの眺め
View from Kami-Daigo

Sakura no Baba) from the main gate. When you enter the front gate, you see the great entrance with its purple hanging curtain with the family crest of Toyotomi. From there you can view the the various rooms: Aoi-no-Ma, the Akikusa-no-Ma, the Chokushi-no-Ma, the *omote shoin* (study-cum-living room), and the Junjōkan, where Hideyoshi enjoyed flower viewing. Beyond the *omote shoin* is a large garden believed to have been constructed at Hideyoshi's directions.

In the *Okushin-den*, you can see the distinctive "Daigo-dana" shelves, a style of shelf construction that is considered one of the three elegant shelf designs of the period, along with the "Kasumi-dana" found in the Shūgaku-in Imperial villa and the "Katsura-dana" in the Katsura Imperial villa.

エリア 6-1 Area 6-1

高野川
Takano River
叡山電鉄
Eizan Dentetsu
赤山禅院
Sekizan-zen-in
修学院離宮
Shūgaku-in
Imperial villa
音羽川
Otowa River
白川通北山交差点
Shirakawa St.-Kitayama Crossing
修学院
Shugakuin Sta.
鷺森神社
Sagi-no-mori-jinja
白川通
Shirakawa St.
曼殊院
Manshu-in
詩仙堂
Shisen-dō
金福寺
Konpuku-ji
白川通北大路交差点
Shirakawa St.-Kitaōji Crossing

エリア 6-2 Area 6-2

エリア 6-3 Area 6-3

エリア 6-4 Area 6-4

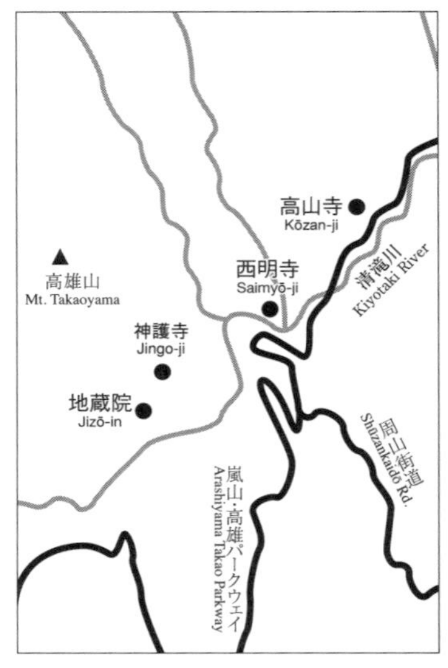

エリア 6-5　Area 6-5

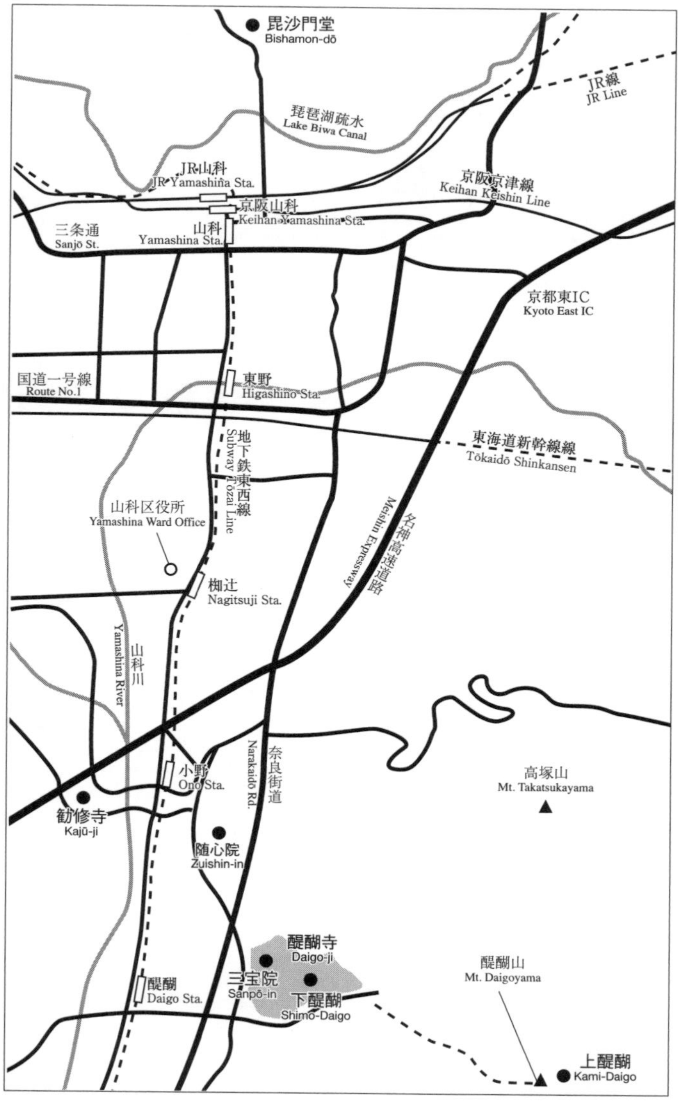

[対訳ニッポン双書]
英語で話す「京都寺社ガイド」
Introducing Kyoto in Temples and Shrines

2020年 3 月10日　第1刷発行

編　者　**紫　紅　社**

発行者　**浦　晋　亮**

発行所　IBCパブリッシング株式会社
〒162-0804
東京都新宿区中里町29番3号 菱秀神楽坂ビル9F
Tel. 03-3513-4511　Fax. 03-3513-4512
www.ibcpub.co.jp

印刷所　株式会社シナノパブリッシングプレス

ISBN978-4-7946-0618-1